About the Author

Khoo Boo Teik was born, bred and schooled in George Town, Penang, Malaysia before studying at the University of Rochester, MIT and The Flinders University of South Australia. He is the author of *Paradoxes of Mahathirism: An Intellectual Biography of Mahathir Mohamad* and an Associate Professor in the School of Social Sciences, Universiti Sains Malaysia.

Beyond Mahathir

Malaysian Politics and its Discontents

Khoo Boo Teik

Zed Books Ltd
London • New York

Beyond Mahathir: Malaysian Politics and its Discontents
was first published in 2003 by
Zed Books Ltd
7 Cynthia Street, London N1 9JF, UK and
Room 400, 175 Fifth Avenue, New York, NY 10010, USA

Copyright © Khoo Boo Teik 2003

Distributed in the United States exclusively by
Palgrave, a division of St Martin's Press, LLC
175 Fifth Avenue, New York, NY 10010, USA

Set in Arial and Baskerville by Foo Ah Hiang
Printed and bound in Malaysia

The rights of the author of this work have been asserted by him in
accordance with the Copyright, Designs and Patents Act, 1998.

All rights reserved

A catalogue record for this book is available from the British Library.

US CIP has been applied for.

ISBN 1 84277 464 6 Hb
ISBN 1 84277 465 4 Pb

Contents

List of Tables	vii
Abbreviations	viii
Preface	x

1 From Paradoxes to Crises — 1
  A Question of Legacy — 2
  The Politics of a Project — 5

2 The Projection of a Vision — 15
  Three Turning Points — 17
  Nationalism and Regionalism: Vision 2020 and 'Asian Values' — 20
  Hegemonic Interlude: The 1995 General Election — 26
  The Futurism of the Multimedia Super Corridor — 30

3 The Anarchy of the Market — 38
  Gambling with Money — 40
  Depreciation, Devaluation and Disinvestment — 47
  Rescue, Recapitalization and Reflation — 51
  Bringing the Crisis Home — 56

4 The Inventions of Anwar Ibrahim — 71
  Between Praise and Damnation — 73
  On the Way to the Assembly — 78
  The Improbability of Succession — 82
  Four Phases and a Contradiction — 86

5 *Reformasi* and the End of UMNO's Hegemonic Stability — 99
  The Meanings of *Reformasi* — 100
  The Trials of Anwar Ibrahim — 108
  Barisan Alternatif and the 1999 Election — 112
  The End of UMNO's Hegemonic Stability — 121

Contents

6 The Cultural Imperative of Coalition Building   134
    DAP and the Pendulum of Minority Politics   135
    The Rise and Rise of PAS?   145
    Keadilan Between Vision and Fulfilment   154
    The Cultural Imperative of Coalition Building   159

7 The Coming of the Second Dilemma   167
    Limits to Personalized Hegemony   169
    Ambitions, Ideals and Discord   174
    Rumours of an Islamic State   181
    Mahathir's Final Dilemma   188

Bibliography   202
Index   211

Tables

1.1	Political Events, Principal Outcomes and Significance, 1981-94	6
1.2	Political Events, Principal Outcomes and Significance, 1995-2002	9
3.1	Malaysia: Outstanding Private Sector External Debt, 1987-97	44
3.2	Malaysia: Portfolio Investment in Shares and Corporate Securities, 1991-97	45
3.3	Kuala Lumpur Stock Exchange, Selected Indicators, 1990-97	46
6.1	DAP's Parliamentary Performance, General Elections, 1974-99	136
6.2	Parliamentary Seats (Proportion of Popular Vote) of Principal/Predominantly Malay Opposition Parties, General Elections, 1978-99	146

Abbreviations

ABIM	Angkatan Belia Islam Malaysia (Malaysian Islamic Youth Movement)
ADIL	Pergerakan Keadilan Sosial (Social Justice Movement)
APU	Angkatan Perpaduan Ummah (Muslim Unity Force)
BA	Barisan Alternatif (Alternative Front)
BCIC	Bumiputera Commercial and Industrial Community
BN	Barisan Nasional (National Front)
BNM	Bank Negara Malaysia
CDRC	Corporate Debt Restructuring Committee
DAP	Democratic Action Party
Dongjiaozong	United Chinese School Committees' Association and United Chinese School Teachers' Association
EPF	Employees Provident Fund
GAGASAN	Gagasan Demokrasi Rakyat (People's Democratic Coalition)
Gagasan Rakyat	Gagasan Rakyat Malaysia (Malaysian People's Coalition)
GERAK	Majlis Gerakan Keadilan Rakyat (Council of the People's Movement for Justice)
Gerakan	Parti Gerakan Rakyat Malaysia (Malaysian People's Movement Party)
IMF	International Monetary Fund
ISA	Internal Security Act
Keadilan	Parti Keadilan Nasional (National Justice Party)
KLSE	Kuala Lumpur Stock Exchange
Malaysia Inc.	Malaysia Incorporated

Abbreviations

MCA	Malaysian Chinese Association
MIC	Malaysian Indian Congress
MSC	Multimedia Super Corridor
NDP	National Development Policy
NEAC	National Economic Action Council
NEP	New Economic Policy
NGO	Non-governmental organization
NPL	Non-performing loan
PAS	Parti Islam SeMalaysia (Pan-Malaysian Islamic Party)
PBS	Parti Bersatu Sabah (Sabah United Party)
Petronas	Petrolium Nasional (National Petroleum Corporation)
PRM	Parti Rakyat Malaysia (Malaysian People's Party)
Reformasi	post-September 1998 reform movement
S46 or Semangat 46	Parti Semangat 46 (Spirit of '46 Party)
SUARAM	Suara Rakyat Malaysia (Voice of the Malaysian People)
Suqiu	Malaysian Chinese Organizations' Appeals for the General Election 1999
UMNO	United Malays National Organization

Preface

Datuk Seri Dr Mahathir Mohamad has been Prime Minister of Malaysia for 22 years. Bolstered by his long tenure in office and his ability to survive political crises, Mahathir's personality, ideas, policies, and even 'style' have fascinated many different types of 'Mahathir watchers', including journalists, politicians, academicians and diplomats.

Among them circulates Mahathir's reputation for being controversial, or even contradictory, in ways that exceed the inconsistencies that are part of a veteran politician's stock-in-trade. As a result, Mahathir appears to be a bundle of opposites which are sometimes amusing, at times alarming but frequently confusing. Reading many journalistic and academic accounts of Mahathir, for example, one may think Mahathir is dynamic in implementing his ideas and projects, but quite possibly out of touch with economic reality. Observers who have praised Mahathir for being a visionary leader seemingly capable of peering deeply into the future were likely to have criticized him, too, for being myopic about the present. And although Mahathir has been prolific in his writing and unrestrained in speech, he can appear to be enigmatic, forbiddingly difficult to comprehend and impossible to predict.

These and other incongruities, which have been attached to Mahathir, man and politician, may or may not withstand scrutiny. Nevertheless they have helped to surround Mahathir with an aura that makes him the centre, the subject, the prime mover, and, in Malay, the *dalang* (puppeteer) of Malaysian politics.

In self-criticism, I should admit to having perhaps contributed to such a perception of Mahathir. My earlier book, *Paradoxes of Mahathirism: An Intellectual Biography of Mahathir Mohamad*, while painting an ideological portrait of Mahathir and approaching him as a man of different personae and paradoxes, may have treated a large part of Malaysian politics merely as the canvas upon which Mahathir drew his actions, initiatives and interventions, if not so when he was a young man, then certainly by the time he was in power.

Of course, Mahathir was 'always there' in the politics of the 'Mahathir era', and surely he took charge of difficult situations and outwitted his rivals far better than his contemporaries. Yet many of the most significant political events that took place during his term in office lay outside Mahathir's control, not least when he struggled to manage their associated economic developments and unsettling social consequences. The limits to Mahathir's writ were especially clear during the period under consideration in this book, that is, the second half of Mahathir's years in office when 'Mahathirist politics' lurched from triumph to crisis and then to uncertainty.

At the crucial moment of the 1997 East Asian financial crisis, for instance, the international money market did not lie within Mahathir's grasp. At another critical point, the Malaysian *Reformasi* defied his domination. Presently, if one takes seriously the notion of a 'second Malay dilemma', of which Mahathir warned when he announced in June 2002 his intention to retire from active politics, then the future is as unclear as ever. In short, these matters and other developments were beyond Mahathir.

Beyond Mahathir is primarily an analysis of politics in Malaysia that arose out of the ambiguous confluences of past social transformation and future developmental plans, of nationalist ambitions and globalizing tendencies, and of the dictates of hegemony and the impulses of recalcitrance. We now know that Mahathir sought to manage but could not master those confluences and their conflictual outcomes. Hence, what happened in Mahathir's final years in power bears implications for Malaysian politics beyond his departure from office.

I commenced writing this book a month after Mahathir announced his intention to retire. But I had thought of writing such a book when I spent sabbatical leave from Universiti Sains Malaysia (USM), between May 1999 and February 2000, as a Visiting Fellow at the Asia Research Centre (ARC), Murdoch University, Perth, Australia. I would like to record here my gratitude to USM and the ARC respectively for the sabbatical leave and the fellowship. I am indebted, moreover, to Richard Robison, Cisca Spencer, Garry Rodan, Kanishka Jayasuriya and Del Blakeway whose friendship, encouragement and interest in my work made memorable my stay at the ARC.

During the past year, I was helped by many people. At the School of Social Sciences, USM, Abdul Rahim Ibrahim was understanding and supportive; Letchimi Devee, Rosni Yusoff and Zaiton Kassim

Preface

lightened my administrative duties; and Wu Yoke Li and Kong Siew Hee provided able research assistance. At The Star Publications, Lee Kam Hing, Ng Poh Tip, Asha Devi and the staff of the library liberally facilitated my access to newspaper records.

For some funding that was made available from the project, *Discourses and Practices of Democracy in Southeast Asia*, I am grateful to Sida/SAREC, Sweden. For their understanding and cooperation while we worked together on that project, I wish to thank Wil Burghoorn, Sven Cederroth and Joakim Ojendal of Göteborg University Center for Asian Studies, Sweden.

In different but equally valued ways, Abdul Rahman Embong, Chang Yii Tan, Chia Ling Eng, Chin Yee Whah, Hwa Mei Shen, Khoo Khay Jin, Francis Loh Kok Wah, Maznah Mohamad, Ooi Guat Kuan, P. Ramakrishnan and Yeap Jin Soo listened patiently to me, lent me materials, answered my questions, and extended their hospitality whenever I had need of it. Cheah Boon Kheng, Low Swee Heong, Mustafa Kamal Anuar, Tan Liok Ee and Toh Kin Woon each read the entire draft of this book and, with good cheer, offered valuable suggestions for improving the manuscript. I wholeheartedly thank them all.

In the production of this book, Jomo K. S. gave unreserved support, critical comments and good advice, Foo Ah Hiang performed the typesetting with admirable competence and forebearance, and Lim Siang Jin generously provided the painting for the cover design. Despite working under harried circumstances, Fong Chin Wei edited the manuscript with skill and care, all the time displaying the sort of perseverance and thoughtfulness only friendship allied to duty inspires.

As I was preparing the final version of the manuscript, my father was dying of cancer. Sadly for both of us, he did not live to see the book in print. But without the expert, devoted and compassionate care given to him by Oo Loo Chan, Ruby Chong and Kevin Hew of Mount Miriam Hospital; Tan Kok Hin of Hospital Pantai Mutiara; my mother, Lim Ah Paik; my sisters, Ai Choo, Ai Poh, Ai Wah and Ai Boey, and my brother, Boo Hin; my wife, Pek Leng; and my children, Teng Jian and Teng Xiang, I would not have been able to complete the manuscript.

Penang
17 July 2003

*To my mother, Lim Ah Paik,
and the memory of my father,
Kay Yeow (1926-2003)*

1
From Paradoxes to Crises

> It is characteristic of the Malays that having once placed their trust and respect in a person they are loath to revise their opinions even under altered circumstances. Thus, it is no longer their convictions that count but those of Dato Onn.
> C. H. E. Det (1950) 'New thoughts on nationality',
> *Sunday Times*, 9 April

> There are people who suggest that Malays be a little rude. This suggestion has been well received. But why be a little rude? Just be downright rude. And so the views that it is unnecessary to feel obliged to the benefactors gained acceptance.
> Mahathir Mohamad, Speech at the UMNO General Assembly,
> Kuala Lumpur, 11 May 2000

Twenty-two years ago, Dr Mahathir Mohamad became the fourth Prime Minister of Malaysia. During his tenure, Mahathir oversaw economic and social changes that transformed Malaysia into a very different place from what it was in 1964, when he was elected Member of Parliament for the constituency of Kota Star Selatan, Kedah. Mahathir was defeated in the general election of 1969. Since 1974, however, Mahathir has been returned regularly as Member of Parliament for Kubang Pasu; he was last elected in November 1999.

Of course, if we were to compare Malaysia today with its colonial past in 1948, the social, economic and political changes it has undergone are even more profound. It was in 1948 that the young Mahathir, a student at the King Edward VII College of Medicine, began showing his ability as an ideologue. Using the pseudonym of C.H.E. Det, Mahathir published the first of his reflections on Malay affairs and Malayan politics in *The Sunday Times*. Since then, no Malay intellectual or politician has written or spoken more extensively on what might be regarded as the Malay social condition and its relation to the rest of Malaysian society and polity, or the 'Malay dilemma', as popularized by Mahathir in 1970.

A Question of Legacy

A career as long as Mahathir's, punctuated so often with controversy and crisis, will attract reviews and assessments with his planned retirement in October 2003. Many of these reviews, undoubtedly, will attempt to compose balance sheets of Mahathir's successes and failures, his qualities and shortcomings, and, above all, try to record his 'contributions to Malaysian society' for posterity.

It should be clarified at the outset that this book contains observations and commentaries, many of which cannot avoid being judgemental of Mahathir. Strictly speaking, however, this book does not evaluate Mahathir's career along the themes indicated above. One reason for not doing so is provided by Mahathir himself who has repeatedly indicated his indifference as to how he might be 'judged by history'. Only two years after becoming Prime Minister, for instance, Mahathir noted, 'It's totally irrelevant to perpetuate oneself in history. You can't determine what kind of judgement history is going to pass on you.'[1] As to how he would like to be remembered, Mahathir said quite simply, eighteen years later, 'I don't care.'[2] If the second statement seems astonishing, coming as it did from Mahathir who has consistently urged Malaysians to be conscious of history, it remains one of those rare Mahathir pronouncements that may be accepted almost at face value. In other words, Mahathir is so convinced of the importance of his work and the correctness of his actions and views that he is not concerned with how others may judge him.

There is a stronger justification for not reviewing Mahathir's 'legacy' here, at least not just yet. As soon as Mahathir announced his plan to retire from office, the domestic and international media gave quick takes on his role in Malaysian history. Many of these instant assessments of Mahathir were unhelpfully partisan. One of Mahathir's advisers, for example, unhesitatingly pronounced his advisee to be the greatest Malay leader of the past 500 years. In like tone, one of the aspirants to the highest levels of leadership in the United Malays National Organization (UMNO), Mahathir's party and the dominant party of the ruling coalition in Malaysia, swiftly declared that a leader of Mahathir's calibre appeared only once in a millennium. At home and abroad, journalists, columnists, scholars, and other commentators rushed to affix Mahathir with such formulaic labels as *Bapa Pembangunan* (Father of Development), modernizer, visionary, and 'the man who set

Malaysia on the world map'. Thus was Mahathir elevated, or, what amounts to the same thing here, reduced to a stock character, an image that could be conveniently imprinted onto the public imagination. Conversely, over the non-state-controlled information superhighway, some of Mahathir's implacable opponents tarred him as the embodiment of all that was wrong with Malaysian society.

In such a situation, where the choice is between unabashed adulation or unrelieved damnation of Mahathir, even 'compromise', an often used term in Malaysia's cultural vocabulary and a presumed virtue of its political system, may not bring about any balance, for it can be just as distorting to seek the mean between someone's glorification and vilification. A politician's legacy is not set the day he or she leaves office; its effects cannot be suddenly arrested and neatly packaged. It may not be known for some time how these effects will work themselves through society. A serious interpretation of a political legacy and its consequences, moreover, cannot presume a settled and unproblematic past. The interpretation must consider a present that is very much in the making, as well as a future that none can accurately predict. This, however, is not cause for despair; rather it is a reason for delimiting responsibility. Here, I would prefer to think that subsequent historians, with the benefit of additional information, the advantage of distance, and probably advances in social analyses, will be better placed to deliver clearer and more enduring verdicts on Mahathir's place in Malaysian history.

Malaysian society has been increasingly burdened with the assumptions, extensively propagated by the mass media, that only good comes from its government and its leaders, that what is bad is due to the defects of its culture or the failings of its citizens. It seems necessary, therefore, to examine the principal events of the final years of Mahathir's premiership, during which most of the damage done to social interests arose from the conduct of different elites or was inflicted by domestic and international actors. In contrast, uncelebrated citizens strove to retrieve what was promising about Malaysian society. In the critical events of this period, Mahathir played a central role but others intervened as well. Although neither Mahathir nor these other actors could force events to develop at will or under conditions of their choice, much happened during these final years of the 'Mahathir era' that was momentous, disturbing or inspiring. Mahathir acknowledged as much when he recounted that, although he had planned to retire in 1998, he felt compelled to remain in office to cope with the instabilities and threats of 1997-98 that had not been satisfactorily managed by Anwar

Ibrahim, who was then regarded as Mahathir's 'anointed successor'. At the same time, several unexpected events occurred that require a re-examination of the conduct of Malaysian politics, if not a redefinition of the parameters of the Malaysian political system. Perhaps, the latest unanticipated development that has been wrought upon Malaysian political economy and society is Mahathir's recent and forceful caution that a 'second Malay dilemma' has arisen. It is a new dilemma, he warned, that demands an urgent resolution to avoid reversing the socio-economic progress of the past three decades of the New Economic Policy (NEP) and National Development Policy (NDP).

When mentioning all this, I also have in mind such crucial events as the 'East Asian financial crisis' of July 1997, the Mahathir regime's resort to capital controls on 1 September 1998, the persecution of Anwar Ibrahim beginning with his dismissal as Deputy Prime Minister on 2 September 1998, the ferment of *Reformasi*, the formation of the Barisan Alternatif (Alternative Front), the results of the November 1999 general election, the 11 September 2001 attacks on the World Trade Center and the Pentagon, and, finally, Mahathir's announcement on 22 June 2002 of his intended retirement. Each of these events brought immediate and chaotic effects, while their cumulative, intertwining and long-term impact will be tremendous, especially for a nation and society as small as Malaysia. Even if the consequences of these events remain imperfectly understood for some time to come, we still require an interpretation of the politics that emerged from the convergence of these domestic and international events to understand the current situation, and, indeed, the politics after Mahathir's departure.

The interpretation offered here begins where my previous book, *Paradoxes of Mahathirism: An Intellectual Biography of Mahathir Mohamad*, left off. Published in 1995, *Paradoxes of Mahathirism* sketched an ideological portrait of Mahathir to examine a worldview that was framed by his core concerns. 'Mahathirism', I proposed, captured a relatively coherent ideology that can be thematically constructed from Mahathir's nationalism, capitalism, Islam, populism and authoritarianism. I did caution, however, that Mahathirism was laden with tensions and contradictions that, among other things, reflected the occasionally tortuous routes by which Mahathir – as man, ideologue and politician – engaged the central social and political issues of his time. Mahathir's nationalism, for instance, had, over the years, evolved from an early form of Malay nationalism, imbued with Social Darwinist insecurities, to a more inclusive Malaysian nationalism that was motivated by aspirations of finding a respectable place in the world for Malaysia.

Mahathir's capitalism, too, underwent changes from its associations with NEP's state interventionism to privatization favouring a new class of Malay capitalists. Mahathir's Islam sought to instill a work ethic necessary for modernization and industrialization but, behind the values and institutions introduced by Mahathir's Islamization policy, we can discern 'the religiosity of the self-made man'. Populism, for Mahathir, basically entailed knowing what 'the people' thought, felt and needed, and expressing what was good for the 'little guys', whether at home, or in the world at large. Yet, Mahathirist populism was always only thinly separated from his authoritarianism. While Mahathir tolerated democracy to a point, he consistently emphasized the necessity, almost the mystique, of governing a nation according to certain qualities of good leadership. It was suggested that, during times of economic and political stress, Mahathir's populism dissolved into authoritarianism. Moreover, *Paradoxes of Mahathirism* approached Mahathir as a series of personae bearing the influences of his youthful experiences in his home state of Kedah and in Singapore, his family background and his father's ethos, and Mahathir's training and practice as a doctor. The conclusion of *Paradoxes of Mahathirism* argued that *Wawasan 2020* (Vision 2020), with its accompaniments of *Bangsa Malaysia* (Malaysian nationality) and *Melayu Baru* (New Malays), was the mature ideological representation of a Mahathirist project that was tentatively constructed during the C.H.E. Det days, elaborated in *The Malay Dilemma* and *The Challenge*, and fully pursued (if modified for the times) in the major economic policies of the prime minister.

Since the discussion of Mahathirism included an analysis of Mahathir's policies and politics after he came to power, *Paradoxes of Mahathirism* covered major political events that unfolded between 1981 and before the general election of 1995, the year in which the book appeared. As an aid, Table 1.1 (pp. 6-7) gives a summary of these events.

The Politics of a Project

The present work, which can but need not necessarily be read as a sequel to *Paradoxes of Mahathirism*, is not a mere extension of my earlier book or another study in political ideology. The core of this book may be regarded as an examination of the politics of a Mahathirist programme of socio-economic development. Conceptually, Mahathir's developmental programme can be regarded as a nationalist project driven by capitalist impulses or a capitalist project imbued with nationalist aspirations.

The project was *capitalist* in several ways. Historically, it built upon a particular structure of capitalism left behind by a colonial state that had defeated the anti-capitalist alternative implicit in the Communist Party of Malaya-led insurrection of 1948. Beginning in 1970 with the implementation of the NEP, much of the project was bound up with the rise of Malay capital. After Mahathir began implementing his Malaysia Incorporated and privatization policies in the early 1980s, one of the project's priorities was the consolidation of a strategic alliance between the state and domestic capital – the latter being, in Mahathir's

Table 1.1 Political Events, Principal Outcomes and Significance, 1981-94

Year(s)	Political event(s)	Principal outcome	Major significance
1981	Hussein Onn retires	Mahathir becomes Prime Minister	Commencement of reformism and liberalism
	Musa-Razaleigh UMNO Deputy President contest	Musa wins and becomes Deputy Prime Minister	Indications of UMNO's factionalism
1982	General election	1st Barisan Nasional victory led by Mahathir	Mahathir's new economic policies
1983-84	Constitutional crisis	Stalemate between UMNO and royalty	Centralization of executive power
1984	2nd Musa-Razaleigh contest	Musa wins, Razaleigh loses finance ministry	Deepening UMNO factionalism
1984-85	Malaysian Chinese Asscociation crisis	Tan Koon Swan becomes MCA president	Culmination of business and politics in MCA
1984-86	Sabah crisis	Rise of Joseph Pairin Kitingan and Parti Bersatu Sabah	Kadazandusun consciousness and federal-state strains
1986	February: Musa resigned as DPM	Ghafar Baba appointed Deputy Prime Minister	Disaffection with Mahathir's leadership
	General election	UMNO's and DAP's triumphs	Mahathir remains in power
1986-87	Musa and Razaleigh formed Team B	Team B prepares to challenge Team A	Peak of UMNO's factionalism

From Paradoxes to Crises   7

Table 1.1 (continued)

Year(s)	Political event(s)	Principal outcome	Major significance
1987	UMNO election	Team A's narrow victory	Purge of Team B and UMNO split
	'Operation Lalang'	Mass arrests of opponents	End of Mahathirist liberalism
1988	UMNO's deregistration as a party	Formation of UMNO Baru	Team B dissidents excluded
	Judicial crisis	Impeachment of Supreme Court judges	Mahathirist authoritarianism
1988-89	Several by-elections: mixed victories	Persistent dissent against UMNO Baru	Inconclusive tests of political strength
1989	Parti Semangat 46 formed	Razaleigh leads Team B in opposition	Basis of new coalitions in opposition
1990	General election	Barisan Nasional's victory	Two-coalition system; PAS's return in Kelantan
1991	Vision 2020	New Mahathirist agenda	National Development Policy
1993	UMNO election; Anwar ready to challenge Ghafar	Wawasan Team victory	Anwar becomes Deputy Prime Minister
1994	Sabah election	PBS's narrow victory, toppled by defections	New federal-state relations

schema, a national capital offering a leading role to entrepreneurs from the state-nurtured Bumiputera Commercial and Industrial Community Malay (BCIC).

The project was *nationalist* in two meanings. It began under Malay nationalists who used the NEP and the BCIC to recompose the Malaysian class structure in ethnic terms, which meant recomposing Malay society in class terms. By the early 1990s, the project had helped to consolidate a Malaysian capitalist class who, Mahathir hoped, would lead the drive of Vision 2020. That the developmental programme was a social *project* and not the accidental outcome of a *laissez faire* economy was indicated by the determined state interventionism of successive post-1970 regimes.

As the nationalist-capitalist or Mahathirist project was not monolithic in its design, uncontested in its implementation, or inexorable in its progress, it led to the various controversies and crises of the 1970s and the 1980s. Even so, the project had advanced along the policy pathways of the NEP, privatization, Malaysia Inc., the NDP and Vision 2020 to a seemingly clear triumph in 1995-96, only to be entangled in the severe crisis of 1997-98. It is my contention that the implications of this sudden reversal in the condition of the nationalist-capitalist project provoked and shaped the politics of the final years of Mahathir's premiership.

Table 1.2 (p. 9) summarizes the period of analysis and its most significant political events. The analysis begins in Chapter 2 with the Mahathirist project's triumphalist phase from the promulgation of Vision 2020 in 1991 to the eve of the July 1997 financial crisis. This chapter explains the Mahathir regime's hegemony over Malaysian society, achieved as a result of the confluence of national economic growth and what the World Bank called the 'East Asian miracle'. Domestically, the victory of the ruling coalition, Barisan Nasional (National Front), in the 1995 general election marked the summit of that hegemonic achievement. Globally, the regime's grandest ambitions were articulated in the form of the Multimedia Super Corridor, whose futuristic conception and bold promotion, rather than its subsequent operational difficulties, signalled the Mahathir regime's most self-assured ever interface with the world. The regime's exuberance (and Mahathir's personal confidence) was anchored in the unprecedented levels of material prosperity reached during this period. For the first time since independence in 1957, many Malaysians glowed in the pride of being Malaysian. Paradoxically, this sense of national unity, which had eluded the elites who headed the Alliance regimes until 1969, and the architects of the NEP, was attained under Mahathir, a politician once adulated by the Malays for being a 'Malay nationalist' and feared by non-Malays as a 'Malay ultra'.

However, the state's comfortable interface with the world was rudely unsettled as the speculative activities of the international money market brought the collapse of the Thai baht in July 1997, triggered an East Asian financial meltdown, and nearly derailed the Mahathirist project. In Malaysia, the meltdown pitted the state against the money market, each blaming the other for the 'loss of investor confidence' that depreciated the Malaysian ringgit, eroded the Kuala Lumpur Stock Exchange's market capitalization, and ended a decade of high growth. As the state-market conflict intensified, the Mahathir

Table 1.2 Political Events, Principal Outcomes and Significance, 1995-2002

Year(s)	Political event(s)	Principal outcome	Major significance
1995	General election	Barisan Nasional's triumph, DAP's defeat	Dominance of Vision 2020
1996	Angkatan Perpaduan Ummah split	Razaleigh and Semangat 46 return to UMNO	PAS threatened in Kelantan
1996	UMNO election	Mahathir and Anwar unchallenged	Anwar regarded as 'anointed successor'
1997	July: East Asian financial crisis	Depreciation, devaluation, disinvestment	State-market conflict, and recession
1998	1 September: capital controls	Capital controls and 'economic shield'	Policies of rescue, recapitalization, reflation
1998	2 September: Anwar's dismissal	Beginning of Anwar's persecution	Anwar calls for *Reformasi*
1998-99	November 1998 – April 1999: Anwar's first trial on charges of corruption	*Reformasi* protests amidst controversial trial proceedings	Anwar convicted and sentenced to 6 years' imprisonment
1999	Barisan Alternatif contests November general election	BN's victory but with major UMNO losses	UMNO's loss of Malay support; PAS returns to power in Kelantan and Trengganu
1999-2000	2nd Anwar trial on charges of sodomy	Continuing protests over equally controversial trial proceedings	Anwar convicted and sentenced to 9 years' imprisonment
2001	ISA arrests of Keadilan leaders and alleged KMM members; DAP-PAS differences; 'September 11'	Keadilan crippled, DAP leaves Barisan Alternatif	End of the alternative coalition
2002	Mahathir announces his intention to resign	UMNO compromise on Mahathir's departure	Transition to Abdullah Badawi's leadership

regime was alone in rejecting the money market's demands for reforms and the International Monetary Fund's (IMF) strategy for overhauling the financial systems of Thailand, Indonesia and South Korea. Chapter 3 charts the terrain of this conflict and explores the diminishing options available to the state to explain the Mahathir regime's decision to erect an 'economic shield' of capital controls and reflationary measures. As there was no proven case for or against the adoption of capital controls then, Mahathir made his decision based on his political intuition and the urgency of saving the nationalist-capitalist project. The regime succeeded with regards to the latter goal but, as Chapter 3 concludes, the temporary withdrawal from the money market, which was carried out on 1 September 1998, signified the end of Malaysia Inc. as the symbol of further capitalist rationalization under Mahathir.

The July 1997 crisis brought a dramatic sequel when Anwar Ibrahim was dismissed from office on 2 September 1998. Chapter 4 shows how Mahathir's bitter conflict with the market drew Anwar, Deputy Prime Minister and Finance Minister, into the fray. There were disastrous political consequences for Anwar and the senior technocrats of the central bank, Bank Negara Malaysia, as they acted to placate Mahathir and the market. On the one hand, the market condemned Mahathir's refusal to reform and wanted Mahathir out of office. On the other hand, Mahathir had no faith in Anwar's policies of reform while domestic political and corporate interests plotted to prevent Anwar from becoming Prime Minister. With the deepening crisis, unsatisfactory economics bred desperate politics. When an ill-disguised attempt mounted by Ahmad Zahid Hamidi, an Anwar ally, to criticize Mahathir for 'cronyism' and 'nepotism' at the 1998 Pemuda UMNO General Assembly failed, Zahid's move brought a counterattack that led to Anwar's fall.

Chapter 4 traces the Mahathir-Anwar split before the immediate events of 1997-98 and takes into account leadership transition difficulties within an UMNO that had been steadily wracked by factionalism since the 1970s. At the same time, Chapter 4 offers a longer view of Anwar's 30-year career of social activism and politics and reflects on Anwar's own contradictions and 'tragic inventions' that led him to confrontation with Mahathir in a time of crisis. Chapter 4 argues that strains of populist and divergent views of 'Asian values' had made Anwar a putative anti-Mahathirist before the calamities of 1997-98 took place.

The ejected Anwar was credibly and powerfully reinvented as the icon of *Reformasi*, a movement of dissent that took its name from the

Indonesian *Reformasi* that brought down Suharto's New Order regime in May 1998. The Malaysian *Reformasi* brought out the most sustained mass demonstrations of anti-regime sentiment in over a generation, although these outpourings of mass disaffection did not match its Indonesian precedent in scale, depth or quality. Chapter 5 provides a detailed analysis of the different meanings of *Reformasi* in Malaysia. At one level, *Reformasi* was an inchoate movement of cultural opposition. It was born of Malay revulsion at Anwar's maltreatment. At a second level, *Reformasi* was the site of dissident voices and alternative media of expression, communication and debate. Especially over the uncensored channels of the Internet, *Reformasi* supporters, individually or in groups, created new and rich forms of social criticism and political defiance. At a third level, *Reformasi* signified a massive erosion of the regime's hegemony over civil society.

The success of pre-crisis Mahathirist politics was contingent on three sets of premises: rapid growth and continued prosperity, nationalist vision and popular support, and strong leadership and managed succession. The July 1997 crisis challenged the regime's claim to being able to ensure rapid growth in pursuit of the prosperity promised by Vision 2020. Anwar's dismissal on 2 September 1998 damaged the leadership's legitimacy and threw UMNO's succession plan into disarray. After that came the tide of anti-Mahathir and anti-UMNO protests that undermined the regime's support and diminished its nationalist vision. In political terms, *Reformasi*'s dissent was real, even if it was amorphous. Since neither the political parties nor dissenting non-governmental organizations (NGOs) could stay aloof and hope to influence the course of such a movement of dissidence, the opposition parties and several NGOs joined efforts, first in the Majlis Gerakan Keadilan Rakyat (GERAK) and then in the Barisan Alternatif (BA). Both became the institutional vehicles for transforming *Reformasi*'s popular dissent into organized electoral opposition.

At the November 1999 election, BN triumphed over BA, but UMNO, the principal target of *Reformasi*, suffered electoral setbacks on a scale it last encountered in 1969. More than specific losses of seats, UMNO's real defeat lay in the readiness of half of the Malay electorate to contemplate installing a federal government that was not led by UMNO. Ironically, it was the solid non-Malay electoral support that sustained UMNO in many key 'ethnically mixed' constituencies. These electoral outcomes were historic developments that held enormous implications for future politics. A political flux seemed to have arisen in which all major parties had to reinvent themselves to survive or to advance. Chapter 5 shows how UMNO was unable to accomplish this task either by internal reform or by resorting to its time-honoured tactic of urging 'Malay unity' against imaginary non-Malay threats. The chapter concludes that *Reformasi* had exposed the fragility of UMNO's claim to being the source of hegemonic stability in the Malaysian political system.

At this juncture, a critical question was whether BA's four-party coalition (supported by a number of NGOs) could build upon the momentum of dissidence created by *Reformasi*. Chapter 6 maps the major post-election tensions between Parti Islam (Islamic Party, or PAS) and the Democratic Action Party (DAP), respectively the BA's most successful party, and and most disappointed party. Although the two parties' main disagreements revolved around PAS's pursuit of an 'Islamic state', they had other difficulties as well. In fact, DAP's difficulties may be traced to the changing character of non-Malay politics that had shifted emphases and sympathies during the Mahathir regime's triumphalist phase. In PAS's case, there was a bifurcation of its political programmes at the national level and at the level of the PAS-led state governments in Kelantan and Trengganu. Concurrently, the Parti Keadilan Nasional (National Justice Party, or Keadilan), the party most closely associated with the now imprisoned Anwar Ibrahim and the weak link in the BA chain, was subjected to relentless repression in 2000-2001. At the time of the 11 September 2001 attacks on the World Trade Center and the Pentagon, the DAP-PAS cooperation had terminated and the regime had incarcerated Keadilan's most energetic leaders without trial under the Internal Security Act. Other Keadilan leaders soon left the party because of internal disagreements or disenchantments. Hence, BA was virtually finished as a second coalition and an alternative front. The regime seemed to have won by repression and by default what it lost at the 1999 election.

Were *Reformasi* and BA then merely short-lived intrusions onto a political system that remains unchanged? The conclusion of Chapter 6 explores this question by locating BA's significance in a cultural imperative of coalition-building that has been peculiarly important to the political history of Malaysia's plural society. In any case, could so many crises involving political economy, undermining hegemony, invoking new strands of ideology, and inspiring novel forms of social experimentation have ended only in a restoration of pre-1998 politics? What are the social and political transitions that have taken place and what are the accompanying changes to the system? What implications might they bear for future politics in Malaysia? Collectively, however, such and other related questions became more pressing when Mahathir unexpectedly announced on 22 June 2002 his intention to resign as UMNO President and retire as Prime Minister.

From Chapter 2 to Chapter 6, each chapter bears its own appraisal of the transitions and changes that have taken place in the major areas discussed in the chapter. The final chapter, Chapter 7, concentrates on four issues that are particularly important in defining the principal directions of 'politics after Mahathir'.

First, there is the issue of leadership. During his long tenure, Mahathir exerted a pervasive influence over politics, policy-making and the state of public institutions. In addition, he attained a personalized form of hegemony based upon a seeming ability to project a grand vision for Malaysian society. Mahathir could accomplish this because of his own ideological and leadership qualities that the UMNO leaders waiting to take over from Mahathir do not possess.

Second, the matter of UMNO's factionalism is significant because it has always been broadly and intimately linked to an axis of discord in the Malay community that has been the source of much instability during the two decades of Mahathir's leadership of the party and the nation. Mahathir's own thoughts, initiatives and policies formed the basis of many of the ruling ideas, which a rising dominant class needed, but the problems of instability have lain with the NEP and Mahathirism's structural weakness of developing a party-bureaucracy-class axis that continually fractured. As Mahathir has been unable to secure the integrity of that axis for long, the issue is whether his successor(s) can restructure Malay capitalism and restore its links to state and UMNO sufficiently to prevent their problems from spilling over to UMNO as the terrain for intra-Malay conflict.

Third, there is the possibility of the secular Malaysian state and constitutional government being replaced by an 'Islamic state' administered under 'divine laws,' which was raised by PAS's rise and UMNO's setbacks in the November 1999 general election. It has since become an integral part of post-September 11 discourses on Islam and politics within Malaysia. Chapter 7 examines the obstacles that stand in PAS's way. The chapter also cautions that there are social conditions under which secular constitutional government, or public faith in it, may be undermined but not necessarily by PAS.

And, fourth, there is the riddle posed by Mahathir shortly after his announcement of resignation that the Malay community now faces a new or 'second Malay dilemma'. What does this re-formulation of the original 'Malay dilemma,' which Mahathir had pronounced to be no longer relevant, mean? Chapter 7, and the book, ends with an interpretation of this second Malay dilemma that links Mahathir's dire prognosis to the prospects of post-Mahathir political economy, and to past mass Malay interventions in Malaysian politics of which, I argue, Mahathir would be keenly aware.

I hope to give the reader a sense of social and political change that departs from mainstream interpretations and standard perceptions of politics in Malaysia as the 'ethnic politics' of a 'divided society'. The transitions of the past few years alone suggest that new ways of analysing politics in Malaysia are necessary in order to understand, much more grapple with, its future. These new ways of understanding rely in turn for guidance on the lessons of the historical conjuncture of 1997-98 that overturned so many assumptions about the immutability of ethnic politics, tried the regime's ability to resolve critical problems of political economy, tested the nationalist-capitalist project's constant need for a stable tripartite balance of power between the state, domestic capital and foreign capital, revealed the vitality of a cultural revolt based on discordant perceptions of 'Asian values' and inspired new struggles against the state's hegemony. The finest dimensions of these popular struggles are to be found in *Reformasi*'s popular re-interpretations of Malaysia's past and present, and its creativity of dissent, as well as the Barisan Alternatif's socio-political experiment.

I have not written this book as an academic exercise. While I have tried to conform my presentations and arguments to the demands of rigorous analysis, I have refrained from entering into academic or theoretical debates. Where it is instructive or useful for clarifying significant points or specific arguments, I have referred to existing academic analyses and other views. Otherwise, I have kept the use of endnotes and citations to a minimum, usually just enough to document the sources of direct quotations. Above all, I intend to engage the lay reader who has some knowledge of Malaysia's history, a grasp of its contemporary developments, a lively concern with its political future, and an intuitive appreciation that politics is too important to be left only to politicians or academic specialists.

Notes

[1] Quoted in 'A Vision for Malaysia: Interview with Prime Minister Mahathir', *Asiaweek*, 23 September 1983, p. 37.
[2] Quoted in 'When You Grow Old, You Face Reality', *Asiaweek*, 26 January 2001, p. 27.

2
The Projection of a Vision

> A new Asia is on the rise, and that is something only the blind and the deaf in mind would fail to notice. Asia cannot be stopped. This New Asia must continue to be an achieving Asia, a continent of progress, bringing massive and comprehensive development to all Asians. This new Asia must be a contributing Asia ... a mover and a shaker, not the object but the subject of international affairs, not a consequence but a cause. ...there must be an Asian Renaissance, a rebirth that will remake Asia and reshape the world.
>
> Mahathir Mohamad, Speech at the New Asia Forum,
> Kuala Lumpur, 11 January 1996

> It is probably fair to say that all organized societies in former times depended (in part) for their cohesion on visions of the past which were not too antagonistic to one another.... What is extremely hard to find in such visions is intense concern about the Future. When nationalism entered the world late in the eighteenth century, however, all this changed fundamentally.
>
> Benedict Anderson (2001)

What does it mean to be Malaysian? For most of the period since 1957, when the Federation of Malaya became an independent nation, the question was probably perplexing to its people and the answers unsatisfactory.

At the level of the nation-state, Malaya's experience with decolonization, which was formalized in the 'Merdeka constitution', did not overcome the ethnic divisions of its plural society. Within six years of independence, Malaya merged with Singapore, Sabah and Sarawak, producing Malaysia. The merger provoked many questions about the character of nationhood, not least due to challenges from abroad. The Philippines objected to the inclusion of Sabah, over which the former claimed a prior sovereignty. Indonesia detected hostile British and American imperialist designs in the Malaysia proposal and responded with *konfrontasi*. Singapore presented no small difficulty. The island's incorporation turned out to be only a brief interlude between its unnatural exclusion from the Federation of Malaya in 1948 and in 1957 (respectively when the federation was formed and when independence was attained) and its anomalous secession from Malaysia in 1965. Since then, Malaysia has congealed as a political unit, although there remains a gulf between 'Semenanjung' (Peninsula), and Sabah and Sarawak that no one knows how to bridge.

At the individual level, complex reasons tied to historical legacies, social divisions and political developments made it immensely difficult to internalize the idea of a Malaysian nationality conceived as a deeply felt and closely held identity. It was a historical irony that the three great currents of Asian nationalism, originating in China, India and Indonesia, had washed over colonial Malaya, without leaving in their wake any ideological synthesis that could truly be called Malaysian nationalism and sustained as such. In the absence of such an ideological synthesis, Malaysia's multicultural society, burdened by its once rigid ethnic division of labour, was easily swayed by insecure or self-serving perceptions of competition among the different races. Nor did the *Rukunegara*, the state ideology prescribed to ease the pain of the 13 May 1969 violence, engender a strong sense of social commonality. The *Rukunegara* was too contrived and superficial to capture the public imagination. Instead interethnic recrimination dominated the politics of the 1970s and 1980s when the implementation of the New Economic Policy (NEP) pitted, as it were, 'Malay nationalism' against 'non-Malay chauvinism'.

Constrained by these two sets of difficulties, 'being Malaysian' frequently took on an inward-looking stance that presupposed the necessity of maintaining national integrity and the desirability of attaining national unity. Considering the real and imagined needs to overcome the fissiparous tendencies of a plural society, it was assumed for a long time that to be Malaysian was to have an identity that was more than, or what comes to the same thing ironically, less than each of the ethnic identities into which Malaysians were born or with which they grew up.[1]

In the early to mid-1990s, however, the same question – what does it mean to be Malaysian? – was recast in unfamiliar ways so that its plausible answers were likewise novel. Then, Malaysians of different ethnicities, brought up, schooled and socialized almost without exception to think of themselves as Malays, Chinese, Indians and 'Others', and too often kept socially and culturally apart, were predisposed, in

Benedict Anderson's famous formulation, to 'imagine' themselves to be Malaysian. Arguably, this was the closest Malaysians had ever come to discovering a genuine pride in being Malaysian. This unexpected phenomenon not only took place shortly after a threat of interethnic violence had loomed in 1987 but also appeared to have been attributable primarily to the leadership of Mahathir, who had been adulated by Malays as a 'Malay nationalist' and feared by non-Malays as a 'Malay ultra' up to the 1970s.

What conditions produced this beguiling outcome? The answer to this question lay in the coming together of economic developments, political initiatives and ideological influences. This confluence emerged during the second decade of Mahathir's premiership and was signalled by a turning point in each of three areas: economics, politics and policies.

Three Turning Points

By the early 1990s, the Malaysian economy had visibly shrugged off its hangover from the economic recession of 1985-86. A trend of high economic growth averaging more than 8 per cent per year began in 1988 (8.9 per cent) and continued to 1996 (8.6 per cent). Net inflows of foreign direct investment were high for most years in the early 1990s, averaging RM3.19 billion per year for 1991-94, before declining to RM486 million for 1995-96. The economic recovery was variously attributed to Mahathir's privatization programmes, curbs on public spending, suspension of the NEP's restructuring requirements, liberalization of the conditions for foreign investment, and attraction of East Asian foreign direct investment.

By the early 1990s, the social effects of the high growth were widely felt. The official unemployment rate fell from over 8.7 per cent in 1986 to less than 4 per cent in 1992 (and to 2.5 per cent in 1996). Generally, there was a rise in income and living standards, and an extensive spread of consumption. Consequently, Mahathir's and Finance Minister Daim Zainuddin's management of the national economy was applauded within and outside Malaysia. Naturally, the loudest praise for Mahathir came from UMNO members, his coalition partners in the Barisan Nasional (BN), the captains of commerce and industry who had benefited most from cooperating with the state, and a mass media linked to major political and commercial interests.

Mahathir's leadership was credited with the turnaround from the difficult days of the 1980s for a compelling reason: Malaysians could not recall a time of greater prosperity. A regional magazine was led to say, rather fawningly, that 'the Malays, like Malaysia's other ethnic groups, are enjoying their greatest period of prosperity since the days of the Malacca Sultanate'![2] The major exceptions in this general experience of material well-being were marginalized minorities, typically of 'native' or Orang Asli origin, and a new underclass of foreign, legal and illegal, unskilled and semi-skilled labour.

In the early 1990s, Mahathir won his political battles over his major foes. Between 1987 and 1990, Mahathir's political survival hung in the balance when he was challenged by Tengku Razaleigh Hamzah within UMNO, in the courts, and again via Parti Semangat 46 (Spirit of '46 Party, or S46). At the 1990 general election, however, BN scored a notable victory over two opposition coalitions formed separately from S46, the Democratic Action Party (DAP), Parti Islam SeMalaysia (Islamic Party, or PAS), the Parti Bersatu Sabah (Sabah United Party), Parti Rakyat Malaysia, and other minor parties. The BN's victory strengthened Mahathir's leadership beyond foreseeable challenge.

Aside from the political parties, the Malay rulers who had fought Mahathir to a stalemate during the Constitutional crisis of 1983-84 were soundly defeated in 1992 when Mahathir and the BN-dominated Parliament seized upon the Sultan of Johor's assault on a hockey coach to enact legislation that partially removed royal immunity from prosecution or legal suits. For a few years during the mid-1980s, the judiciary had unwittingly served as an independent terrain for contention between the executive branch of government and a range of political dissidents, and between conflicting factions within UMNO. But after the impeachment and dismissal of the Lord President of the Supreme Court and two other Supreme Court judges in 1988, the judiciary accommodated itself to a regime of executive supremacy.

Many of the non-governmental organizations that had forged solidarity movements during the 1980s to protest the many crises and scandals associated with Mahathir's administration remained active but they had to make do without the wider support they enjoyed before 1990.

These political developments were proof of Mahathir's determination and ability to remain in power and signs of an increasing concentration of power in the executive. But, crucially for Malaysians who had lived through the crises and tumult of Mahathir's first decade in office, the same developments signified a much-needed return to normalcy.

There was a third turning point related to national development policy. For two decades, the year 1990 – when the NEP was scheduled

The Projection of a Vision

for termination – had cast rancour over ethnic relations, as no one knew whether the NEP would or should be extended. In late 1986, in response to the recession, Mahathir had taken a political risk by deciding to 'hold NEP in abeyance'. Yet neither he nor any other leading politician had set official directions for post-1990 development policies.

When a new National Development Policy (NDP) and its accompanying Second Outline Perspective Plan, 1991-2000 were finally promulgated in 1991, they more or less resolved the question of the NEP's termination. The NDP would implicitly retain some measure of the NEP's two basic objectives of 'poverty eradication irrespective of race' and 'restructuring to abolish the identification of race with economic function'. Of the two objectives, the 'affirmative action' objective of 'restructuring' Malaysian society had been more contentious by far, and it had continually provoked suspicion and recrimination between the Malay and non-Malay communities..

In Mahathir's assessment, however, the NEP had accomplished much since 1970, especially when the NEP's progress was measured against the record of failed social engineering elsewhere in the world. With no small measure of satisfaction, Mahathir noted that 'when all is said and done, the NEP must be acknowledged as one of the greatest policies of independent Malaysia, enabling it to prosper without the blatant injustices of a totally materialistic society'.[3] In particular, there had been significant Malay advancement, measured by the NEP's own criteria. The Malay share of corporate ownership had risen from about two per cent in 1969 to just over 20 per cent in 1990, while state-owned enterprises holding assets 'in trust' for the Malays and private Malay companies dominated the commanding heights of the economy. The extent of the 'abolition of the identification of race with economic function', conceived more broadly, was already evident from the emergence of an economically and politically influential Bumiputera Commercial and Industrial Community (BCIC), a combination of Malay capitalists, professionals and middle class elements.

Mahathir argued that the BCIC should no longer require further state-imposed quantitative boosts in their share ownership, business, educational and employment opportunities. It was necessary, though, for BCIC members to acquire management and entrepreneurial skills and fortify themselves with a value system that would raise 'the quality of their participation in the economy'[4] and render their participation 'permanent [and] sustainable'.[5] The BCIC, Mahathir enjoined, had to reject the temptation of an 'indiscriminate distribution of wealth which [was] immediately frittered away' because that would only cause 'lasting damage by creating a very dependent society which [could] not manage without continuous government support'.[6] Instead the BCIC had to demonstrate a capacity to 'retain their share', 'force themselves to learn and learn fast', and 'go fully into the marketplace to compete'.[7] Here, Mahathir introduced a critical distinction between the state's past and current perspectives on restructuring. Whereas the NEP's 'stress on quantity had resulted in Bumiputeras owning 100 per cent of continuously losing companies', the NDP's insistence on the 'quality of participation' meant that 'they will be better off owning 10 per cent of profitable companies'.[8] However else that point could have been interpreted, Mahathir's argument held out the promise of meaningful Malay-non-Malay business cooperation in which 'non-Bumiputera partners must find genuine Bumiputera partners willing to risk their capital and involve themselves in the day-to-day running of the business'.[9] Commenting on the structure and performance of the urban retail sector, for example, Mahathir urged that 'Bumiputera retailers should … de-emphasize their Bumiputera character and aim for the larger market'.[10]

It was a cautious way of implying that 'the NEP is no more', which was exactly what Mahathir said a few years later, after he had revealed not just a new policy but also a fresh vision.

Nationalism and Regionalism: Vision 2020 and 'Asian Values'

Whether one was an enthusiastic Malay supporter or, conversely, a suspicious non-Malay critic, of the NEP, one could argue even then that an NDP free of ethnic quotas could potentially pave the way for Malay gains exceeding the NEP's original targets. That this line of argument was not made explicit was evidence of Mahathir's success in recasting the future of Malaysian political economy and society in post-NEP terms. Or, as Mahathir outlined in a paper, 'The Way Forward', Malaysia's future lay in a new national goal of attaining 'developed country status' by the year 2020. By 'developed country status', he meant Malaysia's eventual membership in the club of rich, modern and advanced economies. Economically, this goal was predicated on steady growth averaging 7 per cent per year over the next 30 years. It was an ambitious target but, in Mahathir's view, an achievable challenge and not wishful thinking. By raising the average annual rate of growth by 0.1 per cent – from 6.9 per cent over the previous two decades – the Gross Domestic Product would double every ten years and make Malaysians in 2020 'four times richer in real terms' than they were in 1990. In 'The Way Forward', Mahathir dwelt upon Malaysia's structural transformation from its previous dependence on primary commodity production to having an industrialized economy that could advance towards post-industrial conditions.

Mahathir's articulation of this new 2020 goal of achieving developed country status in 30 years was a tacit admission that the NEP's long-term goal of national unity had to some extent been reached. Certainly Mahathir's statement was immediately understood by most Malaysians to be a significant departure from the old NEP concerns. Probably buoyed by his own recent triumphs, Mahathir was only a little short of being infectiously optimistic about reaching this 2020 goal. Yet, neither Mahathir's optimism, nor mere national pride over past achievement, nor any crass anticipation of future wealth could adequately explain how this Mahathirist agenda, packaged as *Wawasan 2020* or Vision 2020, came to seize the popular imagination in Malaysia. Within a short period, Vision 2020 was ideologically dominant in a way that no one was likely to have foreseen. At the 1993 UMNO party election, for instance, Vice-President Anwar Ibrahim led Najib Tun Razak, Muhammad Muhammad Taib, Muhyiddin Yassin and Rahim Tamby Chik in forming a 'Wawasan Team' to edge out the incumbent Deputy President Ghafar Baba, and Vice-Presidents Abdullah Ahmad Badawi and Sanusi Junid. The success of the Wawasan Team reflected a rather slick extraction of political advantage out of the popularity of Vision 2020. In the 1990s, it also became fashionable for shops and commercial enterprises to incorporate 'wawasan' or 'vision' or '2020' in their names or the brand names of their products. This was a mundane but telling example of how deeply Vision 2020 had reached into Malaysian society. It was inconceivable that anyone would have named a business after the NEP or *Rukunegara*.

Not everything about Vision 2020 was new or novel. Much of it came from earlier Mahathirist ideas, as *Paradoxes of Mahathirism* explained. In ideological terms, however, the popularity of Vision 2020 owed a great deal to its subtle negotiation between past, present and future which somehow, in Mahathir's own words, 'articulated the best aspirations of our citizens', 'shifted the mindset of our nation from less productive pastures to the making of a more promising future', and 'pointed to where we needed to go as a nation'.[11] In John Hilley's insightful expression, Vision 2020 '*contextualise*[d] popular understandings of modernisation, social mobility and cross-ethnic prosperity as part of an "inclusive" national framework',[12] thus helping the regime to build 'a strong popular association between the *idea* of "collective economic development" and Vision 2020 as a signifier of future rewards'.[13] Six years after presenting 'The Way Forward', Mahathir claimed, with justification, that 'the unity of the Malaysian people behind Vision 2020 is historic and unprecedented' because Vision 2020 had

> laid to rest the gremlins that lurked within the darkest corridors of our history. It settled many of the unresolved issues of the past. It took from our backs some very heavy baggage of history which had greatly hindered us in the past.[14]

It was then that Mahathir categorically pronounced that 'the NEP is no more'. Vision 2020, he explained,

> made perfectly clear what Malaysians needed to do in our second generation as an independent country, so that this present generation of Malaysians will be the last generation of Malaysians to live in a society that is called 'developing'.[15]

Not all the rhetoric of Vision 2020 was Mahathir's. The public, too, accepted the 2020 challenges to be theirs as well. But in a curious tribute to Mahathir's ability to articulate popular aspirations, mainstream public imagination regarded the vision to be Mahathir's and his alone. Thus one might say that 'Mahathir's vision' gave the NEP an almost perfect way to end, not with a bang as was often feared, nor a whimper over 'many unresolved issues', but with a collective intuition, *pace* Albert Camus, that Malaysian society's 'real generosity towards the future lies in giving all to the present'.[16] Somehow Malaysians were inspired by Vision 2020 to discover their ability to imagine themselves as a community, and to do so with a sense of the 'ineradicable Goodness of the nation'.[17]

Yet it took more than the terminology of Vision 2020 to intoxicate many sections of Malaysian society, and especially the business, professional and middle-classes to whose vastly improved socio-economic conditions Vision 2020 spoke most directly and forcefully. Had Mahathir's vision been disembodied from the historical context in which Vision 2020 was propagated, it would have sounded like the bravura of many an underachieving leader of an underdeveloped country. But the prosperity of the 1990s supplied the material base needed to authenticate Mahathir's vision and help the Mahathirist agenda gain an unparalleled hegemonic effect. It was not only the already rich owners and controllers of public companies who became extremely wealthy by speculating and cashing in on the Kuala Lumpur Stock Exchange's (KLSE) ascent to giddying heights, beginning in late

1992 and continuing the whole of 1993. Under the spell of an unprecedentedly strong bull run, many ordinary Malaysians who had cash to punt speculated on the stock market. They thereby joined and frequently boosted the transformation of speculative investment into outright gambling. Along the way, they quickly absorbed the vernacular of the market. They learnt to talk of corporate captains and helmsmen, of their fleets and flagships, and institutional buyers and foreign funds. They exchanged news and rumours of mergers and takeovers, and of Initial Public Offerings and Second Board listings. They kept track of trading days and margin calls, volumes, yields and P/E ratios, and so on. With gusto they lived the beneficence of dazzling wealth effects issuing from every kind of market as economic growth averaged an annual rate of growth of 8.6 per cent from 1991 to early 1997. The share market soared, the property market boomed, and the market for durable goods expanded to the extent that, for example, used cars could cost as much as new ones when demand for the Proton cars outstripped the manufacturer's capacity to supply the 'national car'.

Never before had consumption been so widely democratized in the country. It seemed that never before had so many Malaysians 'had it so good' such that 'many Malaysians in the mid-1990s saw nothing else but wealth'.[18] Among young professionals, for example, it was accepted if not axiomatic that economic opportunities in Malaysia were so abundant and lucrative that offshore employment in places like Singapore (hitherto a favoured destination for young graduates and skilled workers) and beyond was no longer alluring. At lower levels in the tightening domestic labour market, the availability of semi-skilled and unskilled work drew increasing numbers of migrant labour, from the Southeast Asian region primarily, into the Malaysian economy. In social terms, the upper classes, middle-class families, and small-scale commercial enterprises, including family-operated informal sector businesses, profited from easy and affordable access to low-wage foreign domestic help and service labour. From another angle, the private sector was privileged as the engine of growth, the source of high remuneration and the site for building fast-track careers. 'Social perceptions of wealth, power and the good life,' observed Halim Salleh,

> suddenly took a new turn: traditional dependence on the government gave way to the material gains promised by the private sector. Private employment and business ventures acquired a new sense of elevated social status.[19]

Graduates and professionals who were likely to think of themselves as being the 'best and brightest' shunned the once prestigious civil service. Indeed more and more senior civil servants, including academicians, who were eligible for 'optional retirement' (then set at the young age of 40) were themselves encouraged to leave the public sector for new corporate or business careers. And if some politicians' claims were to be believed, Malaysia's success was even tempting many 'NEP emigrés'[20] to gaze longingly homeward. At different layers of society, then, the public mood was pervaded by so much optimism and such a strong sense of economic well-being that it was hardly believable that Malaysian society had been wracked by a serious recession only a few years earlier. At times, it seemed as if Mahathir was right to claim that inflation could be reduced to 'zero' amidst high growth,[21] that the economy would not overheat, and that nothing was fortuitous about its achievements.

In short, it appeared as if Malaysia was capable of extraordinary feats, especially when its economic performance basked in the world historical significance of East Asia's extraordinary industrial accomplishments. Malaysia's booming stock market had caused it to be included among the emerging markets whose potential profitability excited global investment fund managers. The Malaysian economy was favourably named in the World Bank's loud proclamation of an 'East Asian Miracle'. The country itself was part of Asia that some observers believed would dominate the world in the 3rd Millenium (by the western calendar). In the prevailing discourses of markets, states and regions, which focused on the continued ascent of Asia, Mahathir defined for Malaysian society an ambivalent position. On the one hand, Mahathir's deep suspicion of western perfidy extended to acts of economic labelling such that 'western' characterizations of South Korea, Taiwan, Hong Kong and Singapore as 'newly-industrializing countries' (NICs) did not impress him at all. On the contrary, he regarded those labels to be part of a ploy to deprive the East Asian NICs of the USA's GSP concessions. The World Bank's ebullience did not move Mahathir either. He kept insisting that no miracle had materialized beyond the hard-earned outcome of careful planning allied to the 'old fashioned way' of depending on a great deal of 'toil, tears and sweat'[22] on the part of East Asians, including Malaysians. Likewise, he rejected any prediction that the 21st century would be an 'Asian century' – 'a tantalizing idea which is most appealing to the Asian ego' but was in fact 'the Yellow Peril all over again, only this time there are tinges of brown'.[23] For Mahathir, predictions of Asian domination only served to justify western trade protectionism and other economic forms of ill will towards the Asian region.

On the other hand, Mahathir himself took too much pride in the reality and continued promise of Asian success not to lend credence to certain Asian elite and popular notions of the supposed superiority of an East Asian model of development that had bred so many robust 'tiger economies'. The diplomatic expression of that pride was a Malaysian proposal to form an East Asian Economic Group (EAEG) that would more directly articulate the economic interests of Asian countries than the Asia-Pacific Economic Cooperation (APEC) framework that was dominated by the USA and other Pacific rather than Asian nations. But opposition within APEC, primarily from the USA, compelled Malaysia to whittle the EAEG proposal down to an ineffectual East Asian Economic Caucus (EAEC). Mahathir was left to express his faith in Asian competitiveness, and to urge that 'it's time Asia be accorded due respect'[24] via the ideological construct of 'Asian values', of supposedly non-western values, that he claimed were responsible for Asia's success and stability. Mahathir's arguments, together with Lee Kuan Yew's views on Asian culture, promptly provoked an international 'Asian values debate' during the mid-1990s. With minor differences in emphases, Mahathir and other proponents of 'Asian values' fastened on a well-rehearsed litany of values.[25] They contended that Asians demonstrated, as it were, a cultural predisposition towards stable leadership rather than political pluralism, preferring continuity to change in government. They suggested, too, that Asians had an intuitive respect for authority and social harmony, and showed a proclivity to consensus as opposed to a tendency towards dissent or confrontation. The point was often extended to suggest that Asians, therefore, preferred a strong, even harsh, government, so long as the government's policies and actions continued to deliver economic prosperity. Thus, Asian leaders such as Mahathir and Lee Kuan Yew maintained that Asians not only tolerated but welcomed a broad and penetrating state and bureaucratic intervention in social and economic affairs because Asians had a greater concern for economic well-being instead of a presumed western preoccupation with civil liberties and human rights. Finally, Asians were supposedly communitarian, not individualist, and accepted that the welfare and collective good of the community took precedence over individual rights. Such values then formed the moral underpinnings of the East Asian model of development.

In the 'Asian values' debate, which involved politicians, ideologues, activists, academics, and journalists, many pointed and telling criticisms were levelled at the ideational validity of 'Asian values' and their crude deployment by authoritarian regimes in Asia. Yet the real significance of the discourse of 'Asian values' lay neither in epistemology nor anthropology but in political ideology. Japan's economy had begun to slide at the beginning of the 1990s, but, no matter, the East Asian elites maintained a secure belief in the region's greatness. Any claim that certain values were immanently, immutably and uniquely Asian can readily be shown to be contrived and flawed. Even so, the Asian elites needed to anchor their beliefs in a populist cultural-philosophical commonality that would gloss over, even if it could not bridge, Asian diversities. Malaysian society was probably not much moved by one or another variant of 'Asian values'. But deluged with repetitive references to Asian dragons and tigers, values and work ethics, models and miracles, and exhortations to draw 'lessons from Japan', 'lessons from South Korea' and 'lessons from Taiwan', Malaysian society was moved by sentiments of Asian triumphalism to discern common cause if not shared destiny with the East Asian high achievers. In that milieu, coincidental rather than crafted, 'Asian values' could serve Asia the way that Vision 2020 served Malaysia.[26] And with Mahathir articulating both ideological strands, it was just plausible in the public imagination to fuse a novel Malaysian nationalism with an incipient Asian regionalism, and to ally a 'Can Do' Malaysia with 'The Asia That Can Say No'.[27]

Henceforth, the nationalist ambition of the one was vindicated by the regionalist triumphalism of the other: Malaysia had a bright future inasmuch as the future belonged to Asia.

Hegemonic Interlude: The 1995 General Election

Before that, the immediate future of Malaysian politics belonged to Mahathir. The April 1995 general election amply proved this in two ways. First, the 1995 election results essentially marked the end of an era of NEP politics that was conducted at very high levels of interethnic disputes. Second, the BN's huge victory, which erased almost all the opposition's gains in 1986 and 1990, was widely regarded to be Mahathir's personal triumph.

During the 1970s and 1980s, the Malaysian political scene was marked by very high levels of interethnic disputes that were linked to the NEP's implementation and cultural disputes continuing from an earlier period. These political disputes reached their height in the August 1986 general election and grew to alarming proportions in late

1987. The disputes spilled into the 1990 election although that election was more complex, given UMNO's split in 1987 and the persistent challenge of Tengku Razaleigh Hamzah and the UMNO dissidents to Mahathir's continued leadership. But in the post-NEP and new Vision 2020 socio-economic environment, interethnic recrimination had steadily diminished because of several factors. The high rates of growth, the accompanying prosperity, and the policy shift to NDP had collectively removed or reduced the immediate economic sources of interethnic contention. Moreover, Mahathir's regime introduced some measures of liberalization and reform in tertiary education, including the corporatization of public universities, privatization of new colleges, and deregulation of the tertiary education sector. These measures expanded opportunities for tertiary education and reduced disputes over the NEP-justified ethnic quotas for admission into public universities. It was typical of the changed policy emphases of the time that these measures, facilitated by the passage of the Higher Education Act 1994, were justified on pragmatic grounds of quickening human resource development to meet labour market requirements and improving the quality of graduates and professionals to service national needs.

A similar sentiment of pragmatism was expressed in areas that were previously susceptible to controversy, namely, language, and the Chinese schools. When he was the Minister of Education in the 1970s, Mahathir had played a central role in implementing the national policy of using the Malay language as the sole medium of instruction in the national school system and public universities. Two decades after its implementation, the national language policy had no detractors but there was worry in various political, administrative and corporate quarters that Malaysian standards of English had seriously declined. Mahathir wanted to amend the national language policy to broaden and deepen the use of the English language in the schools and universities. Once again, he offered practical reasons for re-emphasizing the use of English, chiefly the need to conduct diplomacy and international commerce, to keep apace with scientific knowledge and technological advancement, and to stay Information Technology-literate. However, Mahathir's plan to revive the use of English could not be implemented systematically, owing to opposition from Malay 'linguistic nationalists'. However, the private colleges whose students were predominantly non-Malay were permitted to teach in English, especially where their programmes involved twinning arrangements with foreign institutions. Finally, there was an unanticipated enrolment of non-Chinese pupils, and predominantly Malay pupils at that, in the Chinese-language schools. In 1995, there was an estimated 35,000 of these pupils. The non-Chinese parents who sent their children to Chinese schools generally believed that the Chinese schools were more disciplined, and offered superior instruction in the 'difficult subjects' of mathematics and science, and hence gave their students better preparation for a future in which the public sector was no longer the principal employer. Given the tumultuous history of the politics of Chinese education, and the bitter debates over the national language policy, the steadily rising but uncontroversial enrolment of Malay children in Chinese schools indicated a change in ethnic relations that was inconceivable during the NEP era.[28] To the extent that ethnic differences and cultural grievances in Malaysia had always had an economic element to them, Mahathir's economic and pragmatic solutions to cultural problems had combined to defuse ethnic squabbles over issues of language, tertiary educational quotas for students of different communities, and the Chinese independent schools.

After the 1990 general election, organized political dissent was located in three major centres – the states of Sabah and Kelantan, and the large urban Chinese-majority constituencies. In Sabah, the staunch support of a Kadazadusun-Chinese alliance had permitted the Parti Bersatu Sabah (PBS) to be in power for a decade since 1984. Sabah's politics had taken on an ethno-regionalist edge because of local resistance to federal encroachment, the rise of Kadazandusun (broadly non-Muslim bumiputera) consciousness, and the reconstitution of the main Muslim bumiputera parties into the Sabah UMNO.[29] The basic Muslim-non-Muslim bumiputera polarization left the non-Muslim and non-bumiputera Chinese in between. The state of Kelantan was ruled by the coalition of Parti Islam (PAS) and Parti Semangat 46 (S46) that had completely shut out UMNO in the state in 1990. Kelantan's politics was almost entirely Malay politics that was variously tied to PAS's Islamic idiom, S46's reversion to Malay causes, and UMNO's claim to represent the ethnic and religious concerns of the Malays. The Democratic Action Party (DAP), although not in government anywhere, had emerged as the leading opposition party. Its strength lay in the large urban Chinese-majority constituencies of Peninsular Malaysia (notably Penang) that played an intricate game of swinging between the ruling coalition and the opposition, depending on the voters' calculations of local economic interests and reactions to the prevailing climate of ethnic relations.

By the February 1994 state election in Sabah, the combined Kadazandusun and Chinese opposition had been divided and weakened to the point that PBS was ousted from its ten-year hold on power by a combination of repression, losses in the state elections and subsequent defections to the UMNO-led BN. By the time of the 1995 general election, UMNO had won back eight seats in Kelantan. PAS still held 24 seats and S46 had eleven. But the PAS-S46 coalition was on the verge of collapse, and just one year later, PAS's position became precarious when S46 was dissolved and Mahathir's formerly strongest rival, Razaleigh Hamzah, led his followers back to UMNO.[30] However, the most spectacular result of the 1995 election was the DAP's loss of eleven of the twenty parliamentary seats it won in 1990. This rout was caused by the desertion of several of its strongholds traditionally rooted in the largest urban Chinese-majority constituencies. In Penang, where the non-Malay electorate was all but ready to hand the state government to the opposition in 1990, the DAP lost thirteen of its fourteen state assembly seats. From being three seats short of forming the Penang state government in 1990, the DAP was left with only one seat. In sharp contrast, the DAP's chief rival for Chinese electoral support, the Malaysian Chinese Association (MCA), which had lost every contest in Penang in 1990 as the non-Malay electorate vented its anger upon this oldest of UMNO partners, won all nine of its contests in 1995. On the whole, the BN won its highest ever share of the popular vote (63 per cent compared with 53 per cent in 1990) and its most dominant control ever of Parliament (84 per cent of parliamentary seats). The results of the 1994 Sabah election and the 1995 general election did not mark the end of ethnic politics. Voting behaviour could not but be influenced by ethnic issues and interests as long as the electoral system was constituted along ethnic lines. Yet the PBS's defeat, the PAS-S46's setbacks, and the DAP's rout marked the declining appeal of older forms of ethnic dissent. Deprived of any contention over the NEP's restructuring, quotas for university admissions, language issues, and Chinese schools, even former supporters of the opposition preferred 'a shift from ethnicism to developmentalism', in Francis Loh's words.[31] And Vision 2020 was nothing if not seductively developmentalist.

The 1995 election, the biggest victory in BN's fourth electoral battle under his command, was a personal triumph for Mahathir. Already the longest serving prime minister, Mahathir became a politician who had no rival, whose vision of the future faced no competition and in whose heir the public had not yet shown much interest. The election in a way brought to a close the era of NEP politics. The ethnic acrimony that almost erupted into violence in October 1987 was mostly forgotten. The overt manipulation of ethnic grievances, too, became less habitual among politicians of both the ruling coalition and the opposition parties. Instead there was hopeful and not just propagandistic talk of the unifying goals of Vision 2020.

Even the Muslim and Chinese calendars lent a hand so to speak. For three years, from 1995 to 1997, there was a rare coincidence of the Muslim New Year and the Chinese New Year. Upon this coincidence was bestowed the catchy term of *Gong Xi Raya* (formed from combining the Muslim *Hari Raya* and the Chinese New Year greeting, *Gong Xi Fa Cai*), thus capturing a fortuitous conversion of the old weakness of ethnic differences into the new strength of multicultural diversity. Subtly but significantly, Malaysian society shed some of its past tendencies towards communalism. The society had gained a form of communitarianism expressed in a Mahathirist ethos of competitive national capitalism joined to an inclusive, that is, Malaysian and not merely Malay nationalism.[32] To the degree that domestic politics was influenced by international events, the ethos of a competitive national capitalism was captivating in the heyday of the 'East Asian Miracle', while the inclusive nationalism was eminently sensible in the light of the terrible ethnic wars in the collapsed former Soviet bloc.

During the immediate post-colonial years, nationhood was to have been the lynchpin of the Alliance's rule but it remained an elusive state. Subsequently, national unity was the ultimate goal of the NEP architects but that, too, was abstract and distant. Under Mahathir in the mid-1990s, nationhood and national unity were as close to being attained as they ever would be. Deputy Prime Minister Anwar Ibrahim might have been liberal with his rhetoric when he pitched his own slogan, *wo men dou shi yi jia ren* ('we are one family')[33] but perhaps not by much.

The Futurism of the Multimedia Super Corridor

If there was one thing Mahathir was persistently anxious to sell to his 'family', it was its future place in the sun, to use an old Mahathir plea, or its niche in a borderless world, to employ the jargon of the day.

On this matter, Mahathir's salesmanship gained a boost from his excitement in technology, especially when the technology was embodied in things that moved: motorcycles, cars, sea-borne vessels, and aircraft. For example, and whether it was to show his mastery of big machines, or his social status, or perhaps both, Mahathir used to ride a Harley-Davidson motorcycle, and he drove a Pontiac when he was a doctor in Alor Star. As Prime Minister, he appeared genuinely delighted to be photographed behind the steering wheels of cars or trucks and even go-karts. Otherwise, Mahathir would happily board ships and yachts, or sit in the cockpits of airplanes. He did not have a pilot's licence but he let it be known he could fly an airplane. Always one to think of spin-offs, Mahathir had initiated the Langkawi International and Maritime Aerospace exhibitions as part of promoting Langkawi as a tourist destination. Adjacent to the new Kuala Lumpur International Airport, the Sepang International Circuit would in time provide a track for Formula 1 races.

More to the point, the Prime Minister was no technophobe, unlike some of his colleagues or subordinates who stayed away from machines or showed no feel for computers. Mahathir remains a technophile whose interest and faith in technology had found earlier expression in the heavy industrialization he had promoted, although to no great success. In short, whereas Malaysian politicians and bureaucrats tended to rehearse their lines about science, technology, R&D and innovations with no conviction, a technology-embracing Mahathir personified the future, at a mere remove from the 3rd Millenium, when a crucial part of being futuristic was to be empowered by Information Technology (IT).

Hence, *Cintai IT!* (Love IT!) – as the state soon exhorted its citizens via public radio and television. No one who loves IT could have helped loving the Multimedia Super Corridor (MSC) which was planned to have the 'world's best physical infrastructure' and to 'leapfrog available information infrastructure':

> the MSC is physically a 15 [km wide]-by-50 km long corridor that runs from the world's tallest buildings, the Kuala Lumpur City Centre, in itself an intelligent precinct, down to what will be the region's largest airport when it opens in 1998. This piece of real estate is almost a greenfield site for the building of state-of-the-art cities and systems. Half-way between the KLCC and the Kuala Lumpur International Airport will be two cities; one, the new administrative capital of Malaysia [Putrajaya], and the other a cyber city where we will locate industries, R&D facilities, a Multimedia University and institutions, and operational quarters for multinational corporations to direct their worldwide manufacturing and trading activities using multimedia.[34]

Conceptually, MSC followed the bold 'premise' of eventually bringing into being:

> a multicultural web of mutually dependent international and Malaysian companies collaborating to deliver new products and new services across an economically vibrant Asia and beyond. And like a spider, it will weave

ever more intricate webs of relationships and synergies amongst participating countries. Such a web could be the new model of development for the Information Age.[35]

To facilitate the operations of the MSC's corporate residents, the state would institute the 'world's best soft infrastructure' – a 'comprehensive framework of societal and commerce-enabling cyber laws on intellectual property, digital signatures, computer crime, distance learning, telemedicine and electronic government'.[36] For that matter, and while speaking to a highly courted American audience, Mahathir, himself never known to be a promoter of civil rights domestically, offered a 'ten-point Multimedia Bill of Guarantees' for companies receiving MSC status from the project's 'fully empowered one-stop shop', the Multimedia Development Corporation.[37]

It was typical of Mahathir's devotion to the task of selling Malaysia as an investment centre around the world that, in the terminology used by public relations consultants, he energetically went on a 'roadshow' to 'showcase' the MSC to foreign investors and university audiences. Besides, it was prescient of Mahathir to invite to the MSC's International Advisory Panel some of the world's best, brightest and richest IT operators and innovators. Like an indefatigable salesman, Mahathir stressed just about every conceivable quality that Malaysia – state and society – possessed to ensure the MSC's success. For example, a three-decade experience of interfacing national developmental priorities with changes in the global structure of industrial production demonstrated the state's ability to plan with care and its financial capability to execute long-term master plans. That the state and FDI had had a mutually satisfying partnership was proven by Malaysia's record in attracting and expanding the scope of export-oriented industrialization in the export processing zones. Even Malaysia's ethnic differences were no longer a liability but an important strength that was to be pressed into the service of promoting the MSC. Malaysia's 'multicultural, multilingual and multiethnic environment … [d]rawn from many Asian civilizations', imparted a 'unique vitality to Malaysian life' and would support 'multicultural links with the biggest Asian markets' to the benefit of companies whose activities (including multilingual publishing or telemedicine) combined many forms of western and non-western knowledge.[38]

Of course, Mahathir followed custom in this kind of campaign by offering investment incentives to foreign investors who would locate or relocate their businesses within the MSC. But even if Mahathir was sometimes coy in his rhetoric before industry leaders, major players and other people whose opinions and decisions mattered, his marketing of the MSC avoided mimicking the pathetically plaintive manner of a typical effort by an underdeveloped host country to offer FDI yet another package of Third World comparative advantages. And even though 'Malaysia is quite conscious that it is not the master of leading edge technologies in any field',[39] Mahathir advertised the MSC with an imagination that was indicative of the confidence with which Mahathirist nationalism was projecting itself before the rest of the world. 'Other plans may sound similar because all of them use "IT", "Cyber" or "Multimedia"',[40] Mahathir cautioned, but only the MSC was 'truly a world first'. At a historic juncture, when the world was poised 'on the threshold of the cyber revolution'; when the road to the information age, digital economy, e-commerce, borderless marketing, the wireless telecommunications industry, and so on, would have to be paved with 'intelligent multimedia'; and when the 'death throes of the industrial era ethos and the birth of another' cried out for a 'giant test bed for experimenting with not only multimedia technology but ... the evolution of a new way of life in the unfolding age of information and technology', Mahathir presented MSC as Malaysia's 'gift to the world'.[41]

Much of the MSC's conceptual content and interest can be traced to Mahathir's own and his regime's concerns that Malaysia had reached the limits of FDI-driven export-oriented industrialization, in terms of what the latter required from or could offer the national economy. Post-Cold War conditions, illustrated by the global market's continual revision of its criteria of national attractiveness, showed signs that Malaysia's openness might not remain a competitive advantage for long. New economic directions and policies might be necessary to achieve further transfers of foreign technology, say, or an indigenous climb up the technological ladder. In any case, the economy could not be allowed to languish in its previous successes in manufacturing computer components and assembling electronic goods. By the calculations of Mahathir and his planners who formulated the two Industrial Master Plans, the Malaysian economy had to shift along a service-based post-industrial direction towards the more lucrative pre- and post-production phases within a value added chain. In practical terms, the MSC, the icon of that directional shift, would accommodate a massive hothouse for R&D work, technological innovation, software engineering, and the development of new IT-based service industries.

The MSC would simultaneously serve as a 'pilot project for harmonizing our entire country with the global forces shaping the Information Age'.[42] Within the ambit of Vision 2020, therefore, an MSC-wired

Malaysia would leapfrog its manufacturing economy into a post-industrial society. The Mahathir regime's presentations of the MSC before international audiences in 1996-97 were replete with the imagery, hyperbole and enticement used by most peddlers of the future. But at a time when the global buzzwords for the future included ideas and knowledge and vision, the MSC possessed a refreshing conceptual boldness.

Much of that boldness was later forgotten as various subsequent problems in execution led to the MSC's being lumped with other 'megaprojects' criticized for being mere white elephants. Presently no one can authoritatively determine whether Malaysia would have actually emerged as a key IT player, had the MSC's implementation not begun just as the nation entered its most severe economic crisis.[43] But one would be niggardly to dismiss the magical futurism that accompanied the birth of this incomparable emblem of a national, if not nationalistic, engagement with IT across space and time, and the grandest projection of the Mahathirist vision.

Vision. Prosperity. Nationalism. Regionalism. Mahathir's ideological persuasiveness drew richly from these four elements and their interactions. If material prosperity authenticated Vision 2020, the vision in turn conferred a mission upon the economic growth. Past experiences of high growth were of course important but they largely served as balm to fractious ethnic bargaining and class control. Before the 1990s, Mahathirist nationalism was burdened with many reminders that Mahathir's own Malay-Malaysian swings were unpredictable. But domestically, Mahathirism now spoke the idiom of a new Malaysian Nationality (*Bangsa Malaysia*), while internationally it was alloyed to an incipient regionalism. Separately, each of those four elements of vision, prosperity, nationalism, and regionalism was not determinative. The result of their timely coalescence, however, was a remarkably triumphalist matrix framed by a growing public confidence in the political leadership, an optimistic assessment of national capability, the reality of regional accomplishment, and the credible promise of eventual reward. Consequently, one might have said of Malaysian society, that looking inwards, it was reassured: Malaysia Boleh! Looking east, it found an economic miracle. Looking to the future, it foresaw its own arrival at the club of developed nations.

Into all this, one may read a narrative of decolonization, inasmuch as such a historic arrival, chiefly in declared intention but partially in deed, is critical to true decolonization because it helps to dismantle the colonization of the imagination.[44] But the arrival is tied to a logic

– of catching up, perhaps getting even, with one's former colonizers – that has too frequently turned awry under different post-colonial situations in other parts of the world. For Malaysian society, the Mahathirist logic of catching up, perhaps overtaking, the West, entailed a contradictory overcompensation of a psycho-social inferiority complex that originated in the colonial subjection of the Malay states, grew with the relative economic backwardness of the Malay community, and extended into the underdeveloped status of Malaysia.

Undoubtedly, the matrix of vision, prosperity, nationalism and regionalism significantly diminished that sense of inferiority so that Malaysia's multicultural society, to employ a cliché, could find some peace with itself. From Vision 2020 to MSC, Malaysian society went a full circle from discarding a past and inward looking obsession with ethnic divisions to adopting an outward oriented strategy of 'harmonizing our entire country with the global forces'. Nevertheless, when that matrix set in, inferiority gave way to a hubris that manifested itself in superlatives: the world's tallest buildings, the world's best physical infrastructure, the region's largest airport, the longest submarine cable, and the MSC as 'truly a world first'. It was as if the previously crippling limits in the worldview of the colonized had to be transcended by securing entries in *The Guinness Book of Records*. Other 'Malaysian firsts' followed: Conquering Everest, Parachuting Over the South Pole, and Circumnavigating the Globe. Or, as Mahathir encouraged young Malaysians: 'We must have the confidence to achieve all our dreams … [these include] climbing the Everest, sailing across the Pacific, conquering the Arctic and Antarctic'.[45] But did not these dreams betray an imagination slaving under a compulsion to respond to the taunts of the 'heroes of the British Empire', most long departed, albeit Mahathir had his own small role in dismantling that empire?[46] Was it not a symptom of a troubled psychology of decolonization that Mahathir, in an otherwise uncharacteristic departure from stern sobriety and disapproval of any 'aping of the West', should urge young Malaysians to attempt 'crazy things' that 'previously only Westerners liked to do'?[47]

Yet Mahathir's vision was not just a personal thing, not even just a winning ideological construct. A shrewd leader who was able to articulate popular concerns and aspirations, Mahathir was, at this important moment of the beginning of the 1990s, articulating the dreams of a Malaysian national capitalist class. Early Mahathirism, up to the NEP days, was dominated by a Malay nationalist perspective that was bent on remaking Malaysian political economy in ethnic terms. But that task necessarily involved restructuring Malay society –

and thus Malaysian society – in class terms. Late Mahathirism centred less and less on popular Malay anxieties vis-à-vis non-Malay encroachments, and more and more on elite Malay and non-Malay capitalist ambitions on the global terrain.

It was no political coincidence that Mahathir did not first present Vision 2020 to the people of Malaysia, to their representatives in Parliament, or even to UMNO. Rather Mahathir unveiled his vision at the inaugural meeting of the Malaysian Business Council in February 1991 before sharing it with the society at large. It was to, and on behalf of, the gathered captains of industry – local and foreign, Malay and non-Malay – and the selected politicians and senior bureaucrats who were organized in that Council that Mahathir spoke of creating their legacy for a future Malaysia.

In retrospect, Mahathir had achieved a breakthrough in the quest to answer the question: what did it mean to be Malaysian? But the full force of living with this double-edged Mahathirist breakthrough was soon tested when the future arrived not in Vision 2020's gratifying picture of managed destiny, but in the rude shape of malignant globalising forces that the MSC was in fact conceived to 'harmonize'.

Notes

1. On this matter, the former Penang Chief Minister, Lim Chong Eu, had a philosophically enticing formulation that 'To be a Malaysian is to be no less a Malay, a Chinese, an Indian, a Kadazan, a Murut, a Dayak, an Iban and so on ...' (Lim 1990: 124).
2. 'The Spokesman', *Asiaweek*, 2 June 1995, p. 52.
3. Mahathir (1993: 429).
4. *Ibid.*, p. 428.
5. *Ibid.*, p. 431.
6. *Ibid.*
7. *Ibid.*, pp. 435-46.
8. *Ibid.*, p. 438.
9. *Ibid.*, pp. 435-36.
10. *Ibid.*, p. 439.
11. Mahathir (1997c).
12. Hilley (2001: 7); original italics.
13. *Ibid.*, p. 6; original italics.
14. Mahathir (1997c).
15. *Ibid.*
16. Camus (1956: 304).
17. To adapt another of Anderson's suggestive ideas on nationalism (Anderson 1988: 364).

18 Halim (1999: 189).
19 *Ibid.*
20 My term for the predominantly non-Malays who emigrated to avoid NEP.
21 Mahathir (1995a).
22 He especially insisted upon this point to 'West Asians' when he noted that a survey showed that in 1994 only Chileans and Koreans worked harder than Malaysians (Mahathir 1997b).
23 Mahathir (1996e).
24 Mahathir (1996c).
25 See Robison (1996: 310-11) and Rodan and Hewison (1996: 47-48).
26 Khoo (1999a).
27 The original title in Japanese of Mahathir and Ishihara (1995).
28 The long and difficult disputes between the state and the Chinese education movement in Malaya are well documented in Tan (1997). The enrolment of non-Chinese (mainly Malay) children in Chinese-language schools is now estimated to be about 65,000.
29 Loh (1997).
30 With one defection from S46 to PAS, the 1996 balance of power in the Kelantan state assembly became 25 seats for PAS and eighteen for UMNO.
31 Loh (2002).
32 One should emphasize 'national' to stress the unifying quality of that ethos and ideology vis-à-vis the rest of the world, because the ethos of capitalist competition in another sense fostered a 'devil take the hindmost' attitude which is the individualist opposite of communitarianism.
33 Significantly Anwar phrased the slogan in Mandarin rather than the official Malay language. Anwar's ideas on multiculturalism, elaborated within his discussion of an 'Asian renaissance', are found in Anwar (1996).
34 Mahathir (1997d: 78).
35 Mahathir (1997g: 41).
36 Mahathir (1997a: 98-99).
37 *Ibid.*, p. 108.
38 *Ibid.*, pp. 104, 106.
39 Mahathir (1997d: 81).
40 Mahathir (1997a: 100).
41 Mahathir (1997f: 66).
42 Mahathir (1997a: 100).
43 For a general contemporary review of some practical problems the MSC might face, see Ong-Giger (1997).
44 See Nandy (1983) and Chen (2001).
45 'PM reminds Everest climbers to be vigilant', *Business Times*, 1 March 1997.
46 *The Heroes of the British Empire* was the title of a Standard 5 history textbook still used in the mid-1960s. Its principal figures included people like Edmund Hilary, James Scott and James Cook.
47 'Wanted: Heroes', *The Star*, 1 March 1997.

3
The Anarchy of the Market

> The only thing that can stop this is if we have order in the international financial system. There is total anarchy.
> Mahathir Mohamad, quoted in
> 'How dare you say these things!', *Time*, 15 June 1998, p. 30

> The economists, by dint of their refusal to see that economic choices are practicable only if the political and social compromises that they imply are acceptable, are encouraging a utopian economism.
> Samir Amin (1993)

When delivering a speech at St Catherine's College, University of Oxford, on 16 April 1996, Mahathir informed his audience, 'We think the market economy is a winning formula. We are convinced by it.' But, he immediately proceeded to ask, 'What is the good of prosperity which is transient? What is the good of prosperity if in the end we are going to return to the status quo ante; to be back to square one, to be poor and miserable again?'[1] One should not misunderstand Mahathir here. He was not lamenting market failures but warning against human frailties. He cautioned that any economically successful society had still to practise good morals and strong ethics to avoid 'being poor and miserable again'. Fifteen months after Mahathir made his St Catherine's College speech, the so-called 'East Asian financial crisis', marked by the severe depreciation of several Asian currencies, did indeed throw some Asian nations 'back to square one'. This time, Mahathir entered an intense ideological and policy battle to determine who and what had caused the crisis – East Asian regimes and their moral imperfections, or the international money market and its cynical manipulations?

The market consensus, voiced principally by the mainstream western, regional and international media, attributed the crisis to the Asian *dirigiste* regimes' violation of the principles of efficient, that is to say 'free market', resource allocation and capital deployment. The market consensus, which was aligned with the neo-liberal 'Washington consensus', charged that the 'East Asian model of development' was riddled with the non-transparent business practices of powerful coalitions of commercial and political interests that encouraged inefficiency, cronyism, and corruption. In other words, the 'tiger economies', made moribund by a 'loss of investor confidence', could only be nursed back to health on a strict regimen of economic reform, market discipline and good governance.[2]

Mahathir, however, attacked the rapacity of western currency traders and hedge fund managers (personified by George Soros) who had conspired to mount a speculative attack on the Thai baht and other Asian currencies, thus precipitating wild currency depreciations and eventual economic collapse in Thailand, Indonesia and South Korea. More broadly, Mahathir blamed the crisis on the international money market whose unregulated operations left small and weak economies defenceless against 'unnecessary, unproductive and immoral' currency trading.[3] Since enormously rich investment funds had subverted the control sovereign nations ought to have over their currencies and economies, it was the international financial system, and not the Asian regimes, that required stiffer regulation and sterner supervision.

The divide between Mahathir and international finance capital captured to some extent the tensions latent in Mahathir's developmental programme when it was forced into a confrontation with the global money market. As was outlined in Chapter 1, Mahathir's developmental programme could be regarded either as a nationalist project driven by capitalist impulses, or a capitalist project imbued with nationalist aspirations. By the 1990s, the project had already advanced along the policy pathways of the NEP, privatization, Malaysia Incorporated (Malaysia Inc.), the NDP and Vision 2020. In the process, the project gained a critical resilience from two structural factors.

The first was a tripartite balance of power – among the state, foreign capital and domestic capital – that maintained a relative stability in Malaysian political economy. The second was a managed interface of national priorities with changes in the structure of the global economy that imparted an overall competitive advantage. But the spreading crisis undercut these two pillars of political economy, diminished the state's capacity for 'governing the market', to use Robert Wade's expression, and endangered the continued viability of the Mahathirist project. No previous recession had exposed the state to such a damaging combination of the actual severity of sudden and drastic currency depreciation, the ideological animosity of neo-liberalism towards Asian *dirigiste* regimes, and declining western empathy with Southeast Asia in the post-Cold War global environment.

To Mahathir's way of thinking, which utterly abhorred social disorder, the crisis which began in July 1997 was not only an economic calamity but virtually a state of anarchy that had arisen from a free market laid bare to 'anarchists waiting to destroy weak countries in their crusade for open societies, to force us to submit to the dictatorship of international manipulators'.[4] But if the currency crisis approximated anarchy, then contrary to Mahathir's and the money market's respective partisan positions, the malaise arose from internal *and* external disorders, as well as the failings of both regimes *and* the market.

Gambling with Money

What has 'no heart, soul, conscience, [or] homeland'? The answer is money, according to a Canadian businessman.[5] To be precise, it is capital in three basic forms: foreign direct investment (FDI), portfolio investment funds, and international loans. These forms of capital operated in different ways and with different impacts upon the nations, economies and communities in whose midst they were to be found, but by the 1990s, all these forms of capital were understood to be mobile in character, roving in tendency, global in reach, and relentlessly profit-seeking.

In Malaysia's encounters with these types of foreign capital, the FDI of the multinational corporations was the most welcome. The FDI, which developed the factories of the export-processing zones in particular, had been relatively long-term and stable, even if some of the FDI had partially de-industrialized their domestic bases and was feared to be footloose in foreign locations. The first major wave of manufacturing FDI came in the 1970s as the state's NEP objectives were partially realized within the 'new international division of labour' that arose from changes in the global structure of industrial production. Another wave of FDI in the late 1980s and early 1990s helped lift the economy out of its 1985-86 recession into a period of very high growth.

For Malaysia, international loans used to be contracted almost exclusively by the state, but the state appeared to have learnt from the Latin American debt crises and its own painful experience of repaying its post-Plaza Accord inflated yen-denominated loans to reduce its dependence on foreign loans as a source of development funding. Beginning in the 1990s, however, the state's liberalization of the domestic financial sector made international loans more accessible to domestic private sector borrowers, especially big corporate borrowers involved in privatized megaprojects. The same process of financial liberalization was implemented when the domestic stock market enjoyed the status of an 'emerging market', then favoured by international fund managers.

Subsequently came an influx of the most mobile form of capital – the portfolio investment funds. This source of 'hot money' was potentially destabilizing because it was speculative and had no compunction about suddenly entering and exiting financial systems.

Even if the state had reservations about this phase in the development of financial globalization, the state hoped to take advantage of it to expand Malaysia's capital market. Already, the state was developing the physical, institutional and statutory infrastructure to transform Malaysia into a regional financial centre. In 1990, an International Offshore Financial Centre was established in Labuan and it accommodated foreign banks that had been granted offshore banking licenses by the central bank, Bank Negara Malaysia (BNM). There were additional plans to establish an International Stock Exchange and Monetary Exchange in Labuan and to use the International Offshore Financial Centre to provide expertise in various forms of Islamic offshore financial products.[6] There was a growing Private Debt Securities market dealing in bonds, warrants and notes that called for the services of another domestic rating agency. By the end of 1996, the Kuala Lumpur Options and Futures Exchange and the Malaysia Monetary Exchange were to be operational. As part of a series of measures of financial liberalization, the country's single largest fund, the Employees Provident Fund, traditionally required to invest its assets with prudence, had already been allowed a greater scope of participation in the capital market. Stock brokering houses could operate unit trust funds and a graduated commission system would offer more competitive brokerage charges, while foreign fund management companies could manage 100 per cent of their funds locally. The Kuala Lumpur Stock Exchange (KLSE) would accept the public listing of large privatized infrastructural projects. In short, the state planned to expand, liberalize and upgrade the KLSE's operations, guidelines and facilities in order to bring the securities industry 'to a greater level of sophistication and professionalism in line with the globalization of securities trading'.[7]

There was a time when Mahathir was not so enamoured with the explosive growth of an international 'paper economy' – decoupled from the 'real economy' – where money was traded in seemingly limitless permutations of financial papers, instruments and derivatives. He was particularly anxious about the trade in currency and the implications of foreign exchange fluctuations on the economies of developing countries.[8] But when the Mahathirist economic programme demanded accelerated growth and larger and larger infusions of investment in different economic sectors, the state's policies to upgrade the domestic capital market and tap it for investment funds constituted a calculated engagement of the state's developmental priorities with the 'globalization of securities trading'. During the 1990s, some official statements hinted at the state's aspiration for an expanded and diversified Kuala Lumpur-based capital market to overtake Singapore or displace Hong Kong after the British colony's return to China in 1997. A particularly enthusiastic industry assessment of the money-making potential in a Malaysian capital market foresaw Kuala Lumpur emerging as 'Asia's Future Wall Street'.[9]

Whatever the true prospects of Kuala Lumpur's development into an international financial centre, the new initiatives of financial liberalization that arose from the meeting of the state and the money market were likely to benefit a class of domestic conglomerates most of all. These conglomerates were best positioned to enter the liberalized areas of financial services and required funds for their own rapid expansion. The domestic conglomerates – Malay-owned, non-Malay-owned and Malay-non-Malay joint-venture entities – had been groomed within the framework of Malaysia Inc., the name for Mahathir's plan to create a post-NEP alliance of the state and national capital.[10] Malaysia Inc. was basically an alliance in which Malay capital could play a major role.[11] However, the privileged advancement of these domestic conglomerates, which enjoyed prime access to an extensive programme of privatization, had several consequences for the economic structure, power alignments, and practices of governance that laid the domestic conditions for the July 1997 crisis in Malaysia.

The Mahathir regime's original rationale for privatization rested on curbing public sector expenditure and dismantling unprofitable state enterprises in favour of a more efficient private sector, a rationale that had been ideologized as 'rolling back the frontiers of the state' in Thatcher's United Kingdom. But as privatization was 'entrenched in the policy matrix', and a *Privatization Masterplan* was formulated in 1991, there was a radical shift of developmental priorities from the public to the private sector.[12] Contrary to the original rationale, the practice of privatization subsequently came to include the sale of profitable state monopolies (in energy and telecommunications, for example), the award of large infrastructural works (the North-South Highway and the Bakun Dam being the largest), and the opening of newly commercialized areas of social services (such as health care and tertiary education) to domestic capital. To the extent that more and more sectors, companies and projects passed into private hands, privatization entailed some degree of 'rolling back the frontiers of the state'. Despite its pro-market justifications, however, Malaysian privatization did not quite operate under market conditions. Huge privatization projects were awarded without open competition and often without any tendering process at all.[13] Within this tightly controlled situation, rent-seeking and money politics were rife, as influential coalitions formed around the domestic conglomerates and powerful politicians competed to become privatization's chief beneficiaries.

To be sure, not every conglomerate started out with a privatized project. Some major corporations had made their name in their chosen fields (while enjoying varying degrees of state patronage) before becoming candidates for large privatization projects. But now a new category of politically connected Malay, non-Malay, or inter-ethnic conglomerates evolved into privileged oligopolies. These conglomerates did not manufacture for the world market, where success relied on technological innovation, research and development, and international competitiveness. Some operated in primary commodity production that could trace its competitiveness to colonial times, or in resource-based industries where local sourcing was an obvious strength. Most of the conglomerates congregated in banking, resource exploitation, construction, property and real estate, gaming, tourism, transport, utilities and services, and selected import-substituting industries. These were sectors in which state policies, protection and patronage could make the difference between success and failure. The conglomerates came to adopt an almost standard business strategy (though not necessarily realized in the following order of activity): deal in property and real estate, build up construction capacity, lobby for infrastructural and utility works, secure a banking or finance arm or a brokerage licence, buy up plantations, diversify into tourism, and enter newly privatized areas like telecommunications and social services. It has been observed of the 'contemporary conglomerate style of growth' that it increasingly involved 'mergers, acquisitions and asset-stripping, with scant regard for relevant experience and expertise' and that it reflected 'the greater attention to financial accumulation rather than the difficult but ultimately necessary development of internationally competitive productive capacities'.[14] By the 1990s, conglomerate after conglomerate had followed a predictable mode of expansion: having a 'flagship' in one area, they relied on corporate takeovers, acquisitions, mergers, or applications to the state to build up a 'fleet' of companies. Accordingly, these conglomerates were turning themselves into ersatz *zaibatsu*, and *chaebol*, respectively the Japanese and South Korean conglomerates whose success had so inspired Mahathir and his idea of a Malaysia Inc., with the critical difference that the typical Malaysian conglomerate was not known for its productivity, innovation and export competitiveness – the performance standards imposed by the South Korean state on its *chaebols*.

This Malaysian trend of corporate expansion was frenzied during the era of high growth. To support their expansion, the conglomerates drew financial support from two main sources: external borrowings, and capital raised on the KLSE. At this juncture in the 1990s, the dalliance between the state and the inter-national money market came into its own. The liberalization made it easier for the conglomerates to raise external loans or internal capital.

Between 1988 and 1990, the private sector's medium and long-term external debt stood at just under RM5 billion (Table 3.1). Thereafter,

Table 3.1 Malaysia: Outstanding Private Sector External Debt, 1987-97

Year	Medium and long-term debt (RM billion)	Short-term debt (RM billion)
1987	5.559	n.a.
1988	4.855	2.464
1989	4.613	3.343
1990	4.943	4.415
1991	6.723	7.171
1992	10.471	13.157
1993	15.498	17.320
1994	24.203	14.244
1995	28.080	16.204
1996	32.973	25.170
1997 (June)	38.650	35.681
1997 (total)	61.089	43.257

Source: Bank Negara, *Monthly Statistical Bulletin* (January 2002: 123, Table VIII.11).

this debt grew at an average annual rate of 33.8 per cent or from RM6.723 billion in 1991 to RM38.650 billion in June 1997.[15] Between 1988 and June 1997, the private sector's external short-term debt also grew from RM2.464 billion to RM35.681 billion (Table 3.1).

The second major source of funds for corporate expansion was the KLSE whose growth was one direct result of a deluge of portfolio investment entering Malaysia between 1991 and the second quarter of 1997, the eve of the financial crisis. As Table 3.2 indicates, incoming foreign funds invested in shares and corporate securities increased by more than nine-fold from 1991 to 1996. Just the first two quarters of 1997 showed portfolio investment receipts of RM69.797 billion.[16] Except for the beginning and end of the period 1991-97, Malaysia received a net inflow of funds invested in shares and corporate securities. These capital inflows greatly boosted the KLSE's market capitalization (Table 3.3) which peaked at RM888.66 billion in February 1997 (compared with RM131.6 billion in 1990, and RM744.47 billion in June 1997). During the 1990s, the KLSE Composite Index rose from 506 in 1990 to 644 in 1992, and then almost doubled to 1275 in 1993, before declining to 971 in 1994, and 995 in 1995. In 1996, the Composite Index increased to 1238 before falling to 1077 in June 1997, and a post-crisis low of 545 in November 1997.[17]

Since the late 1980s, there had been reforms of the Malaysian financial system but these were typically made to liberalize the capital market, support its growth, and introduce some competition.[18] The new legislation giving Bank Negara broader powers of supervision (Banking and Financial Institutions Act 1989) and establishing the

Table 3.2 Malaysia: Portfolio Investment in Shares and Corporate Securities, 1991-97

Year	Receipts (RM million)	Payments (RM million)	Net inflow (RM million)
1991	13,645	15,524	−1,879
1992	33,324	26,481	6,843
1993	116,743	92,076	24,667
1994	129,953	115,521	14,432
1995	90,987	85,642	5,345
1996	127,590	120,899	6,691
1997 (to June)	69,797	78,279	−8,482
1997 (total)	113,212	138,675	−25,463

Source: Bank Negara, *Monthly Statistical Bulletin* (February 1998: 117).

Table 3.3 Kuala Lumpur Stock Exchange, Selected Indicators, 1990-97

Year	Composite Index	Turnover (RM bn.)	Number of listed companies	New share issues (RM bn.)	Market capitalization (RM bn.)
1990	505.92	29.522	285	8.6496	131.66
1991	556.22	30.097	324	4.3914	161.29
1992	643.96	51.469	369	9.1815	245.82
1993	1,275.32	387.276	413	3.4326	619.64
1994	971.21	328.057	478	8.5479	508.85
1995	995.17	178.859	529	11.4376	565.63
1996	1,237.96	463.265	621	15.9244	806.77
1997	594.44	408.558	708	18.2247	375.80

Source: Bank Negara, *Monthly Statistical Bulletin* (February 1998: 68-69, 72).

Securities Commission in 1993 were attempts at regulation and institutional reform (especially after the 1986 deposit-taking cooperatives' debacle). By and large, however, the conglomerates escaped the scrutiny and regulation that should have accompanied liberalization. This was partly because the power of the technocrats and bureaucrats had been curtailed under Mahathir's administration. Under the Tun Abdul Razak government, the technocrats and bureaucrats in such agencies as Bank Negara, the Treasury, and the Economic Planning Unit, played key roles in planning, implementation and regulation. Under Hussein Onn's premiership, the non-financial private enterprises and state economic development corporations enjoyed their status as 'social enterprises'. Even if one were critical of their actual performance and their ethnically coloured motives, the bureaucrats who regulated capital under the NEP probably did so with a sense of mission. Under Malaysia Inc., however, they were instructed to cooperate with the private sector, or more crudely, serve capital (not least, Malay capital) which, Mahathir was fond of saying, paid the salaries of the civil service.[19] Thus the power balance between bureaucracy and business shifted: 'With increasing Malay hegemony in the 1970s, the role of the predominantly Malay bureaucracy was significantly enhanced, only to give way to an increasingly assertive executive and a more politically influential rentier business community in the 1980s'.[20]

Even if there had been stringent and consistent regulation or good governance, the bureaucracy would not have been very effective when pitted against the growing power of the conglomerates. This power was reflected not just in the conglomerates' multiplying assets, and their political connections but also the influence they wielded by being part of several high-level forums (the Malaysian Business Council being the most important) that institutionalized government-business consultations within Malaysia Inc. Certain corporate leaders were reputed to be particularly influential but, on the whole, Malaysia Inc. gave big business an almost equal footing with government so that, according to former Deputy Prime Minister Musa Hitam, matters 'got to the stage when the private sector was dictating terms, telling government what to do based on their links to leadership'.[21] The notable exception in this trend of declining bureaucratic influence over big business was the Prime Minister himself, who had so centralized, if not personalized, decision-making and policy formulation that the business circles took it as a truism that gaining Mahathir's confidence was a necessary element of good business practice.

Thus, an intensifying concentration of wealth and power in what Terence Gomez and Jomo K. S. called the 'politicized oligopolies'[22] created various problems: the absence of a strong regime of corporate governance, lack of transparency in government-business relations, and rampant rent-seeking behaviour. To these could be added: a persistent current account deficit, the threat of overheating, the probability of declining export competitiveness, mounting indebtedness, and an emerging asset bubble, both in the property sector and the stock market. This latter set of structural problems was among the primary reasons initially offered for the speculative attack on the Southeast Asian currencies in mid-1997.

Depreciation, Devaluation and Disinvestment

In hindsight, not even the cynical foresaw that it would fall to the lot of the international money market to show that the Malaysian nationalist-capitalist project was living on borrowed time and not just borrowed money. The 'contagion' of the 'East Asian crisis' that began in Thailand in July 1997 threatened the viability of that project from two principal directions. Global market forces, manifest in a loss of investor confidence among currency traders and fund managers, drastically depreciated the Malaysian ringgit and greatly reduced the KLSE's market capitalization. Moreover, an abrupt end to almost a decade of high growth compelled the state to confront the agony of International Monetary Fund (IMF)-type structural adjustment and market reform and the urgency of preserving the Malaysia Inc.-led project.

In April 1997, the ringgit enjoyed a peak exchange rate of RM2.493 to US$1. By July 1997 and January 1998, however, the exchange rate had fallen to RM2.636 and RM4.595 to US$1 respectively.[23] As BNM reported:

> The initial response of BNM to the contagion pressures on the ringgit arising from the floating of the Thai baht was to intervene in the foreign exchange market to stabilize the exchange rate. However, the result of this intervention was much higher interest rates. The subsequent actions of BNM showed that it decided to accept the volatility in the foreign exchange market in order to maintain the stability of domestic interest rates.[24]

Having so decided, BNM removed the ringgit's quasi peg to the US dollar, and the ringgit slid to an average July 1997 rate of RM2.636. Although significant, the scale of depreciation of the ringgit was not yet alarming and some analysts expected the ringgit to trade between RM2.70 and RM3.00 to US$1.[25] It was unlikely BNM had a better alternative. The cost of BNM's 'initial response' to the foreign exchange volatility was not just higher interest rates but large losses of foreign reserves. Any further defence of the ringgit risked depleting those reserves, as had happened to Thailand's foreign reserves after the Thai central bank's unsuccessful defence of the baht. Parallel to the ringgit's depreciation, the KLSE's market capitalization fell from RM806.77 billion to RM375.80 billion between 1996 and 1997 (Table 3.3), primarily because global fund managers were departing the East Asian region's 'submerging markets' to avoid foreign exchange and share losses.

As the crisis unfolded, those who led the state in Malaysia were forced to negotiate a new stance vis-à-vis the money market. Their initial attempts backfired. In August 1997 the KLSE banned the short-selling of 100 index-linked stocks, hoping to arrest the decline of share prices. In September, the regime announced it would establish and use a RM60 billion fund to buy stocks selectively from Malaysian companies or shareholders but not from foreigners.[26] These measures – which *The Economist* described as a conversion of 'nasty words [and] mere bluster ... into economic deeds'[27] – failed. They were swiftly reversed or modified after share prices plunged, as fund managers who feared being locked into a falling market dumped their stocks. As one report put it,

> Stunned by the government's decision to restrict short-selling of the index-linked stocks, investors hammered the market to its lowest level in four years; the composite index closed at 812.18, down 4.2%. The Malaysian ringgit also came under a fresh speculative attack, sinking to

2.9020 to the U.S. dollar, its weakest level since the ringgit was officially floated in 1973.[28]

Deputy Prime Minister and Minister of Finance Anwar Ibrahim and Daim Zainuddin (appointed executive director of the newly established National Economic Action Council) then attempted to placate investor confidence. The 1998 Budget, presented by Anwar in October 1997, showed fiscal restraint, made budget cuts, and adopted some IMF-type structural adjustment measures.[29] But the budget forecast a growth rate of 7 per cent, which the market considered to be wholly unrealistic. In December, Anwar announced stricter austerity measures that included lowering the 1998 current account deficit to three per cent of GNP, cutting the Federal Government's expenditure by eighteen per cent, reducing the projected 1998 growth rate to between four and five per cent, and deferring non-strategic projects.[30] This December package, akin to an IMF package without the IMF's intervention, seemed to restore some confidence.[31]

A month later, the Foreign Investment Committee amended the corporate takeover rules to permit United Engineers Malaysia to acquire 32.6 per cent of its parent company, Renong Berhad (UMNO's holding company), without making a general offer to shareholders.[32] The market's response was to send the ringgit and the KLSE's Composite Index to their lowest levels. In March 1998, the national oil company, Petronas, took control of Malaysian International Shipping Corporation, while the latter acquired the shipping assets and debts of Konsortium Perkapalan Berhad which was 51 per cent owned by Mahathir's son, Mirzan Mahathir. When further plans were announced to rescue debt-ridden banks and companies, capital flight hardened into a capital strike: the market would not return if the state, under Mahathir, could not be disciplined.

It was a mystery to many that Mahathir should have been so provocative towards the market when he needed above all to soothe jittery investors with prudent statements and confidence-building measures. After all, 'Malaysia [was], arguably, the strongest among the latest generation of Asian tigers'[33] and its 'pre-crisis macroeconomic fundamentals were sound'.[34] In particular, Tan Tat Wai has shown that the economy had more favourable 'key characteristics' at the onset of the 1997 crisis than at the start of the 1985-86 recession. He has argued that 'had there been a well managed publicity campaign backed by specific actions to build domestic and international confidence, there should have been no massive erosion of confidence'.[35]

The question could be posed more starkly: had Mahathir said and done the wrong things at the wrong time to convert an orderly departure of some investors from Malaysia into a resentful retreat of international capital? At various international forums and in numerous press statements and interviews, Mahathir elaborated on his criticisms of the trade in money and the need for an overhaul of the international financial system. He insisted that states should be permitted to exercise control over their currencies but he had no illusion that they could do so without extensive regulation of the global money market. Mahathir's plea for reform of the international financial system received no more than curt dismissals from the IMF and mocking rebuttals by mainstream western and international media, both of which chose to interpret the 'East Asian meltdown' as a failure of state economic interventionism and a confirmation that the market was ultimately correct.[36] But the more Mahathir railed at George Soros, or condemned western machinations, or censured IMF insensitivities,[37] or hinted at a 'Jewish agenda',[38] or warned that 'people who sabotage the economy must be made to pay the price',[39] the more the currency and shares fell – and the faster was capital's exit from Malaysia, which was disastrous for an economy that had been chronically dependent on large infusions of foreign investment.

The money market suspected that Mahathir's diatribes against a 'free market' dominated by 'an international dictatorship of manipulators' were the prelude to the imposition of capital controls in Malaysia. The harshness of Mahathir's rhetoric and ineffectiveness of the state's policy flip flops paled before the scale and suddenness of economic collapse in Thailand, Indonesia and, almost unbelievably, South Korea. As these countries were forced to seek the IMF's rescue and submit to its 'conditionalities', the IMF, the money market and economic orthodoxy were adamant that the only solutions to the crisis were currency floats, higher interest rates, restrained liquidity, market liberalization, (domestic) financial sector reform, and good governance.

In a sense, it was beside the point if Mahathir's words and actions bordered on insanity[40] or heralded a reckless collision with the money market. Any one of the market's or the IMF's recommended remedies, stringently applied, would have been bitter medicine for the leading Malaysian conglomerates. Taken together, they would have been fatal to Malaysia Inc.: a free market would govern a non-interventionist state!

Rescue, Recapitalization and Reflation

On the whole, the sharp currency and share price falls of 1997-98 spared few, whether they were corporations taking advantage of cheap loans to expand, businesses dependent on imports, middle-class punters who had channelled savings into the KLSE, or students abroad whose state or family-borne expenses were paid for in major foreign currencies.

The leading domestic conglomerates seemed destined to collapse first and spectacularly. They had developed quickly in well protected, non-tradable sectors yielding predominantly ringgit cash flows but their expansion had been fuelled by international and domestic borrowings and market capitalization. The crisis left the conglomerates overexposed to bloated and mostly unhedged external loan repayments. The KLSE's severe devaluation reduced their asset values. For the conglomerates that had relied on the KLSE for corporate mergers and acquisitions, 'as the stock market [fell] and finance institutions force[d] the selling of shares used as collateral, the companies, businesspersons and finance institutions concerned suffer[ed] a permanent destruction of wealth'.[41] The money market's capital flight ruled out a quick restoration of the conglomerates' wealth by way of further loans, loan extensions and a recovery of share prices. Indeed, it has been estimated that 58 per cent of the companies belonging to ten major conglomerate groups, and 42 per cent of other public listed companies suffered losses exceeding RM500 million each between 1997 and 1998.[42] The plight of the conglomerates and of other businesses affected by contracting consumer demand, stalled projects and tightening credit – the signs of an impending recession – imperilled in turn the financial system.

On this issue, BNM offered little relief. BNM had to juggle between calming market sentiment that affected the national economy heavily and placating conglomerate interests accustomed to receiving state protection. BNM was thus caught between trying to boost investor confidence and having to keep the IMF at bay. Evidently, with the support of Anwar Ibrahim and Daim Zainuddin, BNM chose to implement monetary policies and measures to improve corporate governance that amounted to an 'IMF package without the IMF'. By early 1998, BNM had limited credit growth, imposed higher statutory reserve requirements for banking institutions, raised interest rates and reclassified non-performing loans (NPLs) according to three months of non-payment instead of six months. Predictably, the percentage of the banking sector's NPLs rose from 4.1 per cent in 1997 to 13.6 per cent in 1998.[43] Most directly affected by this change in the basis of

NPL classification were many of the leading conglomerates, which faced imminent insolvency.

Given the state's achievements in the past and its ambitions for the future, it was equally difficult for the state to reorient economic planning towards slower growth, lower consumption, and stricter regulation. The austerity budgets and structural adjustment measures announced in October and December 1997 had not prevented the economy from contracting during the first quarter of 1998. The tried but time-consuming route of inviting FDI to engage in long-term productive activities could not be of much use in rescuing the economy from impending disaster. The other route of welcoming FDI from East Asia, successfully followed in the late 1980s, was simply out of the question. Initial hopes of an 'Asian solution' to an 'Asian crisis' by creating an 'Asian Monetary Fund' were dashed when Japan could not assert the regional economic leadership it had been urged to assume for many years over the opposition of the USA, the IMF and even China.[44] Consequently, Mahathir despaired to know how else to restore confidence when market demands, over the course of a year, had changed from a prudent management of economic fundamentals to acceptance of the IMF's conditionalities, to the forced closures of domestic financial institutions, to the opening up of domestic corporations to foreign equity and control, and, ultimately, to changes in government.[45]

On 1 September 1998, the state demonstrated a desperate resolve: BNM instituted foreign exchange control mechanisms that ended the free convertibility of the ringgit.[46] The ringgit, which traded at RM4.0960 to US$1 on that day, was pegged at RM3.800 to US$1 the next day. Holders of offshore ringgit accounts were allowed a month to repatriate their funds to Malaysia: beginning 1 October, the ringgit could not be traded overseas. For the money market, the most serious controls were those that prohibited non-resident correspondent banks and stock brokering firms from obtaining domestic credit facilities, and residents from obtaining ringgit credit facilities from non-resident individuals. Non-residents were required to deposit their ringgit securities with authorized depositories and to hold the proceeds from the sale of such securities in external accounts for at least one year before converting them to foreign currency. BNM insisted that the controls would curb currency speculation but would not affect the 'general convertibility of current account transactions' and 'free flows of direct foreign investment and repatriation of interest, profits and dividends and capital'.[47] Had the state not acted, in the words of

BNM's Acting Governor, to 'bring the ringgit back into the country',[48] the currency would have collapsed. Instead, the capital controls halted the trend of capital flight, if only by trapping remaining foreign funds for a year, and even reversed the flight, if only by forcing the return of some offshore ringgit funds. For the time being, the currency peg ended the volatility of the ringgit and gave domestic businesses and foreign direct investment a measure of stability by which to plan, contract and manage.

Mahathir and Daim's political priority was to save strategic economic sectors and the conglomerates by domestic initiative and resources: they did not have a more promising remedy. In 1998, the net capital outflow from Malaysia was RM21.7 billion.[49] And capital was still on strike. When the regime planned to issue new bonds, the international rating agencies, Moody's, and Standard and Poor's, downgraded Malaysia's credit worthiness and the plan was abandoned. Thus, the capital controls presaged a policy regime of rescuing local business, recapitalizing the financial sector, and reflating the economy.[50] To that end, the state established three institutions to deal with the financial system – Danaharta (an 'asset management company'), Danamodal (a 'special purpose vehicle') and the Corporate Debt Restructuring Committee (CDRC). Danaharta took charge of 'remov[ing] NPLs from the balance sheets of financial institutions', thus 'free[ing] the banks from the burden of debts that had prevented them from providing loans to their customers'.[51] In 1999, Danaharta purchased RM45.5 billion in NPLs from banks and financial institutions. Danamodal recapitalized the financial sector by giving credit injections totaling RM7.59 billion to some of the leading banks. The CDRC managed 67 debt-restructuring applications involving RM36.3 billion. The best-known applications were those involving the UMNO-owned Renong, the state-owned Bank Bumiputra, and Sime Bank. Recapitalization largely depended on three sources: public funds (notably the Employees Provident Fund and Petronas's reserves), external loans (from Japan and the World Bank) and the international bonds that were eventually issued by the government and Petronas in 1999. After September 1998, BNM increased liquidity and facilitated bank lending to the corporate sector partly by lowering the banks' statutory reserve requirements, from 13.5 per cent in February 1998 to four per cent in September 1998. The base lending rate was reduced from 12.27 per cent in June to 6.79 per cent in October. In September 1998, the classification of NPLs was returned to six months of non-payment from three months. BNM directed a higher target for bank lending and, by offering terms more favourable than those in existence in July 1997, made credit more readily available to support such key sectors as the automobile industry and the property market. The capital controls of September 1998 generated a controversy around the world that has not found and will probably never find a settled resolution in terms of economic theory and analysis. While the controversy was fresh, proponents of the free market predictably heaped scorn on the capital controls. Some of them, by citing China and India's capital control problems of 'bureaucratization and leakages, leading to corruption and capital flight', dismissed the controls and currency peg as being impracticable.[52] Others warned that 'even if controls on capital outflows can buy time in a short-term panic, it is time bought at a high long-term price', and that 'even if the controls are explicitly designed to exclude foreign direct investment, as Malaysia's are, history suggests investors shy away nonetheless'.[53] In any case, foreign investors did keep away when Morgan Stanley Capital International removed the KLSE from its index. Celebrated economists, such as Paul Krugman and Joseph Stiglitz, expressed some support for the capital controls as a temporary solution to the havoc in the money market. On the other hand, Jomo K. S. disputed the efficacy of the September 1998 capital controls, even as he maintained that 'capital controls may well be the most acceptable alternative to the destabilizing effects of capital flows on inadequately regulated financial systems characteristic of developing economies'.[54] Jomo contended that the controls were too late to avert the crisis, penalized 'investors who had shown greater commitment to Malaysia', and were ambiguous in their contribution to economic recovery.[55]

Perhaps the most important gains from the capital controls were political and ideological rather than economic ones. The state's programme of recapitalization, rescue and reflation – implemented behind what the defenders of the capital controls called an 'economic shield' – was at odds with the reforms the money market and international agencies had demanded of the Asian crisis-stricken regimes. But the recapitalization, rescue and reflation allowed the economy to avert a collapse – without IMF intervention. Unexpectedly, therefore, the capital controls served as a bold example to many different quarters who rejected any vision of an unfettered money market that would '"lock in" neoliberal reforms' and 'sever the nexus between government and business that has been so characteristic of East Asian development'.[56] There were critics of the undemocratic treatment of Anwar, for example, who nonetheless supported the 'independence' of the capital controls. And even if the 1999-2000 economic recovery was significantly attributable to fortuitous developments – chiefly, a region-wide recovery and an expansion in exports of mainly electronic goods to the USA — the regional crisis had turned, except for Indonesia where the malaise was at its worst. By late 1999, Malaysia's trade surpluses had built up the country's reserves and the reflationary policies had helped to generate sufficient growth to maintain unemployment at its low pre-crisis levels. Share prices recovered from their lowest levels of 1998, no doubt supported by domestic institutional funds.

Critically, it was partly this semblance of a return to economic stability (in contrast to the continuing violence and turbulence in Indonesia which profited no one) that led the state and the market to negotiate a new compromise. The state had relaxed its capital controls as early as in February 1999 to permit the repatriation of foreign funds subject to a graduated exit tax. The state continued to do so until essentially only the currency peg remained. This dismantling of most of the original capital controls, however, did not stop certain investment funds (notably Templeton) from pointedly staying away from Malaysia, even after September 1999 when trapped foreign funds could exit without penalty. Nevertheless, the state was able to return to the market, albeit aided by the quiet backing of the Japanese government and burdened with punitive premiums. In late 1999, the government and Petronas were able to issue their bonds of US$1 billion and US$500 million respectively in the international money market. In short, and in the interests of conducting business despite disagreements in principle, the state and the money market reached a rapprochement – almost exactly as the chief investment officer of a foreign company had predicted in September 1998 when he said, 'In six months to a year, investors will probably come round to accepting the new rules of the game.'[57] A concrete indication of such a rapprochement was Morgan Stanley Capital International's re-incorporation of Malaysia in its index in early 2000 that paved the way for fund managers to re-enter the KLSE. An ideological sign of the state-market compromise was supplied by the *Asian Wall Street Journal* editorial of 23 June 1999 which cajoled Mahathir: 'Now that the pressure of the Asian crisis has abated, it's time to declare victory and rejoin the global economy.'[58]

There was another plausible reason for the state-market rapprochement. The imposition of capital controls was not merely a choice of the most effective way to contain a crisis of regional, if not global, capitalism but a desperate move guided by sheer political intuition.

But, as harried political calculations went, Mahathir's move was made under global circumstances that were not entirely unfavourable.

As the 1997 crisis worsened, the orthodoxy of the money market was discredited, even by supporters of global capitalism, as the self-serving dogma of an 'IMF-Treasury-Wall Street Complex',[59] or 'a phony Washington consensus',[60] and by Joseph Stiglitz, whose criticisms of the IMF led to his departure from the World Bank. Across Asia, if not the world, IMF intervention became synonymous with arrogance and failure. In 1998, moreover, the sudden currency depreciation in Russia, South Africa, and Latin America were openly blamed on contagion from the disease of currency speculation. Around the time Mahathir's capital controls were imposed, the East Asian financial crisis was unabated, the Indonesian economy and politics were in turmoil, Russia had defaulted on its external debt, Hong Kong defended its currency peg and its stock market, while China and Taiwan appeared exemplary in their maintenance of currency controls.[61] Malaysia had never exemplified the East Asian model of development. This was partly because Malaysia had not reached the heights of late industrialization, unlike South Korea or Taiwan, and partly because Malaysia's class and ethnic complexities were unlike those experienced by the other Asian NICs. To some degree, however, East Asian states seemed to hedge their bets on the Malaysian experiment: not many would openly defend it, but not all wished it ill.

'Call me a heretic', or 'a pariah, if you like', said Mahathir,[62] but he had seized upon a regional resentment at a Western-dominated money market to speak for East Asian economic nationalism.[63]

Bringing the Crisis Home

'Why', it has been asked, 'would a comparatively small economy like Malaysia risk incurring the wrath of influential external actors like the International Monetary Fund (IMF) or the increasingly powerful financial markets?'[64] The preceding discussion suggested an answer grounded in the imperatives of a nationalist-capitalist project that took refuge in temporary and partial withdrawal from the international money market when the state could no longer meet the market on the latter's terms. But a fuller answer must go beyond a state-versus-market narrative because the imposition of capital controls brought to a head policy disagreements between a loosely formed 'Anwar Ibrahim camp' and an equally roughly defined 'Mahathir camp' that had been simmering for about a year.

Generally the state's technocrats in BNM, with Anwar's backing, searched for economistic solutions to the crisis. Others performing regulatory functions, in the Securities Commision, for example, wanted to make good corporate governance a reality. Together, the technocrats and regulators hoped to restore investor confidence in the Malaysian financial and securities market. Small businesses were more prepared to be critical of Mahathir and big business for the economic disaster.[65] In particular, small Malay businesses having ties to UMNO, who had been hurt by the market conditions, and given no assurance of protection, were not indifferent to arguments opposing the state use of public funds to bail out selected conglomerates. At least part of both the Malay and non-Malay middle-classes were offended by the lack of accountability in privatization, the rentierism and money politics rampant under Malaysia Inc., and Mahathir's refusal to admit any government failure. Yet others were quite alarmed. Not only did Mahathir appear to be rather irrational in the face of the market's turmoil, he was rumoured to be considering declaring a state of emergency to deal with the crisis and threats to the national economy. The more disillusioned, or even the more self-confident, among those sceptical of Mahathir's rhetoric and stances, might even have thought that only the IMF's intervention, or a full blast of globalization, could really cleanse the Malaysian political economy of its ills.[66]

In this situation, BNM's role became crucial when its assessment of the crisis and its views on crisis management placed the senior technocrats at odds with Mahathir. At the height of the crisis, Mahathir had said derisively: 'Hoping for market forces to create a stable currency exchange, a stable economy and stable politics is the same as doing nothing and leaving everything to fate'.[67] As the Minister of Finance, Anwar Ibrahim did not intend to do nothing or leave things to fate but Anwar seemed more willing to trust matters to BNM's finance technocracy. In its *Annual Report 1997*, the last BNM report issued when Anwar was still the Minister of Finance, BNM explained its attempt to manage the foreign exchange regime after July 1997 thus:

> Since a central bank in an open economy cannot simultaneously determine both the exchange rate and domestic interest rates, attempts to stabilize the exchange rate will transfer the volatility to domestic interest rates. Therein lies the challenge for monetary policy. A balance in judgement is required to limit the volatility in the exchange rate or in domestic interest rates.[68]

No policy-maker or senior advisor in government in 1997-98 could have remained unperturbed by the pressures of foreign exchange volatility on the national economy and domestic businesses. BNM itself had suffered unspecified foreign exchange losses in its initial defence of the ringgit. Subsequently, the BNM's 'balance in judgement' was anchored in a conservative acceptance of 'the volatility of financial prices' as an unavoidable outcome of the 'growing global integration of both the financial markets, as well as the real economy'. Logically, BNM argued:

> It does not imply that volatility of interest and exchange rates due to external shocks should be avoided through economic isolation or capital controls. Rather, there is a general recognition that sound domestic economic management is an important element in reducing the risks associated with this volatility.[69]

Looking back, it is clear that BNM had addressed the key issues of crisis management with a cautiously detached tone and a professional stance that could have formed an eminently useful counterpoint to Mahathir's florid charges. For all that, the senior BNM technocrats earned not Mahathir's gratitude but his wrath! When the external volatility grew wilder and domestic interest rates were driven up, Mahathir demanded what BNM's economic orthodoxy could not deliver, that is, stable foreign exchange *and* low interest rates. And while Mahathir cast around for restrictions to place on speculation, BNM remained very much concerned with improving investor confidence and imposing good governance:

> Greater transparency in policy-making can also remove much of the uncertainty that is associated with private decision-making. A government that has clear objectives and shows a commitment to achieving those objectives earns credibility.[70]

To that degree, BNM's economistic stance was touchingly innocent, if politically naive because, rightly or wrongly, BNM's views could less and less be distinguished from those of the IMF and the money market. Ominously, BNM's stricter regulation of the financial sector – by way of tighter liquidity, higher statutory reserve requirements, limited credit growth and more stringent classification of NPLs – began to resemble a harsh IMF prescription that would have a dire impact on shady loans as well as legitimate businesses. Previous experiences of banking collapses, loan scandals and financial crises in Malaysia had revealed that domestic banks and finance companies were not above making enormous loans on dubious grounds to powerful individuals and companies. For the international mass media, chiefly the financial press, the swift collapse of Bank Bumiputera and Sime Bank was strong evidence of a repeat of past experiences. It was symptomatic of the uncertainty of the times and lack of accurate knowledge of such 'shady loans' that even post-1999 official figures on NPLs were inconsistent. Hence, unofficial but seemingly rising estimates of NPLs – likely to have been influenced by the scale of financial collapse in Thailand, Indonesia and South Korea – coloured media and business perceptions of the health of the financial sector in Malaysia. On the one hand, it was certain that the BNM's stricter reclassification of NPLS would saddle lenders and borrowers with more bad loans. On the other hand, even legitimate businesses untainted by dubious practices had been buffeted for a year by market volatility; they could have no use for the BNM's brand of 'sound domestic economic management' if that effectively meant a credit squeeze, possible loan recalls and eventual recession. For example, a conservative economist turned banker, who was critical of the 'anti-market pronouncements, an unwillingness to consider a market solution and conflicting statements on megaprojects [that] aggravated the crisis', concluded that the BNM's pre-September 1998 'imposition of a regime of stringent credit control led to an overkill'.[71] A former BNM economist turned steel manufacturer who disapproved of the 'severe disagreements within the government on how to handle the crisis', argued that the 'initial drive to emulate the International Monetary Fund policies, and especially the two-pronged attack to cut expenditure and force an immediate contraction of loans, greatly worsened the crisis'.[72]

The two views noted above were not those of the regime's so-called cronies although the views reflected the relief that most businesses gained from the currency peg, recapitalization and reflation, and were congruent with those of the Mahathir camp. Mahathir's interpretation of the origins of the crisis as well as his management policies were obviously crucial to the survival of the conglomerates. But Mahathir's insistence on providing assistance to business in general was welcome to other big domestic business interests and other social groupings. Of this last category, some were being 'patriotic' while others were being 'realistic'. The conglomerates, other established businesses, (those prominent in the various Chambers of Commerce, for example), and 'patriotic' social groups baulked at the prospect of any IMF intervention or further liberalization for fear of an eventual transfer of local corporate assets to foreign purchasers. The businesses saw in credit loosening, a lower interest rate regime, and even asset sales short of a transfer of control to foreign hands, the means to help them weather the economic crisis.[73] Others, roused to reduce imports and 'buy Malaysia', did not necessarily embrace Mahathir's conspiracy theory of the crisis but the unsatisfactory experiences of Thailand, Indonesia and South Korea would have alerted them to the dangers posed by the IMF's conditionalities. As such, home grown alternatives to the transfers of domestic equity to foreigners were to be preferred, including tapping the resources of the rare cash-rich corporations in the name of 'national service', selling non-Malays a part of Malay equity, and, for that matter, using public funds, such as the Employees Provident Fund.

No one, of course, expressed as much contempt as Mahathir did for any advice about 'following the IMF prescription' closely:

> If we were to follow the IMF any closer, we would bankrupt all of our companies. If you look at all the companies in the countries with the IMF, technically they are bankrupt. What the IMF wants us to do is to increase the interest rates, to reduce credit, to increase taxes. Now all three of these things would bankrupt our companies. When you reduce the currency by 50% and the share prices by more than 50%, then all of the companies find they cannot pay their debts, because they borrowed using their shares as collateral, on the basis of 80% of the value of the shares. Now the fall in shares has made the borrowing much bigger and they have to top up. Now how do you top up in a situation when the economy is not doing well? It is never easy to top up. If you cannot top up, our regulations say you will be considered to have a non-performing loan after six months – the IMF says no, it must be three months. But in three months they cannot pay. But if we do not follow the IMF, the result will be a loss in confidence and down goes the currency. So we have to follow. The result is a lot of loans that would not be non-performing become so. And once they become non-performing, companies cannot borrow. And when they cannot borrow, they cannot do business and we get worse.[74]

The divergence in views between the executive and its senior technocrats was overshadowed by disagreements among those who led the state. The disagreements led to policy skirmishes that were not initially portentous but they consigned Mahathir and Anwar to opposite ends. For example, Mahathir bitterly criticized the IMF, but Anwar maintained that 'We have an excellent rapport with IMF officials' (although he added, 'and they have said that Malaysia does not need an IMF rescue').[75] Mahathir directed the use of state funds to rescue several prominent conglomerates he considered blameless in their near collapse. Anwar (with Daim's support sometimes) expressed his opposition to bailouts and reassured the market:

The Anarchy of the Market

We want more transparency. We want to emphasize corporate governance. We will put our foot down and punish those who break the rules. Irrespective of the profile or connections of corporate players, if they break the rules, they won't go unpunished.[76]

Mahathir ordered changes to the KLSE rules to protect local interests and punish foreign speculators; Anwar reinstated the rules, only to have Mahathir overturn his reinstatement! Whereas Mahathir wanted to discipline the market and angrily threatened to curtail trade in the ringgit, Anwar sought to pacify market sentiment: 'We will have to convince investors that we need them. I think we should be in the league with the international system and its commitment to further liberalize. There's no question of a reversal of public policy.'[77] So many additional examples of 'policy debates at the top of government' abounded that some foreign observers described the situation as a 'policy gridlock'.[78]

Nevertheless, one should not overstate the divide in policy-making the way that Mahathir, Daim, the National Economic Action Council and other regime spokespeople did, by conveniently blaming only Anwar and BNM for 'the wrong turns taken during the initial stage of the crisis'[79] and indeed for 'sabotage'.[80]

There are many reasons to be sceptical of such a one-sided account of Anwar's culpability in the deterioration of the economic situation, and to be wary of 'Mahathir's historical revisionism', as Jomo K. S. dubbed the post-September 1998 attack on Anwar's economic management.[81]

First, those 'wrong turns' had been clarified by Anwar in December 1997 to be 'neither mine nor Dr Mahathir's [but] the collective decision of the cabinet'.[82] Anwar repeated in mid-January 1998: 'I categorically make clear that these measures are endorsed by the Cabinet and we will continue to support the liberal regime.'[83] It may have been in Anwar's interest to claim the Cabinet's collective responsibility for policies that could seal the fate of the national economy but then neither Mahathir nor Daim, nor any other Cabinet minister demurred when Anwar made his claim.

Second, there was never a formulaic or linear path of progress towards a resolution of the crisis, barring the much criticized IMF's 'one size fits all' approach. The search for an effective end to the crisis yielded unwieldy, unworkable or unpopular proposals. Of these, perhaps the strangest proposal made to the National Economic Action Council was Mahathir's:

> to increase the income of everybody and raise the prices of everything in order to neutralize the devaluation.

If the value of the currency fell by 100 per cent in terms of exchange rate then we raise income by 100 per cent. This would result in the purchasing power remaining the same.[84]

Mahathir later admitted that the NEAC immediately rejected his recommendation, although he then made a virtue of his error. The search was torturous and required policy reversals along the way. Thus, Jomo K. S. has suggested that 'as Mahathir's policy initiatives and rhetoric caused the situation to deteriorate, Anwar became more receptive to the community and business media, and to foreign, including IMF, policy advice' for which 'Anwar was 'strongly, but quietly supported by many other government officials'.[85] Hence, although 'Anwar approved of the tighter fiscal and monetary policies from late 1997, in line with market expectations as much as IMF recommendations', Anwar by mid-1998 was looking to use public spending and reflationary measures to offset the adverse impact of the October and December 1997 austerity programmes.[86]

As the crisis was prolonged, the state faced unpalatable policy choices. Not conceding to market demands for 'reform' would invite a capital strike until 'market forces are at last being allowed to work'.[87] Acceding to radical reform and full liberalization might mean 'the total opening of national capital markets' and a 'resulting predatory rush to take over absurdly depreciated assets'.[88] Mahathir asked, 'Why do we raise interest rates – and we have raised interest rates – why do we squeeze credit?' and he himself answered, 'Because we are frightened'[89] – of offending the IMF and the money market, he meant. There was an element of truth to that. When the crisis began, the consensus was that while the Malaysian economy and its financial system were in need of structural reforms, they were sound compared to Thailand's and Indonesia's. Even Mahathir's market critics believed so, as implied in their complaint that Malaysia's basic problem was a self-inflicted erosion of investor confidence brought about by Mahathir's bluster and interventions that alarmed investors. One line of criticism argued, ironically, that Mahathir could afford to be 'reckless ... because, after Singapore, Malaysia has Southeast Asia's strongest banks. Balance sheets are firm, non performing loans are low, and the quality of banking supervision is at least a notch above the regional norm'.[90] If that was the case, and the IMF concurred by ruling out any need to rescue Malaysia, then, rationally, one thrust of damage control was to prevent Mahathir from becoming a 'menace to his own country', to use Soros's words.[91] It fell to Anwar's lot to compensate for Mahathir's outbursts with 'clarifications', 'reassurances' and 'spin-doctoring'. It was BNM's task to institute confidence-building measures to placate a market that refused to believe that its own failures had greatly contributed to the crisis. Mahathir might have been right in implying that Anwar and the BNM technocrats were 'frightened' into imposing tighter monetary policies and stricter prudential standards. If so, the accusation was perhaps exoneration itself: Anwar and BNM were not the IMF's stooges, but they strove to keep the IMF at bay by consolidating the financial system, while hoping that its 'stronger fundamentals' would allow Malaysia to escape the fate of other economies. One can speculate that the senior technocrats especially were unprepared through a blend of circumstances, personal temperaments and institutional conservatism to contemplate 'economic isolation and capital controls' as a viable solution for an 'open economy'. Tragically, for these technocrats, a faith in the fundamentals of theory, as Heikki Patomäki lucidly observed, entailed a form of denial:

> Indeed, with hindsight and a firm commitment to orthodox theory, it is always possible to find a variety of arbitrary explanations or a list of deviations from the sound free market principles. 'The fundamentals were, after all, wrong, even if we did not see it beforehand.' Perhaps there were hidden problems in the balance of payments or exchange. Perhaps political compromises between different nationalities within the state meant that parts of the economy were over-subsidized. Perhaps capitalism in those countries was 'crony', meaning that some firms and banks were favoured over others. Perhaps there was also straightforward corruption. Or perhaps the state was, after all, involved too much in crucial investment decisions and everyday practices of banks and firms. The rate of taxation might have been too high as well. Or it may be that there were underlying weaknesses in the state budget, even though they went unnoticed for a long time. Or perhaps there were weaknesses in the way the state had liberalized its trade or financial markets.[92]

Should one have called upon the senior BNM technocrats, who were raised in economic orthodoxy and in the past praised for fiscal and monetary conservatism, to abandon the well-tried tenets of central banking?

Matters were different for a politician used to setting his own course and refusing, at critical moments, to abide by existing rules. During the years of rapid economic growth, Mahathir was widely applauded for his role in industrializing and modernizing the economy. Yet his economic ideas, being a syncretic mix of modernization theory, structuralist arguments, conservative dependency theory, 'Third Worldism' and 'looking East' for lessons in late industrialization, were never clearly defined or developed. By the 1990s, Mahathir was stubbornly clinging to an East Asian model that privileged the role of state-supported conglomerates. Faced with disaster, Mahathir relied on the clarity and flexibility of true desperation. He had no orthodoxy to defend, only interests to protect. He had no theories to prove, only a project to preserve. And, if it needed saying at all, he had his career and reputation to save. Capital controls tied to fixed exchange rates were the norm of the international financial system before the United States abandoned the Bretton Woods arrangement. Could capital controls now end East Asia's currency turmoil and stabilize its financial systems? In 1997-98, no one genuinely knew the answer, as may be inferred from the Bank for International Settlements's equivocal response to Malaysia's capital controls:

> Malaysia's recourse to capital controls has given further impetus to the debate on whether full-scale capital account liberalization is premature for most emerging market economies. In particular, support has grown in recent years for measures to slow the inflow of short-term capital until markets, institutions and regulatory frameworks have been sufficiently strengthened. Measures to contain capital inflows, such as reserve requirements which tax shorter-term inflows more heavily, can be useful. If carefully designed, they may help avoid a domestic lending boom and the asset price bubble which is often associated with it, while allowing a liberal attitude to be maintained towards longer-term inflows such as foreign direct investment.
>
> Much less acceptance has been won for the imposition of controls on capital outflows, in particular where a more liberal regime is already in place. A frequent argument in favour of such controls is that they can give the authorities the necessary room to formulate and implement adjustment programmes that could help restore investor confidence. The counter-argument is that controls can also be abused, either to maintain an inappropriate policy stance for too long, or to delay the restructuring of a weak financial sector. Moreover, the effectiveness of capital controls on outflows declines as loopholes are found and exploited. To plug them, a process is often set in motion of ever more complex and broad-ranging controls, to the point where useful economic activity may be severely damaged. Another counterproductive aspect is that the introduction of controls on outflows may send a negative signal discouraging capital inflows at a critical moment. If this loss of confidence affects neighbouring economies that have similar problems (but have abstained from restrictions), capital controls in one country could be particularly harmful to others. Finally, the potential loss of confidence and policy credibility which controls on outflows could entail is likely to raise the cost of international borrowing for much longer than just the duration of the crisis.[93]

To put it differently, opposing positions on the desirability of capital controls, when they were not dictated by vested interests, were based on unproven theory, sentiments and sheer conjecture. Neo-liberal and money market voices were apt to disparage the practicality of capital controls, when in fact they opposed the controls as a symbolic or real hindrance to a 'free' global money market. In that, they failed to anticipate that, when forced, Mahathir would have the courage of his conviction to take a potentially deadly political risk.

July 1997 was a time of crisis for global capitalism, of speculative currency trading, and even of 'East Asian' ways of conducting business. In Malaysia, the crisis was above all a malaise of Malaysia Inc. and the domestic conglomerates that suffered near demise at their very first collision with global forces. Mahathir persisted in depicting the conglomerates as good and well managed companies sabotaged by immoral manipulators. Such a defence strained public credibility since nothing was said about how Malaysia Inc.'s predilection for foreign funds, which the conglomerates indulged and the state facilitated, smacked of corporate adventurism and incompetent management. As conglomerate after conglomerate became insolvent, it became apparent that the claims of the new Malaysian capital – Malay and non-Malay – to being able to hold their own in the world economy were hollow. One did not have to be a market fundamentalist (then or now) to believe charges that the state's principal measures of crisis management had been aimed at rescuing key conglomerates belonging to UMNO or the regime's so-called 'cronies'. Who could not see that the conglomerates possessed not a visionary but a self-serving 'economic nationalism'? While the conglomerates prospered, they presented themselves as the paragons of the virtues of privatization. When the conglomerates were mired in debt, they were not above socializing their losses.[94] If the conglomerates who had not quite lived by the market were not to die by the market, so to speak, Malaysia Inc. had to erect its 'economic shield'.

In so doing, Mahathir signalled that neither he nor Malaysia Inc. could be the flag bearer of capitalist rationalization in Malaysia any longer. The early Mahathir regime, with its '2M administration' (so named after Mahathir and his deputy, Musa Hitam), embodied an impetus towards modernization and rationalization. Later the Mahathir-Daim combination firmly imposed fiscal discipline and privatization upon the bureaucracy and its public enterprises that were extensively and too often unprofitably involved in business. The high point of this push towards capitalist rationalization came in 1986 when

Mahathir boldly suspended the NEP's restructuring requirements and relaxed the conditions for foreign direct investment. Subsequently came the moves, overseen by the finance ministries of Daim and then Anwar Ibrahim, to liberalize and upgrade the financial system 'in line with the globalization of securities trading'. In their time, each of those sets of measures – bureaucratic reform, privatization, and liberalization – was a significant departure from existing policies. After July 1997, however, Mahathir, in detecting only the dastardly hand of the currency speculator, failed to respond to fundamental shifts in the global economy that held grave implications for the viability of the East Asian model of capitalism and for Malaysia Inc. itself.

However politically motivated it might have been, the soon-to-be doomed Anwar camp briefly supplied the drive towards further rationalization. On 27 August 1998, the BNM Governor, Ahmad Mohd. Don, and his deputy, Fong Weng Phak, persisting in their opposition to the capital controls, resigned their positions. On 2 September, Mahathir dismissed Anwar from all the latter's posts in government. Anwar's dismissal demonstrated that there would be no more concession to the pro-market reforms that accorded with the global money market's ideas for revitalizing the crisis-stricken Asian economies. Instead Mahathir, Daim and the NEAC, the remaining BNM technocrats, and the newly established crisis management vehicles braced themselves to implement programmes of rescue, re-capitalization and reflation. Before and even after this resort to 'economic isolation and capital controls', the options that were implicit in the earlier policy skirmishes did not merely involve a choice between adopting IMF-styled structural adjustment and market-dictated governance, or allowing key economic sectors and strategic businesses to collapse. There was at least the basic option of tying specific rescue plans, bailout measures and reflationary policies to a strict restructuring of the politically linked conglomerates. Subsequently, Danaharta, Danamodal and CDRC rescued such conglomerates and restructured their equity shareholdings. But, whereas there was some corporate restructuring of big businesses after September 1998,

> the repeated bailouts of the Renong group, the purchase of Malaysian Airlines shares from its major shareholders at double the then prevailing market price [and] the reluctance to let the steel mill, Perwaja, fail ... have been held as clear illustrations of Malaysia's will to protect failing businesses at any cost.[95]

Only a month into the imposition of capital controls, Mahathir said that 'the problem of NPLs and the liquidity crunch was initiated largely by BNM's attempt to please the IMF' and that 'with the exchange controls and a return to a more sensible financial regime, the problem of NPLs has been mitigated'.[96] In other words, the post-September 1998 capital controls and the reflationary programmes were not committed to fundamental reform of mismanaged conglomerates and to loosening their grip on Malaysian political economy. With continued protection, the alliance between the state and the conglomerates survived but Malaysia Inc. was finished as the code for capitalist rationalization. As the Mahathir regime claimed credit for having reversed 'the wrong turns taken during the initial stage of the crisis', it was obvious that Anwar had replaced Soros and the IMF as the scapegoat for all that was wrong with Malaysian political economy before September 1998.

And so, as it had happened during the late 1980s, it happened in September 1998: economic crisis precipitated political battle. This time, Anwar's sacrifice at the altar of capital controls let loose what Mahathir unsurprisingly called 'anarchy'. Others named it *Reformasi*.

Notes

[1] Mahathir (1996b: 204).
[2] For example, see *The Economist*, 7 March 1998.
[3] Mahathir (1997g: 64).
[4] Mahathir (1997e).
[5] 'To be in business, your first mandate is to make money, and money has no heart, soul, conscience, homeland', said Frank Stronach, chair of Magna International, a Canadian auto-parts maker; quoted in Suzanne Billelo, 'Free-Trade Pact Stirs Emotions', *New York Newsday*, 7 August 1992, cited in Henwood (1997: 113).
[6] Abbott (1999: 197).
[7] This summary of the state's measures, planned or introduced in the mid-1990s, is drawn from Mahathir (1995b).
[8] Khoo (1995: 59-60).
[9] McCarthy (1994).
[10] Mahathir was prone to depicting this alliance in benign terms, as a 'smart partnership' of government and business, excluding a role for organized labour (Mahathir 1996d).
[11] Khoo (1995: 129-36).
[12] Adam and Cavendish (1995: 135).
[13] See Jomo (1995: 44-48) for a discussion of the cases of the North-South Highway, Sistem Televisyen (Malaysia) Berhad, Sports Toto, Pan Malaysian Sweeps, Totalisator Board of Malaysia, Jalan Kuching-Jalan Kepong Interchange, Indah Water Konsortium, Bakun Hydroelectric Project, Food Industries of Malaysia, and Peremba Berhad.

14 Gomez and Jomo (1997: 179-80).
15 Bank Negara Malaysia, *Monthly Statistical Bulletin* (February 1998: 103). In comparison, from 1987 to 1997 (June), the government's external debt never exceeded the 1987 level of RM44.767 billion; public sector external debt totalled RM41.530 billion in June 1997. This was due to the government's holding down its debt since the 1985 recession, and not any lack of international lender confidence.
16 Bank Negara Malaysia, *Monthly Statistical Bulletin* (February 1998: 117). For 1996 and the first half of 1997 respectively, there were, additionally, RM14.995 billion and RM18.627 for bonds, money market instruments and financial derivatives.
17 Bank Negara Malaysia, *Monthly Statistical Bulletin* (February 1998: 72).
18 Mohamed (1996: 328-31).
19 For Mahathir's criticisms of civil service prejudices against the private sector, see Mahathir (1996d).
20 Gomez and Jomo (1997: 179).
21 Jayasankaran and Hiebert (1998: 14).
22 Gomez and Jomo (1997: 180).
23 The lowest rate at which the ringgit traded was RM4.88 to US$1, in January 1998.
24 Bank Negara Malaysia (1998: 80).
25 Lim (1998: Preface)
26 Lopez (1997).
27 *The Economist*, 6 September 1997, p. 14. See also Appell and Lopez (1997).
28 Lopez and Pura (1997).
29 These included reducing Federal Government expenditure by two per cent, postponing 'megaprojects', reducing the current account deficit, reducing corporate tax by two per cent, limiting credit growth to fifteen per cent by the end of 1998, and consolidating the prudential standards and regulations covering non-performing loans, liquidity within the banking system (Malaysia 1998: Chapter 1).
30 See *ibid.* for these and other measures, including stricter criteria for approvals of reverse investment, enhanced corporate information disclosure, and closer regulation of corporate restructuring.
31 *Business Times*, 9 December 1998.
32 Lim (1998: 45-47, 130-35); 'UEM's waiver reinstated: Anwar', *Business Times*, 12 January 1998.
33 Hiebert and Jayasankaran (1997: 62).
34 Rajah (2001).
35 Tan (2003: 31).
36 *The Economist*, 27 September 1998.
37 Pura (1997); 'Dr M: We have evidence Soros did it', *New Straits Times*, 27 August 1997.
38 'It could be a Jewish agenda, says PM', *The Sun*, 11 October 1997.

The Anarchy of the Market   69

39 'Local funds set to enter the market in a big way', *New Straits Times*, 29 August 1997.
40 In late 1997, I was asked more than once by regional journalists if Mahathir 'had flipped' which was evidently not a question asked by journalists alone but by 'business circles', too.
41 Tan (2003: 35).
42 *Ibid.*, p. 36, Table 3.6.
43 Bank Negara Malaysia, *Monthly Statistical Bulletin* (January 2002: 42, Table III.15); the figure of 13.6 per cent was based on a non-payment of interest for three months.
44 *The Economist*, 27 September 1998. p. 84. 'The crisis has been mismanaged from the start by the world's two largest economic powers, the United States and Japan, both of which wield influence in the region dwarfing that of any other country' (Godement 1998: 28).
45 *New Straits Times*, 13 June 1998. Mahathir put it thus: 'Anything we do in the direction of recovery is seen as wrong and will cause a loss of confidence' (*Time*, 15 June 1998).
46 The features of the capital controls outlined here were drawn from *New Straits Times*, 2 September 1998.
47 *Ibid.*
48 *Ibid.*
49 Mahani (2000: 185).
50 Malaysia (1998).
51 Mahani (2000: 186).
52 Tripathi and Saywell (1998: 52).
53 *The Economist*, 12 September 1998, p.93.
54 Jomo (2001a: 201).
55 *Ibid.*, pp. 204-07.
56 Beeson (2000: 348).
57 Alan Brown, of State Street Global Advisors, London, quoted in 'Executive Action', *Asiaweek*, 11 September 1998, p. 36.
58 'Malaysia needs to end isolation', *Asian Wall Street Journal*, 23 June 1999.
59 Bhagwati (1998).
60 Sachs (1998: 19).
61 *Asiaweek*, 18 September 1998.
62 Mahathir (1998a).
63 Higgott (2000).
64 Beeson (2000: 335).
65 Hiebert (1998: 14) reported that an UMNO delegate to the party's general assembly said, 'There's a lot of unhappiness against the prime minister. Small traders blame him for mismanagement of the economy and selective bailouts. People are getting fed up with his constant attack on foreigners. It's beginning to hurt us.'
66 RAM (1997).

67 Mahathir (1998a: 21).
68 Bank Negara Malaysia (1998: 80).
69 *Ibid.*
70 *Ibid.*
71 Thillainathan (2003: 12-13).
72 Tan Tat Wai (2003: 31).
73 *The Star*, 1 July 1998
74 'How dare you say these things!', *Time*, 15 June 1998 (http://www.pathfinder.co...malaysia_interview.html).
75 'A Difference in Style', *Asiaweek*, 19 December 1997.
76 *Ibid.*
77 'What is Success Without Freedom?', *Time*, 6 October 1997, pp. 23-24.
78 Saludo and Shameen (1998: 44).
79 Malaysia (1998: no pagination, Box 1).
80 'When stability is vital for growth', *New Straits Times*, 23 August 2000.
81 Jomo (2001b: xviii).
82 'A Difference in Style', *Asiaweek*, 19 December 1997.
83 'Camdessus accepts DPM's invitation to visit Malaysia', *New Straits Times*, 10 January 1998.
84 Mahathir (2000b).
85 Jomo (2001b: xx).
86 *Ibid.*, xxiv
87 *The Economist*, 7 March 1998, p. 7.
88 And this 'will be viewed by many as a form of thievery' (Godement 1998: 28). Yet even the opening of the financial system to foreign penetration was being contemplated, as see the Deputy Minister of Finance's statement about the need to reconsider raising the limit on foreign equity in financial institutions beyond 50% (*New Straits Times*, 30 July 1998).
89 'How dare you say these things!', *Time*, 15 June 1998 http://www..pathfinder.co...malaysia_interview.html).
90 'Mahathir Mohamad's Very Bad Bet', *Fortune*, 24 November 1997, p. 23.
91 'Mahathir vs. Soros', *Far Eastern Economic Review*, 2 October 1997, p. 32.
92 Patomäki (2001: 11).
93 Bank for International Settlements (1999: 47).
94 Lim (1998: 125-29, 142-45).
95 Tan (2003: 38).
96 Mahathir (1998c: 86).

4
The Inventions of Anwar Ibrahim

Question: Are these allegations directed at Datuk Seri Anwar Ibrahim?
Answer: Yes ... apparently because people think that he is likely going [*sic*] to succeed me. An attempt is being made to paint him black so that he won't succeed. That's all.
Question: You are saying that this is to damage Datuk Seri Anwar's reputation?
Answer: I don't think it will damage. Unless somebody is very stupid to believe such ridiculous accusations against him.
Excerpts from an interview with Mahathir Mohamad,
New Straits Times, 25 August 1997

It's unfortunate because my views on corruption, on corporate governance, on ground rules for privatization, on cronyism, nepotism, on human rights were not directed at a few people but at creating a better society. But they thought these issues were too radical. (Some people also) felt I was going to challenge Mahathir. No amount of assurances I gave satisfied them.
Anwar Ibrahim, quoted in 'I Never Threatened the PM',
Asiaweek, 18 September 1998, p. 50

The international media has shown considerable interest in the purported differences between Anwar and Mahathir – in terms of their personalities, styles, opinions and policies – ever since Anwar toppled Ghafar Baba from the UMNO deputy president's position in 1993 and was appointed Deputy Prime Minister shortly thereafter. The media's interest turned into a persistent question during the run-up to the 1996 UMNO party elections: would Anwar challenge Mahathir for UMNO's presidency? In the end, there was no contest between Anwar and Mahathir. Anwar stated repeatedly that he would not challenge Mahathir, who Anwar considered to be his mentor and was like a father to him. Mahathir insisted he would abide by UMNO's choice of his deputy in the party and government. After the 1996 UMNO party elections, Mahathir and Anwar trivialized further talk of their differences. From May to July 1997, when Mahathir went on vacation, he officially appointed Anwar as Acting Prime Minister for the first time. Most observers understood the arrangement to be not only a test of Anwar's ability but also a sign of Mahathir's confidence in his 'anointed successor'. When Mahathir returned to Malaysia at the end of his vacation in mid-July, he pronounced himself satisfied with Anwar's two-month management of the country. It was also indicative of Mahathir and Anwar's closeness and of Anwar's deference, besides, that the Prime Minister and the Acting Prime Minister had been in regular contact during the two month period, with Anwar consulting Mahathir, when the former thought it necessary.[1]

Mahathir was abroad when the currency crisis began in Thailand in July 1997. When Mahathir returned to Malaysia, the crisis was almost three weeks old. In the year that followed, Mahathir and Anwar played down their differences, referred to common views and spoke of implementing collectively determined Cabinet decisions in the national interest.[2] In June 1998, seemingly exasperated by unrelenting press probes into his relations with Anwar, Mahathir remarked: 'Do I have to kiss him on the street before people will stop saying there is a rift? We get on together, we manage this country together. I admit we have differences, but in the end a common view prevails.'[3]

Late in the afternoon of 2 September 1998, the Prime Minister's office tersely announced, without providing any reason, that Anwar had been sacked from all his posts in government. In the early hours of 4 September the UMNO Supreme Council decided to expel the party's twice-elected deputy president. The enormous shock that followed Anwar's dismissal and expulsion was aggravated by media revelations of allegations of his 'sexual misconduct', Anwar's dramatic arrest on 20 September, his assault by the Inspector-General of Police while in police custody, his controversial prosecutions, convictions and imprisonment, and the shabby treatment (which continues to this day) of Anwar's supporters and opposition quarters, whether by police, media or electoral methods.

Much of what happened to Anwar after his dismissal will be explored in the next chapter as part of an analysis of the course and political implications of the dissident *Reformasi* movement that began with Anwar's defiance of Mahathir and UMNO. Here a fundamental question has to be addressed: how did a long and warm political relationship that seemed to have addressed some of the most difficult problems of Malay and Malaysian politics come to such a destructive end? Mahathir had parted ways with an old comrade, Musa Hitam, following differences that had developed between them in the midst of the 1985-86 recession and other political crises. Even though Mahathir very narrowly defeated his most determined rival, Tengku Razaleigh Hamzah, over a period of several years, Razaleigh returned to UMNO in 1996. Mahathir has not visited upon either Musa or Razaleigh the persecution that Anwar has suffered.

Part of the answer lies in Mahathir and Anwar's differences in economic policy and management, as discussed in the previous chapter. But economics, especially when limited to the circumstances of the July 1997 crisis, can only provide a one-dimensional analysis. What is required is a multi-faceted answer that reaches into the shadows cast by external events and interventions, the personal calculations intrinsic to desperate struggles for political power, UMNO's tortured experience of leadership succession, and, finally, the contradictions of Anwar's career as activist and politician.

Between Praise and Damnation

It was one thing for Mahathir and Anwar to have differences of opinion, worldview and predisposition; it was another for the differences to erupt into the devastating showdown of 1998. After all, Mahathir and Anwar had worked well together from 1981 to 1997. Ever since Mahathir brought Anwar into UMNO in 1982, Anwar had loyally fought Mahathir's major causes within and outside UMNO, the Constitutional crisis of 1983-84 and the UMNO election of 1987 being two prominent instances. Mahathir had reciprocated by providing Anwar ample opportunity to rise in the party and the government. How then did this web of personal allegiance and amity, spun from a long experience of mutual dependability, come to be so rapidly ripped by sudden mistrust? The calculations and manoeuvres that Mahathir and Anwar made under intense pressure were crucial. But it did not help that their decisions were coloured by the two sides of an 'information coin' whose prophecies of rift and effective urgings towards a clash became more compelling during the 1997-98 crisis than under non-crisis conditions.

One side of this 'information coin' was represented by the leading English-language organs of the international media. While Malaysia's heavily controlled domestic media did not have a free hand in reporting any purported deterioration in Mahathir and Anwar's so-called 'father-and-son' relationship, the international media faced no such constraint in highlighting the Mahathir-Anwar 'policy gridlock' and much else besides. Indeed, the more Mahathir clashed with the market and disagreed with the international agencies, the more frequently the voices of the market ran Mahathir down and not so subtly signalled their preference for Anwar.

Anthony Spaeth of *Time* magazine, for example, wrote that 'Anwar assured the world that no matter what Mahathir declared, his deputy would be making rational decisions behind the scenes. But that hasn't always been the case, and a Jekyll-Hyde leadership has developed'.[4] Spaeth, though, was certain that 'the world, meanwhile, increasingly sees an entrenched Prime Minister ... who is trying to protect his associates. At the very least, Dr M. is out of step with the new tune being played by the global economy'.[5] On 1 September 1997, exactly a year before the Mahathir regime instituted the capital controls so dreaded by the market, *Newsweek* noted that:

> Pundits the world over gave Mahathir an F on his economics, for Soros couldn't have brought down the baht alone. But the pundits missed the point. Mahathir's fight with Soros is less about currencies than about whose values will prevail in Southeast Asia.[6]

According to the same *Newsweek* article, 'the only man in Malaysia with anything near enough power to check Mahathir is Anwar,' and, luckily, the magazine insinuated, 'he is coming into his own'.[7] Less than three weeks later, the *Far Eastern Economic Review* of 18 September editorialized, with no sense of incredulity, that, 'from where we sit, Malaysia would do best to take a page out of Indonesia's book and press on even harder with market reforms'. The editorial condescendingly continued:

> To have erred is natural. To make up for it resolutely as Dr Mahathir appears to have started, will require him to take his country more swiftly down the road of market liberalization than originally planned. There is much to make up for in last month's lapse in judgment.[8]

On 27 September, *The Economist* reported that 'businessmen in Kuala Lumpur, traditionally among Dr Mahathir's greatest fans, fear his unorthodox approach might now bring political uncertainty and financial disaster', concluded that 'Dr Mahathir has lost the plot', and recalled, no doubt incongruously, that 'for years the only significant questions in Malaysian politics have been whether the prime minister will hand over to Mr Anwar, and when'.[9] In like vein, *Time* observed on 6 October that 'Mahathir is being blamed for mishandling the Malaysian economy, and the once-lauded architect of Malaysia's boom is looking dangerously out of touch with modern economic realities'.[10] On 24 November 1997, *Fortune* was full of regret at Mahathir's 'very bad bet':

> A more prudent government might react [to the crisis] by squeezing its budget, tightening liquidity, deregulating industry, and welcoming foreign investors. Malaysia will have none of that.
>
> Like everywhere else in Asia, Malaysia needs deep reforms. Unlike everywhere else in Asia, Malaysia denies it.[11]

Mahathir refused to undertake 'radical reforms', the market and the media noted, and 'whenever he can, Mahathir flays the world for its unbridled power and callousness'.[12] Fortunately, 'Anwar's philosophy is vastly different'[13] and Anwar thought that 'we should not be apologetic in stating the fact that we have to undertake these reforms. We have to be more transparent and have a committed resolve to combat corruption and excesses of power.'[14]

Mahathir reflexively blamed foreign manipulators. Anwar, who declared that 'in politics I am a liberal but in economics I am a conservative', mused thus about the crisis:

> The great lesson we have learned, which is actually a major transformation and a revolution by itself, is that it has called for greater transparency, greater accountability and for greater democracy.
>
> Now people assess what the markets say, what people perceive, whether awards and grants are given to your party supporters or to friends and family. These are openly debated, without exception. I see this as very positive.[15]

Hence, the market and its media began to suggest that only Anwar could 'save Malaysia from too much Mahathir and also bring new ideas to the region'.[16] Anwar, since he appeared to want to wed liberal politics to neoliberal economics, seemed like the new leader the market should do business with:

> People in my generation would certainly like to see greater liberty, access to literature and knowledge, less censorship. We don't have an obsession about the need for order and political stability. We did not experience the same turbulence that our elders encountered.[17]

It seemed logical that Anwar, who professed to belong to 'a new generation that has no hang-ups about the colonial experience', should want to 'emphasize the issues of civil society, fundamental liberties and the trust and wisdom that the public, with exposure to education and knowledge, should be able to exercise.'[18] In short, Anwar was 'lionized by the media abroad' as 'a sobering voice through the recent financial crisis', unmistakably 'at Mahathir's expense'.[19]

For all that, the market and its media were not blind: 'Anwar and his supporters also know that a new generation can't rise until the old one shuffles on'.[20] But was it not a matter of time before someone told the 'old generation' to 'shuffle on'? One week before the 1998 UMNO General Assembly, Barry Wain, writing in *The Asian Wall Street Journal* of 12-13 June, bluntly asked, 'Why doesn't Mahathir bow out?'[21] Wain's question probably articulated a deep wish that had been on many minds of the international media for about a year.

For the record, the international media was never implacably anti-Mahathir; otherwise the media would have shunned him, as it had shunned the truly unacceptable leaders of regimes the western powers castigated as 'pariahs'. Knowing Mahathir to be, ultimately, a friend of the west, and a protector of western commercial interests in Malaysia, the media had learnt to transform Mahathir's testiness and superficial critiques of the west into newsworthy 'controversial opinion'. On Mahathir's part, even though he has frequently reviled the international media or complained of its unfair treatment of him, the Malays, and Malaysia, Mahathir had frequently spoken to, been interviewed by, and written for the international media throughout his career. Mahathir astutely values the international media's reach that has enabled him to acquire a statesmanlike stature out of proportion to Malaysia's humble position in the world. Thus, Mahathir and the international media had developed the proverbial love-hate relationship. That each took occasional pot shots at the other only enhanced their credibility among their constituencies.

After July 1997, however, as Mahathir grew increasingly intransigent towards the international money market's demands for reforms, the international media significantly altered its attitude towards Mahathir. In doing that, the media was being perspicacious: there was no likelier time than an economic crisis for turning even minor disagreements between Mahathir and Anwar into serious splits. The media was also being pernicious: 'wondering whether Anwar's rise is setting the stage for a leadership challenge in 1999,'[22] the media virtually welcomed a Mahathir-Anwar confrontation as an embodiment of the disagreements between the state and the market. And in relying on the insecurity of the one and the ambition of the other to ignite a clash between 'No. 1' and 'No. 2', the media was being perverse. The interests of the money market and the neoliberal agenda of unfettered capital flows were being advanced in the name of a free press covering the political developments of a less-than-free nation.

Others who had a direct interest in a Mahathir-Anwar rift were no less partisan but not quite as sophisticated. The international side of the 'information coin' that circulated in 1997-98 had the advantages of openness, legitimacy and authority. Its flip side, minted from shady, presumably domestic, elements, had the habit of being hidden, unlawful and scurrilous. This domestic source of 'information' – mostly *fitnah* (slander) and *tohmah* (baseless accusation) – appeared in many forms, the most well known being the *surat layang* ('flying' or poison-pen letter).

The favourite topics of the political *surat layang* were corruption and sexual misconduct among politicians, and mostly UMNO ones at that. Since a good part of the art of UMNO's infighting was conducted as *wayang kulit* (shadow play), the *surat layang* typically made a stealthy appearance before or during the UMNO general assembly, party elections, and the general election. It was a rare contender for UMNO's highest posts who escaped being the subject of a *surat layang*, aimed at bringing a rival into disrepute or an antagonist down. Not all *surat layang* were, reportedly, entirely false in their contents! Yet the *surat layang* as a genre of calumny and character assassination was too indirect to be an effective weapon – unless the misconduct it exposed was too widely known and too serious to be overlooked.

Since the 1980s, perhaps because of the ineffectiveness of anonymous vilification, the slanderous rumours and libellous *surat layang* were sometimes overshadowed by the emergence of privately published but openly marketed books whose authors did hatchet jobs on selected targets. An infamous example of these books was *Challenger: Siapa Lawan Siapa?* that vilified Musa Hitam before the 1987 UMNO party election.

In August 1997, Anwar became the subject of 'already seven, eight letters from various parties ... some signed, others not'[23] – and some sent directly to the Prime Minister – which accused Anwar of immoral behaviour, specifically his alleged sexual escapades, heterosexual and homosexual. The appearance of these letters was generally taken to mean that:

> a few of Anwar's opponents within UMNO have already resorted to extreme measures to keep the deputy premier in check.... Few believe the letters, but the affair is graphic evidence of the desperate lengths to which Anwar's enemies are prepared to go.[24]

The most prominent person who did *not* believe the letters or their authors was Mahathir himself. At a press conference held on 24 August 1997, Mahathir categorically dismissed the letters as 'just the usual *fitnah*' employed here to 'sabotage' Anwar 'apparently because people think he is likely going [sic] to succeed me'.[25] The authors of some of the letters, presumably to enhance the credibility of what they wrote, disdained to conceal their identities or their aims. Two such writers who sent letters about Anwar to Mahathir were Ummi Hafilda, the sister of Anwar's private secretary, Azmin Ali, and Azizan Abu Bakar, Anwar's former driver. Mahathir laughed off one effort to discredit Anwar:

> The writer denied the contents.... Yes, the person wrote the letter. Somebody dictated the letter. The letter was written in a language beyond the capacity of one of the writers. Obviously somebody has been moving around and talking about last rites (*talkin*) for someone. It is totally political. There is no truth in it.[26]

But Mahathir had no doubt about the political motives of the unseen hands that had set others to 'paint a bad picture of Anwar so that he doesn't succeed me'.[27]

While the contents of various *surat layang* irritated or titillated the various participants in UMNO's internal disputes, serious investigations were rarely carried out to determine their veracity. Perhaps because the anti-Anwar material was openly aimed at the prime minister's 'anointed successor', and 'this time it's been more planned, organized and meticulous',[28] as Anwar observed, there was a police investigation. Mahathir, who was concurrently Minister of Home Affairs, announced that 'the police looked into this [matter] but since then we have found that there is no case.'[29] The flow of anti-Anwar literature was not stemmed. There were books as well – *Talkin Untuk Anwar Ibrahim (Requiem for Anwar Ibrahim)*, and Khalil Jafri's *50 Dalil Mengapa Anwar Tidak Boleh Jadi PM* that purported to give '50 Reasons Why Anwar Cannot Be PM'. At the time, there might have been 'no case' against Anwar. Yet observers already suspected that 'neither [were] the attacks likely to cease: Insiders [said] an all-out effort could yet be mounted to prevent Anwar from rising to the top.'[30] This was indeed a conspiracy, as confirmed by an ex-deputy prime minister, Musa Hitam, who was not aligned in the Mahathir-Anwar split:

> I do know there are individuals involved who were planning and who in fact told me what will be done against Anwar to make sure he will be toppled. So in that sense, yes, there was a political conspiracy definitely.[31]

On the Way to the Assembly

Anwar's position was precarious: the international media praised his 'virtues', while the anti-Anwar letters and books exposed his purported 'vices'. The two sides were not literary or informational opposites that balanced each other. On both counts, Anwar was damnable, as long as someone was inclined to find fault with him. Unhappily for Anwar, Mahathir was so inclined by the time of the UMNO General Assembly in June 1998.

One reason lay in the practice of *realpolitik* required to maintain oneself in power. Ghani Ismail suggested that Mahathir's concern to divide potential challengers explained why Mahathir supported Musa Hitam against Razaleigh Hamzah in their 1981 battle for the UMNO deputy presidency, when Razaleigh should have slipped into the position and become the deputy prime minister.[32] Musa explained that he resigned as Deputy Prime Minister, after Mahathir had accused Musa of privately discrediting the Prime Minister in order to 'bring him down'. Musa denied being party to 'anti-Mahathirist activities' but Mahathir just said that 'too many senior government officials and journalists have reported it.'[33] Later, a wiser Musa advised Anwar never to give Mahathir cause to doubt Anwar's loyalty.

Another reason for Mahathir's change in attitude towards Anwar was related to Mahathir's temperament and experience that would have made him extremely uneasy over what he believed Anwar's intentions were and Anwar's relations with the media, money market and the IMF. If we were to consider Mahathir's expulsion from UMNO in 1969, the attempt to frame him for being a 'communist' during the 1976 UMNO witch hunt, Musa's 'disloyalty', and Razaleigh's nearly successful challenge, it would be apparent that Mahathir's political career has been deeply etched with ideological antipathy and suspicion towards different sets of enemies.

After Mahathir reached the pinnacle of political power, the most sensitive issues that could be posed to him involved his successor and the timing of his retirement. Mahathir had not said he would never retire but he had warned he would not be pushed out on someone else's terms. Understandably, Mahathir's distinction has been ignored as he tenaciously resisted being replaced, even when his popularity in UMNO waned, for example, during the 1985-86 recession and when UMNO split in 1987-88. In the midst of the 1997-98 crisis, one that Mahathir regarded as being externally manipulated, there was no question then of Mahathir retiring. Obviously, Mahathir meant to protect interests important to him. Even so, he could claim a 'grander' motive: 'Mahathir had given 17 years of sustained effort to building economic prosperity, Vision modernity and UMNO hegemony, none of which he intended to see sacrificed in a moment of domestic uncertainty'.[34]

Mahathir had been too extensively involved with the management of the crisis and immersed in a battle with the money market. To retreat would only have meant defeat and disrepute. Let alone being edged out like Tunku Abdul Rahman after the interethnic violence of May 1969, it would have been unimaginable to Mahathir that he should share the fate of ex-Indonesian President Suharto who was deposed in May 1998. It was scarcely conceivable that Mahathir would consider it mere coincidence that Anwar 'followed the IMF prescription too closely' and articulated the sentiments of a 'new generation' by employing such terms as transparency, cronyism, good governance, and creative destruction. Part of the vocabulary of an international media hostile towards Mahathir, these were 'fighting words'. When In-Won Hwang interviewed Musa Hitam after Anwar's sacking, Musa recalled that he had:

> personally been talking to Anwar saying that 'you will be in trouble'. But he always said that 'no, I have talked to the PM, I told him everything. I don't keep him out of touch with my thinking'. That was more reason that I was worried because that was exactly what I said when I was DPM.[35]

One is not apologizing for Mahathir by inferring that a man with his temperament and experience and with his back to the wall would have considered the coincidental as conspiratorial. After his dismissal, Anwar said that 'it would have served no purpose to challenge [Mahathir], especially at this juncture when the economy was turning bad'; however, Anwar admitted that:

> I also wanted [Mahathir] to understand the undercurrents in the country. I indicated that we should either make adjustments now or let a smooth transition take place eventually. But I never threatened him. I wanted to let him determine the time frame for transition. He thought I was too much of a nuisance or obstacle.[36]

'Undercurrents', 'adjustments', 'smooth transition', 'time frame' – could these words have held any meaning for Mahathir other than disloyalty, challenge, threat and succession whenever they were uttered, let alone in 1997-98?

The die was cast at the Pemuda UMNO (UMNO Youth) assembly of June 1998, held one day before the main UMNO General Assembly. Despite Mahathir's warnings to UMNO members not to be swayed by foreign attacks on Asian 'cronyism and nepotism', Ahmad Zahid Hamidi, Pemuda UMNO President, criticized the practices of 'cronyism' and 'nepotism' in the management of the economy. By then, many people, in and out of UMNO, were extremely worried about Mahathir's handling of the crisis. According to unconfirmed reports, even senior politicians wanted Anwar to 'stop the old man', while others appealed to Anwar to 'lead us out of this darkness'.[37] Even so, it is not established whether Anwar actually directed Zahid and the Anwar camp in UMNO to launch the clumsy criticism of Mahathir's economic management. But however moderate, nuanced or contextualised Zahid's speech before the Pemuda UMNO assembly might have been, it came too close on the heels of the Indonesian anti-KKN (*kolusi, korupsi* dan *nepotisme*, or collusion, corruption and nepotism) *Reformasi* movement that toppled Suharto in May, a month earlier. Mahathir counter-attacked with a typically unabashed claim: his 'cronyism' and 'nepotism', he said, had helped 'six million cronies', meaning the NEP's Malay beneficiaries. Official data released to the press showed that Zahid and members of Anwar's family were among the NEP beneficiaries. Zahid's caper fizzled, without any sequel from Anwar or visible support within UMNO. That in itself raised questions as to whether the Anwar camp was prepared for the consequences of Zahid's move, or whether it had decided to pull back nervously when Zahid's move failed to produce its intended effects.

Afterwards, Anwar professed his loyalty to Mahathir in vain. Was Anwar innocent or complacent? Had Anwar been misled or pressured? For Mahathir, the circumstantial was conclusive: Zahid's speech was proof of a plot to discredit Mahathir at the UMNO General Assembly, maybe to the extent of causing Mahathir to resign.[38] And Zahid was 'Anwar's man'. Writing for the *Mainichi Daily News* of Japan in January 2000, Mahathir accused Anwar of 'building a personal following in preparation to overthrow myself as the president of Umno and Prime Minister'.[39] Later Mahathir would recount that:

> the conspiracy by Anwar to topple the Prime Minister is very much public knowledge. A lot of information has been passed on to me on Anwar's conspiracy and I also knew he was the culprit who made Zahid Hamidi to (*sic*) hurl accusations at me.[40]

Subsequently, Mahathir claimed that 'I still wished to see Anwar take over my place because I had decided to quit after 1998'. But Mahathir made this statement at the UMNO General Assembly in 2000. Later still, Mahathir gave an elaborate account of Anwar's plot:

> This man had been brought up by me, pushed up until he became my deputy, was all along working for himself. His inclination would have been to join PAS. But he joined UMNO because he foresaw no future for PAS. There was no way PAS could ever make him prime minister. He came into UMNO because he thought he would be able to turn it his way. All along he was plotting. I underestimated his capacity for creating trouble.[41]

When asked if he did not bring Anwar into UMNO 'because you needed to give UMNO an Islamic face', Mahathir continued:

> I brought him into UMNO to keep him from joining PAS and creating mischief. Once you are in UMNO you must accept UMNO's struggle, and not make use of UMNO for your personal purpose. He built up cells in every organisation, in the police, in the armed forces, in the civil service, among the students, among the university teachers, abroad. He was building up personal loyalty to himself, using his power. Once he became deputy prime minister his next step was to overthrow me. [42]

Mahathir concluded: 'I could not imagine that a person I helped would do that.'[43] But why then did Mahathir not sack Anwar on those grounds of 'plotting' and 'betrayal' and face UMNO on that terrain? For that matter, why did Mahathir not extend the charges to include an accusation that Anwar was a stooge of foreign interests? Perhaps, after Zahid's caper, a resentful Mahathir, refusing to be humiliatingly pushed out, reinterpreted his association with Anwar in the light of the latter's 'betrayal'. Perhaps, in a bitter reconstruction of the past – the kind that happens frequently during falling-outs – Mahathir underwent a change of heart that made him believe the very allegations of Anwar's 'immoral conduct' that he had dismissed barely a year ago.

The point was, the *50 Dalil* book was packed into the briefcases that were distributed to the delegates at the 1998 UMNO General Assembly. Those who had sponsored the composition and distribution of the *surat layang*, the signed letters to the Prime Minister, *Talkin Untuk Anwar Ibrahim*, and the 'star publication', *50 Dalil*, could not have hoped for a better fulfilment of their hopes: their agenda was now Mahathir's.

The Improbability of Succession

Between the General Assembly and National Day (31 August), rumours circulated that Anwar would resign as Deputy Prime Minister. The rumours were proven wrong, and crucially so. Mahathir, and some of his intermediaries, including Daim, privately asked Anwar to resign or face serious criminal charges. No one has revealed other conditions for Anwar's resignation, including how he would have been politically disabled thereafter. Anwar refused and the rest can be subsumed under *Reformasi* history about which much has deservedly been written.

Anwar's dismissal also brought about a quiet, traumatic shock that UMNO, Malay society and Malaysian politics felt at losing the *third* deputy prime minister under Mahathir, at the sudden departure of a man widely hailed as Mahathir's 'anointed successor' to both UMNO's presidency and the premiership. In that sense, Anwar's dismissal confirmed the deep and tormented history of the problem of leadership succession within UMNO.

Anwar's sobriquet of 'anointed successor' had not been carelessly employed by UMNO leaders and the media chiefs. Anwar's 'anointment' was not only most strenuously upheld by his supporters, it had also been legitimized by the results of UMNO's 1993 and 1996 elections. As such, the anointment had assuaged the uncertainties caused by years of UMNO infighting that precluded an assured transfer of leadership from Mahathir to someone else, if only because that 'someone else' kept disappearing from view. Mahathir's first deputy premier, Musa Hitam, resigned in 1986 and failed afterwards to retain his previously strong influence in UMNO. Mahathir's first Minister of Finance, Razaleigh Hamzah, unsuccessfully fought Mahathir for UMNO's presidency in 1987, and was forced into marginal opposition in 1988. Ghafar Baba, whom Mahathir appointed as Musa's replacement in government, narrowly defeated Musa for UMNO's deputy presidency in 1987. But Ghafar was defeated by Anwar in 1993. In the mid-1990s, therefore, only Anwar, via two consecutive party elections, had secured the depth of party support that signalled that a successor had arrived. Mahathir seemed to have accepted as much, since once, when irked by persistent media speculation over his retirement, he said that Anwar 'can step into the job if for some reason I should drop dead or become disabled'.[44]

It was expected that Mahathir, having been in power since 1981, would step down before too long, but that Anwar would be loyal to Mahathir until then. But whether or when Mahathir would depart office, or whether Anwar would patiently wait his turn or whether he would be pressured by his supporters into challenging Mahathir, were major questions that hung over practically all developments concerning UMNO between 1994 and 1995.[45] Mahathir and Anwar protested this line of thinking, evidently to no avail. Perhaps many preferred to believe that both men protested too much. Rumours then took on a new twist: Mahathir would undermine Anwar's influence in UMNO by backing a new contestant for the party deputy presidency. The would-be challenger was sometimes said to be Anwar's 1993 ally, Najib Tun Razak, the Minister of Education. At other times, as improbable a candidate as Mahathir's old foe and returnee from Parti Semangat 46, Razaleigh Hamzah, was mentioned.[46]

Whatever the truth of the rumours, the major riddle of the 1996 UMNO election was whether Anwar could extend his influence over the party. Mahathir answered the riddle by having the Supreme Council pass three new rulings regarding the impending election. The first ruling took its cue from the 1995 UMNO General Assembly that had resolved that the two top party posts should not be contested. The party's divisions could only nominate Mahathir for president and Anwar for deputy president. Any other nomination or configuration of nominations for the party's two top posts would be rejected. The second ruling stipulated that candidates for the three posts of vice-president, and the twenty-five Supreme Council seats, as well as for all posts in Pemuda UMNO and Wanita UMNO, were required to register their candidacy five months ahead of the general assembly. This stipulation significantly departed from UMNO's tradition of allowing contenders to engage in diverse forms of campaigning long before they declared their candidacy. Most contenders had previously resorted to this form of concealment, partly for the tactical advantage of throwing off their opponents and partly not to offend a presumed Malay cultural distaste for a premature display of personal ambition. Razaleigh had used a late declaration to great effect in 1987; more pertinently, so had Anwar against Ghafar. And then, just five days after the official starting date for campaigning, the Supreme Council banned further campaigning. In Mahathir's words, the ban was:

> the party's way of ensuring fairness to all because there are some candidates who can afford to campaign while others cannot. Members have come up to some candidates who are clean and said we will not support you if you don't give us money. Banning campaigning is one way to level out the opportunity for all.[47]

As it turned out, the Anwar camp swept the Pemuda UMNO and Wanita UMNO elections. Ahmad Zahid Hamidi emerged as President of Pemuda UMNO while critical support from the Anwar camp enabled Siti Zaharah to win the Wanita UMNO presidency against the incumbent Rafidah Aziz. Against predictions, however, there was no sweep by the Anwar camp at the parent body's election. For the vice-presidential contests, no key Anwar ally was returned. Najib Tun Razak and Muhammad Muhammad Taib were re-elected, while Abdullah Badawi regained the seat he had lost in 1993. Najib and Muhammad were members of the 1993 Wawasan Team but Abdullah Badawi, a former Musa associate, was a popular figure in his own right. Significantly, Muhyiddin Yassin, identified as a staunch Anwar man, was not re-elected despite having received the highest vote for vice-president in 1993. Mahathir loyalists dominated the new Supreme Council.

The crowning glory of Mahathir's performance in 1996 was not just his control over his party. It was that he had shifted the burden of the succession question away from himself onto Anwar! Mahathir made it clear that he would continue as party president and prime minister and refused to set a 'succession timetable':

> Why should I give a clear timetable? The moment you give a timetable, you are a lame duck. That's what happens to Western leaders. ... No, I have given nothing. I have said nothing. I can go any time now or 10 years later or whatever. Depends on what the situation is like. I told you whoever is in place as my deputy will succeed me. [48]

Following the 1996 election, Anwar's chief concern was to secure his 'No. 2' spot. UMNO's 1996 election had proven Anwar's control of the party to be less powerful than speculated. But time seemed to be on Anwar's side as he set out to spread his influence over the party. Indeed, by 1998, as the UMNO divisions completed their elections, both of office-bearers and delegates to the 1999 general assembly, it was widely believed that the Anwar camp commanded a plurality of the delegates. Such strong support, if supplemented by support from other party factions, might have enabled Anwar to mount a successful campaign against Mahathir in 1999, should a contest for the presidency take place.

Up to mid-1997, a smooth transition from Mahathir to Anwar was not an implausible scenario.[49] However, July 1997 wrecked that scenario.[50] Anwar's dismissal became the most drastic failure in UMNO's 41-year history of leadership transition. From 1957 to 1976, the party generally heeded the prerogative of its president-cum-premier to determine his successor. It is a moot question whether this tacit acceptance of the leader's prerogative was a vindication of a democratic observance of established procedures, or a confirmation of UMNO's and Malaysia's 'semi' or 'quasi' democracy. In any case, an uncontested exercise of the leader's prerogative had facilitated relatively smooth transitions under diverse circumstances. These were the bloodless palace coup against Tunku Abdul Rahman after May 1969, the sudden death of Tun Abdul Razak in 1976, and the voluntary retirement of Tun Hussein Onn in 1981.

During the subsequent period, from 1981 to 1987, UMNO's problem of leadership transition became sharply contentious as unrestrained competition among UMNO's rival centres of power coincided with the ability of the party to exercise a mandate to determine Mahathir's successor. It is likewise moot whether the party's mandate, arguably a democratic improvement over the leader's prerogative, was to be preferred, since the price of someone securing the mandate was the party's own institutional instability.

In a third period, from 1993 to 1996, the shifting balance of power between the leader and the party at large appeared to reach a stalemate. For all his politically circumspect statements, Mahathir no longer trusted the party on the matter of his succession that was synonymous with his own survival in a time of economic crisis.

At the critical juncture of 1998, Mahathir's actual mastery (or possession) of state power rendered Anwar's reputed control of the party a dispensable formality. In expelling Anwar, Mahathir and the Supreme Council sought to roll back the party's history. They pre-empted an Anwar comeback via a Musa Hitam-style separation between being Deputy Prime Minister – an appointment that could be terminated by the Prime Minister – and being UMNO Deputy President – that should be undone only through another party election. In early 1999, the Supreme Council indefinitely postponed the 1999 party election.

Anwar's assumed plurality of delegates having come to naught, he was compelled to continue his opposition outside UMNO. Thus commenced what many observers have called the reinvention of Anwar Ibrahim. Looking back on Anwar's personal history, though, the reinvention had its seed not in the *Reformasi* he inspired but in the contradictions of a 30-year trajectory of social activism and politics.

Four Phases and a Contradiction

In his activist and political career up to his dismissal by Mahathir, Anwar may be said to have gone through four different phases. During the first phase, which straddled the watershed year of 1969, Anwar was a student leader at the University of Malaya. There, in the milieu of a still vibrant and relatively autonomous campus student politics open to a broad ideological spectrum, Anwar led the Persatuan Bahasa Melayu (Malay Language Society) and Persatuan Kebangsaan Pelajar-pelajar Islam Malaysia (National Union of Malaysian Muslim Students). Anwar's second phase began after his graduation in 1971. With a few others, Anwar founded Angkatan Belia Islam Malaysia (ABIM, or Malaysian Islamic Youth Force) and built it into an important vehicle of an Islamic resurgence, which was all the more powerful for being the voice of a new generation of Malay-Muslim youth. The third and longest phase found Anwar in UMNO and government. Between 1982, when he was elected Member of Parliament for Permatang Pauh, Penang, and 1998, Anwar rose from being co-opted into the early Mahathir regime to emerging as Mahathir's 'anointed successor', and did so with a dizzying rapidity that alarmed many of his rivals in UMNO. The present phase is the post-September 1998 phase when the persecution of Anwar, the latter's defiance and popular dissent combined to reinvent Anwar as the icon of *Reformasi*.

What does this outline of Anwar's activist involvement, career advancement and political fall say about him? One thing is immediately striking. In three out of his four phases, Anwar took an anti-establishment stance. To state matters plainly, Anwar was anti-Tunku Abdul Rahman after 1969, he was anti-Barisan Nasional in the mid-1970s, and he has been anti-Mahathir and anti-UMNO since September 1998. Only during that long third phase was Anwar a leading figure of the establishment.

Anwar's ideological commitments in those anti-establishment phases seem varied enough when they are viewed separately. His 'Malay nationalism' of the late 1960s was associated with an earnest if sometimes melodramatic promotion of the Malay language as the national language. It also embraced the kinds of economic concerns that soon came under the purview of the New Economic Policy. Anwar's Persatuan Bahasa Melayu stance, activities and image drew him to someone like Mahathir, newly expelled from UMNO and widely admired by Malays as a self-sacrificing 'Malay nationalist'. Almost three decades later, Anwar still recalled a 1970 trip he had made to Kedah to visit Mahathir as 'a great meeting', and he had then thought of Mahathir that 'this was one Malay intellectual who can articulate the Malay position and has the guts to do it'.[51] Anwar himself became something of the isolated Mahathir's ally on the University of Malaya campus, from which Anwar and his colleagues 'gave the entire university system to Mahathir as a forum'.[52] On his part, Mahathir let Anwar read drafts of what was later published as *The Malay Dilemma*.

During the 1970s, Anwar's commitments within ABIM were initially expressed via Yayasan Anda's educational activities in aid of Malay-Muslim students and via the nascent campus *dakwah* movement that was emerging both at home and in some foreign universities to which many Malay students had been sent. In a sense, ABIM was just one step removed from Anwar's earlier on-campus attempt at 'uniting the Malay nationalist and Islamic streams in Malay student politics'.[53] But as the NEP's implementation vastly expanded the Malay student population – at home and abroad – Anwar's increasingly high profile and charismatic leadership helped to take ABIM into broader social and political activities. Subsequently, ABIM's programme became more varied but Islam remained the principal fount from which Anwar and ABIM drew certain Malay, Muslim and moral criticisms of the Barisan Nasional government's policies and their outcomes, impacts and abuses. Indeed Anwar's own stand on poverty, economic inequality and social dislocation under NEP led him, with other politicians and students, to Baling in 1974 to support the large-scale Malay farmers' demonstrations, and thereafter to the Kamunting Camp for 22 months of detention without trial under the Internal Security Act.[54] In the final years of Anwar's Islamic phase, before Anwar joined UMNO, ABIM led a nationwide coalition of societies – what would be better known as non-governmental organisations (NGOs) today – in a major campaign against proposed and more restrictive amendments to the Societies Act. Finally, between 2 September 1998, when he was sacked from government and expelled from UMNO immediately after, and 20 September, when he was last a free man, Anwar inspired a popular movement for democracy, reforms and social justice. Imprisoned since 20 September, Anwar has been able to provide only a symbolic leadership to the multiethnic dissident movement that led to the formation of the Barisan Alternatif just in time for the November 1999 general election. The image of Anwar's raised fist and battered face and swollen eye, however, has been evoked by every defiant chant of *Re-for-ma-si!* heard since late 1998.

Anwar's ideological and personal commitments of his three 'anti-establishment phases' have never been fully spelt out, which is one reason he was often thought to be malleable, if not outright opportunistic. Taken collectively, however, it can be seen that Anwar's commitments contained three notable threads.

One thread was drawn from the ethnic strands of the different phases. This thread began with Anwar's campus Malay nationalism. It was then modified by ABIM's brand of non-ethnic civil activism. It has since then been grafted onto *Reformasi* to inspire an experiment in multiethnic politics. This first thread captures Anwar's shift, albeit a gradual shift, from 'Malay nationalism' to an ideological position on ethnic relations in Malaysia that was most liberally called multiculturalism in the 1990s.

A second ideological thread developed from ABIM's moral critiques of economic inequalities, social injustice and the restrictions imposed on civil liberties. Over time, the critiques expanded from the defence of the Baling farmers to the national campaign against the Societies Act. After Anwar's sacking, these critiques were dusted from the shelves of his UMNO days and meshed with Barisan Alternatif's opposition to cronyism, corruption and nepotism.

There was an important third thread that was not so much formed by what Anwar stood for, as with whom he most comfortably stood, and who, in his moments of severe tribulation, would firmly stand by him. These were students, youth and civil society. Students, especially college and university students in and out of the country, and 'socially concerned youth' featured prominently in all the phases of Anwar's anti-establishment activism. Civil society was visibly important in his Islamic and *Reformasi* phases. Following Anwar's sacking in September 1998, this third thread supported Anwar and permitted him to re-invent himself as a political activist and re-establish an old affinity with groups and people who, in social and political terms, tend to constitute floating, transient and marginalized constituencies.

Spun together, these three threads not surprisingly made up an ideological fabric laced with cultural motifs, the concerns of civil society and aspirations of moral renewal. This was precisely the intellectual fabric of *The Asian Renaissance*, the book that Anwar published at the peak of his establishment phase.

Rather intriguingly, Anwar's UMNO phase was marked by deep contradictions virtually from start to finish. When Anwar decided to join UMNO in March 1982, he split ABIM, not least because many ABIM leaders and members either abjured direct political involvement or assumed that their natural ally among political parties was the opposition Parti Islam. Taking part of ABIM along with him, Anwar helped to split UMNO, largely because of previous ABIM-UMNO hostility and Anwar's use of his ex-ABIM allies to build up his influence within the party. For the ABIM Anwar, Islam had hitherto nourished a moral critique of Malaysian society under capitalism. But in UMNO, Anwar fell in with Mahathir, for whom Islam meant above all else a work ethic to serve Malaysian capitalism. In leaving ABIM for UMNO and the anti-Societies Act movement for a place in government, Anwar effectively deserted civil society to enter the state. But, 'call me *Saudara*', he liked to speak as if the state could be made to behave like a 'caring civil society'. To his former allies and comrades in civil society, Anwar had justified his co-optation by Mahathir as an individual mission to 'change things from inside the system'. The imperatives of state power, however, left no room for youthful idealism and personal promises: nothing – not the Societies Act, Internal Security Act or Official Secrets Act – was changed from inside.

Nothing changed except perhaps Anwar's mission was personalized as so often happened when a rising star reached for the political firmament. And so, for sixteen years, between 1982 and 1998, Anwar settled down in UMNO and steadily rose within its hierarchy. That meant acculturating himself to the party's politics as it grew murkier by the year. At the time Anwar joined UMNO, he might not have expected that the party's factionalism and infighting were just whirling out of control. UMNO as political terrain had been transformed into an unforgiving arena where considerations and configurations of state power, party influence and corporate wealth determined where one stood. Factions and teams within UMNO were assembled only to be re-assembled. To survive, let alone prosper, one increasingly valued friends to the degree that they were the enemies of enemies. With Mahathir's support, Anwar defeated Suhaimi Kamaruddin for the Pemuda UMNO presidency in 1982. Anwar was a key Team A lieutenant in the 1987 party election that split UMNO. By 1993, when Anwar led his 'Wawasan Team' to victory in the UMNO election, and became the party's deputy president, Anwar had unquestionably become a veteran of UMNO's factional politics.

Where in this kind of a heartless world was one to find a haven for one's soul? Speaking politically, not spiritually, Anwar might have thought he could chart a haven by negotiating a space between unstoppable political imperatives and unattainable personal impulses. For example, Anwar was aware he could not alter the course of Mahathir's programme of late industrialization but Anwar would try to put a benign face to the programme. Anwar could not prevent all kinds of social, economic and political injustices, particularly those inflicted upon the weak and meek, but he would offer them his sympathy. He could not quite control the rapacity of Malaysia Inc.'s corporate bosses during their heyday but he made to spare a thought for the rest of society. Sceptics would call all this hypocrisy. A neutral way of looking at it is to regard most of it as the politics of an uneasy conscience that is often practised by those who have 'joined the system' but believe that they 'have not sold out'.

Even if one wanted to, however, one could not continue to play the political game at the apex of party and state and be able to switch off the ostentation and insincerity of 'Kay-el' (Kuala Lumpur) on demand, and *balik kampung* to rustic simplicity and grassroots warmth! In good times, one was apt to sound like a wimp. In tense situations, one was called a 'non-team player'. When the chips were down, one could be suspected of being a turncoat. Then one would be taunted in UMNO parlance: *Mahu makan taukeh ke?* (Do you mean to do in the boss?) Surely none of this was new to Anwar. Indeed, at Mahathir's side, Anwar had watched Musa fail in that kind of a game where 'No. 2' played a different fiddle from 'No. 1' and probably played dissimilar tunes before diverse audiences. For example, Musa, according to supporters and detractors alike, appeared to be liberal and approachable in contrast to the authoritarian and blunt Mahathir. Musa, too, had a habit of going back to the 'grassroots' and paying attention to their mundane or local difficulties, whereas Mahathir was inclined to spend his time hobnobbing with the *tokoh korporat* on mammoth projects.

With Anwar repeating Musa's 'habit', the latent problem of a Mahathir-Anwar rift was there long before matters degenerated into the tragedy of September 1998. Like Musa before him, Anwar probably never quite shared Mahathir's conception of the nationalist-capitalist project. At least, Anwar probably did not pursue the project with the same drive. Mahathir's intensity of purpose, sense of historical mission and immense personal pride meant that he would never apologize to anyone for devoting himself to the hardnosed preoccupations of the corporate world, the money market and the global economy. Between the 1960s and the 1990s, Mahathir had come a very long way from being 'a man of the people' to being the captain of the captains of industry, and the patron of the movers and shakers of Malaysia's business and political world. For the Mahathir of Vision 2020, people were stirred by boundless ambition, goaded into ceaseless competition, and inspired by actual achievement – or else, they were destined for failure.

Anwar appeared to apologize on Mahathir's behalf, so to speak, by dabbling in a vague moral economy, or what might roughly be called 'Anwar's agenda'. There was fundamentally not much more to this agenda than a hope that a helping hand might stop the devil from taking society's hindmost. This was not necessarily an insincere hope, even as Anwar rose in prominence and even if no one kept a tally of the real achievement of Anwar's agenda as opposed to the rhetorical satisfaction it provided from expressing concern with popular access to low-cost housing and low-cost healthcare, helping the poor, and assisting the dislocated. Presumably Anwar, again like Musa before him, thought that this was a way of balancing different approaches, as Wan Azizah suggested after Anwar's sacking:

> We had such a good thing (going) for our country. Okay, (the) PM – tallest building, tallest this, tallest that. Okay, he has the vision – great for our

country, why not? And then you have Anwar talking about the masses, low-cost housing, taking care of your workers, this and that. Why not? This is a good combination. That's how our country should work.[55]

For that matter, after July 1997, mostly out of necessity but not therefore out of character, Anwar wanted to minister to the financial needs of the 'little guys' of the economic system – including allocating funds to small farmers, extending micro-credit to hawkers, traders and small entrepreneurs, providing assistance to 'the poorest', improving rural and urban health facilities, and securing funds for rural infrastructure and facilities.[56] One final instance revealed something novel. In the salad days of Malaysia Inc. and Vision 2020, Mahathir regularly took on his official travels the heads of many domestic conglomerates and urged or helped them to conquer foreign markets in far-flung places. Minister of Finance Anwar had his share of rubbing shoulders with the corporate elite. Yet Anwar seemed genuinely excited at the prospect of sending Yayasan Salam (Malaysia's incipient version of the USA's Peace Corps) to poorer nations. In Anwar's scheme of things, one might speculate, would that be akin to using the state to spread ABIM's Yayasan Anda to needy corners of the world?

In other words, Anwar's common threads were, arguably, woven across his UMNO phase as well, with the consequence that he led, as it were, a contradictory coexistence of pro-establishment and anti-establishment parts. For most of Anwar's sixteen years in UMNO and the government, he supported the Mahathirist agenda. Anwar himself did not have, or had not yet had the opportunity to present, a clearly defined alternative socio-economic programme. Anwar relied upon Mahathir's Wawasan 2020 project and largely followed in his mentor's footsteps. Anwar was not fundamentally opposed to Mahathir's nationalist-capitalist project, even if Anwar eschewed its anti-western dimensions and much preferred to look to its interethnic ambitions. Likewise, Anwar never regarded Mahathir's economic solutions to Malaysia's cultural questions to be anathema, only Anwar himself tended to offer cultural solutions to questions of political economy.

One could say that Mahathir's nationalism was severely economic. It was an older strain of anti-colonialism re-expressing itself as competition with the western states in the post-Cold War period. Anwar's nationalism chose to search for common historical, philosophical and cultural roots among the Asian nations. To that extent, perhaps the reality of an 'East Asian miracle', replete with material wealth, excited Anwar less than the possibility of an 'Asian Renaissance', unique in its cultural enrichment. Within Malaysia, Mahathir believed that only economic success could truly resolve interethnic disputes. Anwar frequently spoke as if he could dissolve such disputes in a multicultural amalgam of Islam and Confucianism, as if he could retrieve the commonalities found in a 'consortium of cultures',[57] revalue the contributions of various Asian thinkers, and ultimately make it feasible for Malaysians of diverse cultural heritages to appreciate that 'we are one family'.

Finally, Mahathir in the early 1990s wanted to establish an East Asian Economic Group and spoke a harsh language of authoritarian 'Asian values'. Anwar, in contrast, published *The Asian Renaissance* and acquired the idiom to go with his moral economy: civil society, universal values, empowerment and sustainable development. As a counterpoint to the selective 'Asian values' of someone like Mahathir, Anwar could offer, without undue contrivance, other 'equally Asian' values:

> Asian values are more than [authoritarianism]. What about virtue? What about abhorrence of corruption? What about regard for the rights of others? What about fundamental liberties? What about an inculcation of knowledge? Those are also essentially Confucian ethics, but this has not been highlighted. What is highlighted again and again is filial piety, respect for elders, respect for authority.[58]

Up to a point Anwar could plausibly explain such differences with Mahathir in terms of the gaps in their ages and social experiences: 'Coming from my generation, I emphasize the issues of civil society, fundamental liberties and the trust and wisdom that the public, with exposure to education and knowledge, should be able to exercise.'[59] Up to a point, Mahathir was even bemused by Anwar's attachment to rhetoric and abstractions. At a critical juncture, Mahathir and Anwar's worldviews diverged dangerously. Mahathir saw only conspiracy in the circumstances of mid-1997 and abhorred its resulting 'anarchy'. Anwar's ideological threads wove for him a perspective on the East Asian 'meltdown' that could contemplate a 'creative destruction that will cleanse society of collusion, cronyism and nepotism'.[60]

Seen in that light, each became the other's Other, and Anwar was a putative anti-Mahathirist before the roof collapsed on East Asia.

There would have been no 2 September 1998 without July 1997, at least not in the way things developed after that. As had been seen before during the 1987-88 UMNO crisis, desperate politics grew out of unsatisfactory economics and policy differences became mixed up with personal suspicions and power calculations. From another angle, state imperatives, UMNO's factionalism and corporate interests were jumbled into a volatile mix. Anwar's fall contained not only drama but also a degree of complexity unmatched by any single event in Malaysian politics. The decisive role was reserved for personal considerations of survival and political power that were preceded, complicated and coloured by international developments. These developments included foreign media interventions and repercussions from the Indonesian *Reformasi*'s overthrow of Suharto. So complex a political crisis had to spawn a complex social sequel. Alas for his detractors, Anwar's plight did not lead to his quick oblivion. On the contrary, the severity of Anwar's humiliation and the audacity of his defiance inspired a political and cultural dissent that gave birth to expressions and blossomed on a scale no one could have foreseen.

Before Anwar's fall, ambitious UMNO and BN politicians and corporate bosses cultivated the Prime Minister-to-be, while wheeler-dealers queued to receive his blessings. Anwar's lieutenants did not flinch from using methods of 'money politics' when they took charge where they could, out-bidding, out-influencing and dominating rivals in the party and government. Anwar's think tankers and academic advisers used public institutions, universities and foundations to conduct politically motivated research. Had Anwar gone on to become Prime Minister, many of these people would have become influential beyond their dreams. Their ways of pushing Anwar's agenda would have been institutionalized. During the first days of September 1998, in Anwar's hour of need, the big-time politicians and the corporate bigwigs who had fought to rub shoulders with the 'anointed successor', and their spouses as well as the BN's women politicians who often *berpeluk-peluk*[61] with Wan Azizah, were conspicuously absent. Out of fright, vulnerability, greed or a combination of these, the powerful UMNO or BN politicians, the corporate bosses and the lords of the mainstream media, who could never find any fault with 'No. 2' before, underwent a Stalinist-type conversion. After 2 September, they remembered nothing of past associations with Anwar except for his failings.

But just when everything seemed lost, when even Anwar himself seemed unsure of his next move, thousands upon thousands of ordinary people – unnamed students, youth, and members of civil society – came to Anwar's defence and rallied to his cause. Confronting Anwar's persecution, these ordinary citizens, too, reinterpreted past and present, except in their case, they gained a level of political consciousness that no amount of propaganda in quiet times could have imbued. As Raja Petra Kamarudin has said:

> Many of those REFORMASI supporters were not even Anwar fans in the past. Many of them even thought Anwar was part of the machinery.

Many even blamed Anwar for being part of the problem. They even say Anwar could have done something about all these excesses and injustices when he was part of the government, but he did not. Some even cynically say Anwar is now a victim of the same system he upheld for 17 years. Why did Anwar not change the system when he had a chance to? Now, 'padan muka', he is a victim of this same system.

But all that is forgotten now. Many have even forgiven Anwar for joining the system rather than fight it. Anwar has redeemed himself for being brave enough to take the heat rather than take the easy way out and retire to a life of fame and prosperity. Anwar has paid penance far in excess of his crimes.

To the people Anwar is 'dead'. Anwar is the symbol of what opposition to Mahathir can do to you. Anwar is the icon of resistance.[62]

In Permatang Pauh when he launched *Reformasi*, Anwar recounted his own understanding of 'who stood where'. He declared that he finally knew who his real friends were. They were not the powerful, political and rich corporate types whom he had helped but who had abandoned him at the drop of a hat. His real friends, he said, were the common folk whose support allowed him to reinvent himself. It later became fashionable in *Reformasi* quarters to call him 'DSAI' for Datuk Seri Anwar Ibrahim. In political terminology, one could call Anwar a populist. Populism is notoriously difficult to define since populists come in many shades and shapes. Some of them project latent fears and prejudices that can be quite outlandish and destructive. The more promising populists purport to articulate the basic interests of common people, of the 'grassroots', and communities in need of aid – in opposition to big business and insincere government, of course, but without demonising others, such as foreigners or minorities of one kind or another. It is possible to see one part of Anwar's populism in his caring civil society: assistance for the poor, compassion for the disadvantaged and moral guidance for lost youth. After 1998, another part of Anwar's populism lay in his anti-establishment criticisms of corruption, authoritarianism and the lack of respect for human rights. With the advent of *Reformasi*, Anwar's populism gave voice to post-crisis social concerns that lay beyond a nostalgia for rapid growth and a high Kuala Lumpur Stock Exchange index, but equally beyond reforms that would restore investor confidence only to the extent of advancing influential domestic corporate interests and foreign investments.

If Anwar's tragic trajectory is worth retracing, it is because its end point condensed into itself what was surely sordid about the Malaysian political system. But, surprisingly, it also uncovered many promising things about Malaysian society that came together in *Reformasi*. Salient among those promising things was the reverberation of the principal themes of Anwar's career: multiculturalism, Islamic dissent, anti-authoritarian claims for 'Asian values', and civil society's interventions in politics. Many people might not have been convinced by this part of Anwar's agenda before his fall. After *Reformasi*, many would believe nothing else.

Notes

1. 'Dr M: Anwar has done a good job as acting PM', *Business Times*, 22 July 1997.
2. 'There is always a difference in style. In our system of government, eventually it's the cabinet that decides (Anwar, quoted in 'A Difference in Style', *Asiaweek*, 19 December 1997).
3. Quoted in 'How Dare You Say These Things!', *Time*, 15 June 1998, p. 30.
4. Spaeth (1998: 27).
5. *Ibid.*, p. 28.
6. 'Asia', *Newsweek*, 1 September 1997, pp. 15-16.
7. *Ibid.*, p. 17.
8. 'Decision Time: Malaysia's Mahathir changes course', *Far Eastern Economic Review*, 18 September 1997, p. 5.
9. 'Mahathir's Roasting', *The Economist*, 27 September 1997, p. 29.
10. Spaeth (1997).
11. 'Mahathir Mohamad's Very Bad Bet', *Fortune*, 24 November 1997, p. 23.
12. Spaeth (1998: 27).
13. *Ibid.*
14. Anwar: Unfair to link economic woes to abuse of power', *The Sun*, 2 February 1998.
15. Anwar to Australian journalist, Greg Sheridan, quoted in 'Crony capitalism in Asia will be reduced, says Anwar', *Business Times*, 29 January 1988.
16. Spaeth (1997: 18).
17. Anwar, quoted in 'Hard Work, Toil and Tears', *Newsweek*, 1 September 1997, p. 16.
18. 'What is Success Without Freedom?', *Time*, 6 October 1997, p. 24.
19. Jayasankaran (1997).
20. Spaeth (1997: 16).
21. Wain (1998).
22. Jayasankaran (1997).
23. 'Fitnah "teratur dan teliti"', *Utusan Malaysia*, 26 August 1997.
24. Jayasankaran (1997).
25. 'Too absurd to be believed', *New Straits Times*, 25 August 1997.
26. *Ibid.*

27 'Surat layang mahu jatuhkan Anwar: Mahathir', *Berita Harian*, 25 August 1997.
28 'Fitnah "teratur dan teliti"', *Utusan Malaysia*, 26 August 1997.
29 'Too absurd to be believed', *New Straits Times*, 25 August 1997.
30 Jayasankaran (1997).
31 Hwang (2001: 241-42, fn. 24).
32 Ghani (1983: 17).
33 Musa Hitam, Letter to Mahathir, 26 February 1986.
34 Hilley (2001: 105).
35 Hwang (2001: 252-53, fn. 63).
36 'I Never Threatened the PM', *Asiaweek*, 18 September 1998, p. 50.
37 From Jomo (2001b: xix): 'I was surprised by the criticisms of Prime Minister Mahathir being made by those gathered who were not identified with the Anwar camp. I still remember one particular appeal to Anwar to "lead us out of this darkness" caused by Mahathir. I was even more surprised by Anwar's response. Although he could have maintained a discreet silence, Anwar tried to explain the reasoning behind some of Prime Minister Mahathir's controversial public remarks and to relate this to his earlier explanations for government policy dilemmas. Just before the meeting wound up, I registered my disagreements with the main thrust of the political discussion. Despite my well-known criticisms of Mahathir's policies and role, I urged unity of the leadership in the face of the challenges facing the country at the time. Although only one other person supported this position, Anwar did not indicate any approval for the majority view before closing the meeting to meet a guest.'
38 *New Straits Times*, 15 December 1999.
39 Mahathir (2000a).
40 Mahathir (2000e).
41 'When You Grow Old, You Face Reality', *Asiaweek*, 26 January, 2001, p. 26.
42 *Ibid.* p. 27.
43 *Ibid.*
44 'Interview: Mahathir on race, the West and his successor', *Time*, 9 December 1996, p. 28.
45 For example, when the 70-year old Mahathir declared, after his 1995 electoral triumph, that he was young 'compared to Deng Xiaoping', his statement was taken to mean that Mahathir would not relinquish his position. On the other hand, when key Mahathir loyalists, Sanusi, and former Finance Minister, Daim Zainuddin, could not win control of their party divisions in Mahathir's home state of Kedah, their failures were attributed to moves made by Anwar's supporters to hurry Mahathir out by showing up his declining influence in the party. See 'A Man in a Hurry', *Asiaweek*, 11 May 1995, pp. 26-31. Also see Kadir Jasin, 'Other Thots', *New Sunday Times*, 15 October 1996.

46 In 1996, S46 dissolved itself and Razaleigh led his supporters back to UMNO.
47 Quoted in S. Jayasankaran (1996: 16). Not coincidentally, perhaps, Anwar's political secretary was among several prominent UMNO leaders who were barred from the elections for violating the campaign ban.
48 Citations from this interview were taken from its full text, 'Prime Minister thrives on no-nonsense policies', then available at http://www.feer.com. For an abridged version of the interview, see Kulkarni, Hiebert and Jayasankaran (1996).
49 Despite Mahathir's refusal to set a timetable for his retirement, I had speculated that Mahathir, in the style of Malay politics, floated a succession balloon in 1994-95 (Khoo 1997: 175-76).
50 It is instructive to recall that Musa's differences with Mahathir, which led to their falling out in 1986, became irreconcilable as the Malaysian economy slipped into recession in 1985 so that the Mahathir-Musa rift reflected a wider dissatisfaction with Mahathir's leadership and policies.
51 Spaeth (1997: 19).
52 *Ibid.*, p. 20.
53 Funston (1998: 20).
54 For some observations of Anwar's experience in detention, see the memoir by one of his fellow detainees, Syed Husin Ali (Husin Ali 1996).
55 'Fighting for a Cause', *Aliran Monthly*, Vol. 18, No. 10 (November): 7.
56 Note the emphasis given to such programmes in Anwar's speech to Parliament on 24 March 1998, reprinted as 'Government committed to fiscal discipline', *New Straits Times*, 25 March 1998.
57 Anwar's usage of 'consortium of cultures' includes an engagement with western culture (Anwar 1996: 43).
58 'What is Success Without Freedom?', *Time*, 6 October 1997, pp. 23-24.
59 *Ibid.*, p. 24.
60 Spaeth (1998: 27).
61 Mutually embrace.
62 Petra Kamarudin (2000: 94-95).

5
Reformasi and the End of UMNO's Hegemonic Stability

> It is dangerous to call a tyrant a tyrant in his face. In the old days, one would be incarcerated in prison and left to rot. The modern equivalent to this is adverse and damaging publicity and news which undermine leaders and nations and stunt their economies and political health.
>
> Mahathir Mohamad, Speech at the New Asia Forum, Kuala Lumpur, 11 January 1996

> What need we fear who knows it, when none can call our power to account?
>
> *Macbeth*, Act V, Scene 1

Tunku Abdul Rahman, Malaysia's first prime minister, tended to think of politics as a matter of culture, ideally an elite subculture of good form and chummy compromise. Economics scarcely held any attraction for the Tunku. His leadership of UMNO and the nation came to end when, among other things, mass economic discontent fuelled the violence of May 1969 that destroyed the viability of the Tunku's Alliance regime.

Mahathir, in many ways the Tunku's *bête noire*, considers politics to be primarily a question of economics, and hardnosed economics at that, which Mahathir has decided is necessary to free the Malay community from its 'relative economic backwardness' and to project Malaysia as a developed nation. Mahathir has little interest in culture, with the principal exception of the 'defects' in the culture of his Malay community, a culture he dreads and has always wanted to rectify. After Anwar's sacking, Mahathir and his regime were rocked by a predominantly Malay revolt that was rooted in cultural sensitivities and that inspired new forms of cultural expression. This revolt, with its far-reaching political ramifications, shall be remembered in Malaysian history as *Reformasi*.

The Meanings of *Reformasi*

Anwar was a free man between his sacking on 1 September 1998 and his arrest on 20 September. Expelled from UMNO, Anwar had no political machinery to push his cause. However, he was buoyed by the spontaneous support visibly expressed by the mass gatherings of supporters and visitors outside his home in Kuala Lumpur. Anwar quickly rediscovered his skills as an activist and demonstrated his mettle as a dissident by addressing mass rallies, mosque gatherings and hastily held *ceramah*. Rallies in different parts of the country drew larger and larger crowds. Some attended out of curiosity as to the truth of the charges against Anwar or out of hostility to Mahathir and his regime but most had sympathy for Anwar's position.

At a massive rally held in his *kampung* of Cherok To'kun, Penang, on 8 September, Anwar issued the 'Permatang Pauh Declaration' (named after his parliamentary constituency) that defiantly called for *Reformasi* – for social and political reforms that opposed Mahathir's 'cronyistic' responses to the financial crisis.[1] In the Malay language, *Reformasi* brought echoes of the Indonesian movement against *kolusi, korupsi, nepotisme* (collusion, corruption and nepotism) that had toppled Suharto's New Order regime just a few months earlier in May.

The culmination of Anwar's short-lived 'roadshow' to spread the message of *Reformasi* was a march of tens of thousands of his supporters across Kuala Lumpur on 20 September, one day before the closing ceremony of the 1998 Commonwealth Games being hosted in the capital.

That same evening, balaclava-clad and submachine-gun-toting commandos broke into Anwar's home, arrested Anwar, and whisked him to the national police headquarters in Bukit Aman, Kuala Lumpur.[2]

After that, Anwar's call for *Reformasi* resonated beyond most expectations as *Reformasi* blossomed into a social movement opposed to Mahathir, UMNO and the Barisan Nasional (BN).

At one level, *Reformasi* was an inchoate movement of cultural opposition born of Malay revulsion at Anwar's maltreatment. The official announcement of Anwar's sacking gave no reason for Mahathir's action. Mahathir's explanation for Anwar's expulsion from UMNO, issued 48 hours later, was terse: 'We find him not suitable, that's all'.[3] That could hardly be all.

Affidavits which 'were not tested in court and incriminated Anwar in a broad range of criminal offence', in Amnesty International's words, 'were improperly made public'.[4] The UMNO-owned and other state-controlled domestic media published purported details of Anwar's alleged adulterous liaisons with a number of unnamed women and homosexual relations with his speechwriter, an adopted brother, a former driver, and another unnamed person.

On 4 September, for example, the *New Straits Times* carried a lengthy affidavit by Musa Hassan (Senior Assistant Commissioner II, Criminal Investigation Department) that contained accounts by 'witnesses' who claimed to have been involved in or subjected to different acts of 'sexual misconduct' by Anwar.[5] Musa Hassan's affidavit, along with affidavits produced by the Attorney-General, the Director-General of Prisons, and an Assistant Commissioner of Police, had just been filed as part of a court hearing in which S. Nallakaruppan had applied to be moved from detention in the Bukit Aman police lock-up to the Sungai Buloh prison.

Nallakaruppan, a director of Magnum Corporation Berhad, and someone Anwar had described as 'an occasional tennis partner', had been named in the *50 Dalil* book as an organizer of Anwar's supposed sexual escapades. Nallakaruppan, in detention since the end of July, was awaiting trial on charges of illegal possession of ammunition, conviction upon which would bring a mandatory death penalty. He was also being investigated for possible breaches of 'national security' since 'his activities could be exploited by subversive elements in and outside the country'.[6]

Musa Hassan's affidavit noted that the continuing police investigation of Nallakaruppan's relationship with Anwar had unearthed official letters and 'cash in mixed currency … totalling approximately RM2 million' in Nallakaruppan's possession.[7]

Two days later, the media reported statements by the Inspector-General of Police that Anwar 'had used his position as Deputy Prime Minister to interfere with investigations into the book, *50 Dalil Mengapa Anwar Tidak Boleh Jadi PM*'.[8]

On 8 September, Mahathir insisted that he had dismissed Anwar because of the latter's 'moral misconduct' and not because of 'whatever differences … over political or economic matters'.[9]

One day before Anwar's arrest, Munawar Ahmad Anees, a speechwriter for Anwar, and Sukma Darmawan Sasmitaat Madja, Anwar's adopted brother, were sentenced to six months' imprisonment each for 'having committed an act of gross indecency' by allowing Anwar to sodomise them.[10]

Other 'charges' against Anwar, were insinuated by UMNO figures. For example, Ghafar Baba, with schadenfreude, one assumes, gave a conspiratorial twist to rumours of Anwar's links to 'foreign powers':

Some of the ambassadors have asked point-blank: When will Mahathir step down? Why doesn't he hand over to Anwar so that he can revive the economy? Some, like the U.S. Ambassador, have been very provocative. When Anwar went to Washington, he was given red-carpet treatment, as if he were already PM. These are signals. We may not have concrete proof that a certain Western power wanted to put its puppet Anwar in place, but we Malaysians are not stupid.[11]

During those fateful days of September 1998, the Malaysian public was surely staggered by the scope and scale of the charges against Anwar in official and unofficial ways. As Anwar said ironically,

Dr Mahathir has succeeded in making me a record-holder. Everything. Women, men, corruption, agent for foreign nations, traitor, selling government secrets to foreign agents. And this is the man he supposedly took and raised as his successor.... He has gone to the extreme of accusing me of heinous crimes against humanity, religion and the state.[12]

Malaysians having been desensitized by frequent rumours and *surat layang*-type exposés of corruption and (heterosexual) philandering among occupiers of high office, it was unlikely that mere insinuations against Anwar for like misconduct would have been politically devastating. Nor was it probable that unproven hints of foreign connections would go far in tainting Anwar. Indeed, not a few people would remember that on the very day Mahathir became Prime Minister, his political secretary, Siddiq Ghouse, was arrested on suspicion of being an agent of the Soviet KGB. The revelation then did not deter Mahathir's continuation in office.

All this may help to explain the special prominence given to Anwar's alleged homosexual liaisons in the litany of his supposed misdeeds. Perhaps Mahathir and the UMNO elite expected that after a 'trial by media,' the tawdry allegations of Anwar's acts of sodomy – a crime under Malaysian law and a sin against Islam – would stun the Malay-Muslim community into a cowed acceptance of Anwar's guilt. It was as if the charge was so unbelievable, it simply had to be true! But Mahathir and the UMNO elite had miscalculated. As supporters streamed to Anwar's house and wherever he made public appearances, it was evident that the UMNO rank-and-file and the Malay community in general were unconvinced by the orchestrated expressions of support for Mahathir and verbal attacks on Anwar. Mahathir and the party leadership 'went to the grassroots' to reassure them that proof of Anwar's 'misconduct' would be forthcoming. To incredulous UMNO members, Mahathir responded: 'Those who don't want to believe (Anwar's moral misconduct) are only deceiving themselves. We will not take such action unless we have sufficient evidence'.[13]

But the first pieces of evidence proferred – the guilty pleas by Munawar Anees and Sukma Darmawan – were, politically, insufficient. Sukma Darmawan and Munawar Anees had been detained under the Internal Security Act on 6 September and 15 September respectively. When the Special Branch police interrogated Sukma Darmawan and Munawar Anees, neither had access to lawyers, family or visitors. On 19 September, they were produced in court where they pleaded guilty to the 'gross indecency' that tied them to Anwar. The circumstances of Munawar Anees and Sukma Darmawan's detention and interrogation, the suddenness and brevity of their trial, and the swiftness of their pleas that were made through lawyers appointed for them offended public sensibilities rather than convert the disbelieving. Only an unmoved anti-Anwar camp remained blind to the fact that the guilty pleas had been obtained under extreme duress.

In the *New Sunday Times* of 20 September 1998, Joceline Tan wrote: 'In reality, the *reformasi* line has washed with very few Malays. Most see it for what it is – a camouflage against the very grave allegations being levelled against Anwar'.[14] The opposite was true. Mahathir's move had backfired and it was precisely the levelling of 'very grave allegations' against Anwar that had washed with very few Malays.

Whether he knew it at the time, Mahathir, who had long shown contempt for many aspects of Malay culture and values, had transgressed a deeply held Malay cultural code. Mahathir, whose 'Asian values' had an authoritarian cast, had no appreciation that 'Asian values encompass[ed] more, much more' than 'obeisance to the ruler' and that 'among the larger rubric [was] the implicit regard for honour and the avoidance of shame, often simplified and perverted as "face"'.[15]

That 'Malay values' were no less 'Asian' in their conception and defence of dignity and honour in the face of arbitrary rule is readily apparent from a passage in *Sejarah Melayu* that has been interpreted to denote an ancient Malay social contract between a ruler and his subjects:

> The subjects obtained the agreement of the would-be ruler that no matter how badly the subjects behaved, even if to the point of deserving to be put to death ... they should just be killed. But on no condition were they ever to be shamed and humiliated. In turn, the would-be ruler asked that the subjects would never *derhaka* (rebel). The subjects gave their assent, subject to the condition that if the ruler were to break his side of the bargain, then they, the subjects, would no longer be bound by their side of it.[16]

In towns and villages across the country, within the civil service, on university campuses, among students studying abroad, among women not accustomed to public displays of political disapprobation, and even at UMNO's lower levels, Malay popular opinion had no hesitation in determining who had broken 'his side of the bargain'.

The bargain had been broken by 'stripping the opponent of every last vestige of honour and esteem',[17] by 'dragg[ing] Anwar to the lowest pit, and that too when he had just been idolized as a national leader'.[18] In addition, politics aside and warts and all, Anwar is the father of six innocent children and a husband whose wife has wholeheartedly defended as 'an honest, deeply religious man'.[19] By one of those incalculable convolutions of culture, Anwar's *aib* (shame) was amplified through the humiliation of his family and distended into the disgrace of an entire community. Woefully sometimes, Malays said to themselves and to others that as Anwar had been left with 'no face', 'it was shameful to be Malay'.[20]

There were many anecdotes of elderly Malays in villages who were so disgusted by the unrestrained media descriptions of Anwar's alleged sodomy and masturbation that they shunned the print and electronic media. It was not an isolated matter of the prudery of the rural elderly. In Kuala Lumpur, Malay youth, middle-aged Malays (who brought their children along), and Malay women demonstrated against the regime in waves and numbers not witnessed since the Baling farmers' protests and university and college student demonstrations of 1974. Protestors clashed with riot police in Kampung Baru, the 'Malay heart' of Kuala Lumpur. A cultural line, which should have been respected, had been crossed and the result was moral revulsion stiffened into political opposition: 'There is just so much a man, a people, a nation can take. Enough is enough.'[21]

In the 'face off' between state and citizen, the baton-wielding 'Red Helmets' (Federal Reserve Unit riot police) and plain clothes Special Branch personnel backed by water cannons stood on one side. On the other were ordinary, unarmed and peaceful protesters, including 'elderly men, middle-aged men and women, young girls ... senior managers in the private sector ... executives or civil servants, teachers, businessmen, lawyers' and 'Rockers in leather jackets'.[22] Their varied backgrounds revealed *Reformasi*'s broad social front along which the regime's legitimacy had been lost.

At a second level, *Reformasi* became the site of dissenting voices and alternative mediums of expression, communication and debate that created novel and innovative forms of social criticism. A young satirist,

Amir Muhammad, mixed political irreverence with literary criticism in his 'Perforated Sheets' column in the *New Straits Times* between Anwar's dismissal and February 1999. A middle-aged diarist, Sabri Zain, moved (usually with his 'significant other') between the streets and the Internet, between participating in street-level demonstrations and dashing home to spread eyewitness accounts via the 'alternative information' superhighway. Sabri maintained an online *Reformasi Diary* that provided the most moving record of the 1998-99 protests and activities, as well as the unforeseen changes in social and political attitudes. National Laureate Shahnon Ahmad, writing as an elderly allegorist, encapsulated the loathing for the 'Anwar affair' in his best-selling novel, *SHIT@PukiMak*. Summoning a scatological imagery linking bodily stench to a miasma of social corruption, this 'political novel that stinks and raises stinks' popularized vernacular profanity as an anti-regime code.[23] A cartoonist, Zunar, stopped working for the mainstream media and turned to creating piercing cartoons of Mahathir.[24]

Despite the utterly ridiculous prohibition of the sale of party newspapers to non-party members, Parti Islam's (PAS) twice-weekly party organ, *Harakah*, rose in circulation from 65,000 before *Reformasi* to over 300,000 copies. The regime's media flagships, such as the *New Straits Times* and *Utusan Malaysia*, were boycotted. By default, *Harakah*, also available online, almost became the standard bearer of truth. New Malay language magazines such as *Tamadun*, *Detik*, *Wasilah* and *Eksklusif*, as well as the online bilingual journal, *Saksi*, brought together writers, analysts and artists, and maintained a steady stream of commentary and criticism.

Overnight, *Reformasi* brought an unintended fulfilment of the regime's slogan, *Cintai IT*! All sorts of *Reformasi*-minded individuals 'loved IT', and especially the Internet, for enabling them to post information, access materials and connect with other people in ways that were free of state censorship, even if the users were not quite liberated from fears of state retribution. Here, the regime's promotion of the Multimedia Super Corridor (MSC) turned out to be a boon for its critics. The information superhighway was difficult to police as the regime could not tamper with or shut down websites, without violating the freedom of expression promised in the MSC's 10-point 'Bill of Guarantees' that Mahathir had offered international investors. There were, therefore, virtually no obstacles to the mushrooming of *Reformasi* websites (although anti-*Reformasi* sites emerged as well).

Some were the websites of established organizations, particularly the opposition parties and non-governmental organizations. Contrary to widely held prejudices about the incompatibility of Islam with the use of advanced technology, the PAS website (*Harakahdaily*) was technically the most sophisticated of the websites of the political parties. Some websites were anonymously maintained, whether in Malaysia or from abroad. Their designations, however, made clear the principal concerns and objectives of those who kept, supported and visited them: *Laman Reformasi* (Reformasi Website), *Jiwa Merdeka* (Soul of Independence), *Anwar Online,* and *freemalaysia*. The webmasters of other sites, for example, Sabri Zain (*Reformasi Diary*) and Raja Petra Kamarudin (*The Malaysian* and *Kini*), were individuals who disdained to conceal their names or goals. Other websites even flaunted such names as *Mahafiraun* (Great Pharoah) or *Mahazalim* (Great Tyrant) that were sneeringly open about the target of their derision – Mahathir himself.

The *Reformasi* websites collectively carried countless postings in Malay and English, and, frequently, translations from one language to the other. The postings were breathtaking in their diversity. They included announcements of *Reformasi* events; reproductions and translations of news reports; unofficial transcripts of Anwar's trial proceedings and transcripts of interviews; press releases and eyewitness accounts of protests and public events; economic and political analyses; summaries of public talks; letters, appeals for support, petitions, and reminders on voter registration; rebuttals of official statements, diatribes against leading politicians, denunciations of senior public officials, and accusations against corporate figures; police reports, copies of official and purportedly official documents; poems, modern fables, photographs, and cartoons; and recordings of speeches and video clips.

Not all the postings were thoughtful. Some were barely readable for want of quality or because they were no better than online *surat layang* filled with fabrications. Judging by the impact of the more serious websites, however, the Internet voices of *Reformasi* did challenge the regime's monopoly of mainstream media. Older Internet discussion lists expanded while new lists emerged. Between them, active forums were initiated that extended the boundaries of 'private-public' exchanges. Moreover, an immeasurable amount of Internet material was downloaded, circulated by email, reproduced in what print media existed for the *Reformasi* movement, and redistributed in the forms of facsimiles and photocopies:

> Copies of Internet articles appeared in parts of rural Malaysia where there isn't even electricity or telephone lines – let alone computers. A British journalist described how pleasantly surprised he was to witness a demonstration and see translated copies of an opinion piece he had written on the Anwar issue being distributed and eagerly grabbed by demonstrators.[25]

In these ways, the borders between cyberspace and geographical space, the distances between town and country, and the digital divide between the IT-empowered and those who were technologically deprived or deficient were bridged. Whatever the means for spreading the 'R-word', the Internet *Reformasi* output was ultimately purposeful: Demand justice for Anwar. Struggle for democracy. Reform the political system.

At a third level, therefore, *Reformasi* signified a massive erosion of the regime's hegemony over civil society.[26] The success of pre-crisis Mahathirist politics was contingent upon three premises: rapid growth and continued prosperity, nationalist vision and popular support, and strong leadership and managed succession. The crisis of July 1997 battered the regime's claim to being able to ensure rapid growth and continued prosperity in pursuit of Vision 2020. The crisis of September 1998 damaged the legitimacy of strong leadership and threw UMNO's succession plan into disarray. The tide of anti-Mahathir protests undermined the regime's support and marginalized its nationalist vision.

It fell to *Reformasi* supporters to mock all three premises of the Mahathir regime. Picking up where Ahmad Zahid's abortive pre-UMNO General Assembly criticisms had left off, *Reformasi* supporters accused the regime of being captive to 'corruption, cronyism and nepotism'. Increasingly, they argued that Anwar was victimized because he stood in the way of the 'cronies'. They wanted an end to Mahathir's leadership and rejected the succession implied by Abdullah Ahmad Badawi's appointment as Deputy Prime Minister. And whereas, before Anwar's fall, Mahathir's anti-speculator, anti-western and anti-Soros rhetoric had a certain purchase among the populace at large, *Reformasi* supporters now focused on domestic weaknesses and abuses as the causes of the July 1997 crisis and after. Such positions were not bound by firm ideological unity since *Reformasi* was ideologically more diverse than any other social movement seen in Malaysia.

In economic matters, for example, although it was generally suspicious of the regime's post-capital controls measures, *Reformasi* counted among its adherents free marketeers, supporters of the New Economic Policy, Keynesians, populists, socialists, and Islamists who wanted a path of 'holistic development'. In political terms, *Reformasi* supporters deplored the state and conduct of key public institutions. As the first Anwar trial proceeded, *Reformasi* supporters rejected the prosecution as a mere tool of the regime and disbelieved the judiciary's claim to impartiality. When the riot police, using tear gas, physical force and chemical-laced water cannons, attacked peaceful demonstrators,

Reformasi supporters condemned the 'unprofessional' conduct of the police force. They boycotted the mainstream media for what they were: organs of regime propaganda. After student protestors were arrested, it was the turn of the university administrators to be criticized for their complicity in 'disciplining' those students and otherwise suppressing freedom of expression on and off the campuses. The economic or financial regulatory agencies were derided for lacking in professionalism and independence. Many Muslim supporters of *Reformasi* spurned state-appointed religious officers for collaborating with the regime.

The regime's leaders viewed the shifts in popular mood and the expressions of protest as bordering on 'anarchy'. The regime's reply consisted of even greater media misrepresentations of the protesters and their activities, stricter policing and fiercer repression. Yet *Reformasi* never had the aim of turning Malaysia upside down, only of turning its body politic inside out, so that its institutional organs were bared for cleansing and restored to health. But since Mahathir personified the emasculation or degradation of key public institutions, *Reformasi* supporters were agreed on a fundamental point which summed up the regime's loss of legitimacy: *Undur Mahathir!* (Resign, Mahathir!). And not even the trials and conviction of Anwar could change that mood.

The Trials of Anwar Ibrahim

Anwar was prosecuted in two separate trials in 1998-99.[27] The first trial began on 2 November 1998. Anwar faced a total of ten counts. There were five counts of corruption – one for 'subverting the course of justice' by using his office to suppress an Anti-Corruption Agency investigation into his private secretary's activities, and four for 'interfering with witnesses' to protect himself from prosecution. There were in addition five counts of sodomy with five men, including Azizan Abu Bakar (Anwar's former driver), Munawar Anees and Sukma Darmawan.

The trial was highly politicized, given the manner of Anwar's sacking, the sensational accusations against him, growing public opposition to Mahathir, arrests of several Anwar associates, and domestic and international protests against the assault on Anwar. Some of the circumstances surrounding the trial, such as the arrest, summary trial, conviction and sentencing of Sukma Darmawan and Munawar Anees, were bizarre. Shortly after, both convicted men recanted their guilty pleas and said their confessions had been obtained under duress when they were in police detention. There was a parallel trial of S. Nallakaruppan, during which his lawyer gave evidence that the prosecution wanted Nallakaruppan to incriminate Anwar.

For many people – some were moved to demonstrate against the regime, others to keep a vigil outside the Kuala Lumpur High Court – the trial was odious. Even before his trial began, Anwar, it was felt, had been ignominiously convicted by Mahathir, UMNO and the mass media they controlled. Moreover, the Attorney-General had blamed the police for Anwar's assault and the Inspector-General of Police had resigned but no one had been charged with beating Anwar. Many sectors of the public were incensed by the prosecution's introduction of certain kinds of evidence – such as a mattress said to be stained with Anwar's semen – and repulsed by media presentation of lurid details of sexual acts allegedly committed by Anwar.

To many observers, the conduct of the trial was unfair to the defence. Justice Augustine Paul's restriction of the defence to answering only the charges laid against Anwar, and his refusal to permit the defence to present its counter-charges of a high-level conspiracy against Anwar belied the political character of the trial. In addition, Paul frequently ruled that the testimony of defence witnesses was 'irrelevant'. At one point, one of Anwar's lawyers, Zainur Zakaria, was sentenced to three months' imprisonment for contempt of court while carrying out his client's instructions.

In the public view, nothing was so prejudicial to Anwar's defence as the prosecution's dropping of the charges of sodomy and sexual misconduct at the end of the presentation of its case. By severing the two sets of charges, the prosecution was in fact no longer required to prove Anwar's sexual misconduct. As if this was not controversial enough, Paul, acting at his own discretion, expunged from the record all evidence given in relation to the discarded charges.

In vain, the defence protested that the doubt its cross-examination had cast upon the credibility of key prosecution witnesses had come to nothing. Paul himself noted that 'further attempts by the defence to go into this issue in the course of the trial were met with rigid sanctions from me'.[28] To some observers, the trial took on an almost surreal character from the melodramatic elements of the proceedings including:

> the remarkable admission by the Special Branch to the techniques of 'turning over' and of at least one senior officer to the willingness to lie in obedience to authority, to the weeks of very public lessons in sex education and anal examinations, and the somewhat more dubious lessons in DNA fingerprinting in which the 'teacher' could not explain the simple

but fundamental concept of variance, the daily fashion parade of one star witness and the lapses of another, only to be followed by the amendment of the charges at the end of the prosecution's case and the expungement of weeks of evidence and the erasure of the daily presence of a mattress, further followed by the 'irrelevance' of the various attempts of the defence at their chosen line of defence.[29]

The trial was dogged by other developments. In February 1999, Anwar gave evidence before a Royal Commission of Inquiry investigating the assault he had suffered while in police custody the previous September. The former Inspector-General of Police, Rahim Noor, through his lawyer, confessed before the Commission to the assault on Anwar. In March 1999, the trial was almost halted when Anwar's lawyers were threatened with arrest upon their refusal to make closing arguments as a protest against the conduct of the trial thus far. When the defence team applied to have Paul remove himself on the grounds of bias in favour of the prosecution, the judge rejected the application.

Anwar's first trial ended on 14 April 1999. Paul found Anwar guilty on all counts of corruption and sentenced Anwar to six years' imprisonment on each count, the sentences to run concurrently from the date of conviction.[30] In the courtroom, Anwar maintained his innocence, praised his lawyers and thanked his supporters. Above all, he urged the continuation of *Reformasi*. Outside the courtroom, in various parts of Kuala Lumpur, Anwar's and *Reformasi* supporters demonstrated against the verdict. Or, perhaps, they were largely protesting the harshness of the sentence – the judge had not made any allowance for the seven months that Anwar had already spent in detention while awaiting trial – because the verdict was for them a foregone conclusion. 'From the reaction of people in the streets, one can infer that they believe in political conspiracy,' commented former judge, Harun Hashim.[31] The 'people in the streets' were repeatedly assaulted and dispersed by riot police.[32]

Soon dubbed 'Black 14', 14 April brought the prosecution the legal decision it wanted. It also brought a political outcome beneficial to Mahathir. Anwar was in prison and politically disabled. Barring a successful appeal against his conviction, Anwar would be disqualified from serving as a Member of Parliament and could not stand for election for five years after serving his sentence. Still, the mass demonstrations in Kuala Lumpur, other nationwide protests, and international objections against the verdict indicated that the conduct of the trial and Paul's judgement had not secured for Mahathir and his regime the moral vindication they needed and that only 'justice' – 'done and seen to be done' – could confer.[33]

When Paul permitted the prosecution to discard the charges of sexual misconduct, he stipulated that during the rest of the trial:

> the amended charges merely refer to allegations of sodomy and sexual misconduct and not to the actual commission of sodomy or sexual misconduct of the accused. The truth or falsity of the allegations is therefore not an issue in this trial. Any evidence or argument that has or is to be directed upon that matter is therefore irrelevant and immaterial.[34]

The judge's ruling lightened the embattled prosecution's burden of proof at the cost of debasing its victory. To a populace previously promised 'incontrovertible proof' of Anwar's immorality, nothing could be more 'relevant' than the 'truth or falsity' of the allegations of sodomy. Nothing could be more damaging than the prosecution's being exempted from having to prove Anwar's guilt on charges of sexual misconduct. Perhaps it was the realization that Anwar's conviction on the amended charges had not repaired the regime's eroded credibility that led the regime to commence Anwar's second trial in June 1999.[35]

Then, Anwar faced squarely the charges of sodomy. As in the first trial, the prosecution tried to exclude any hint of political conspiracy from the second trial, seeking only to prove the 'actual commission of sodomy'. Likewise, as it argued during the first trial, the defence linked the 'truth or falsity' of the charges to political conspiracy.

The second trial was as troubled if not more bizarre than the first trial. Inconsistencies in the testimonies of its principal witnesses compelled the prosecution to amend the dates of Anwar's alleged offences *twice*, before the prosecution settled for unspecified dates and times.[36] In September, the trial was abruptly adjourned when the defence produced international expert certification that Anwar suffered symptoms consistent with high levels of arsenic poisoning.[37] The veracity of the test results could not be immediately corroborated or refuted. Nor could alarm over Anwar's condition or safety be contained, given Rahim Noor's previous assault on Anwar. As suspicion grew that Anwar had been poisoned in jail, mass demonstrations broke out again in Kuala Lumpur. The judge ordered Anwar to be delivered into the care of the Universiti Kebangsaan Malaysia's hospital for medical tests and check-ups. Eventually, the tests pronounced Anwar free of arsenic poisoning but the medical personnel involved could not explain the persistence of some of Anwar's symptoms.

While the trial was on, Anwar lodged several police reports, accompanied by copies of official documents, alleging corruption on the part of several of Mahathir's closest political associates, including Daim Zainuddin, Rafidah Aziz and Rahim Tamby Chik. These police reports, ignored by the mainstream media, found their way into the Internet.

On the other hand, Murad Khalid, a former assistant governor of Bank Negara – someone supposedly 'close to Anwar' and who was being investigated for corruption – made a statutory declaration implicating Anwar and many individuals and organizations (all opposed to the regime) in the maintenance of 'master accounts' and 'slush funds'.[38] The media publicized Murad's statutory declaration and the director of the Anti-Corruption Agency declared his agency ready to investigate the allegations made in Murad's statutory declaration. Murad, however, departed for an undeclared destination, with several defamation suits filed against him by those he had 'implicated', notably Chandra Muzaffar and the non-governmental organization, Aliran Kesedaran Negara.

Anwar's trial was again adjourned, initially because the judge had a bad back, and after that, indefinitely. The second adjournment coincided approximately with the advent of the 1999 general election. Anwar was held in seclusion: his stream of communications from prison, police reports, courtroom remarks and off-the-cuff statements came to an end. But by then *Reformasi* had moved onto the terrain of direct politics.

Barisan Alternatif and the 1999 Election

Thus far, *Reformasi* has been discussed as a predominantly 'Malay phenomenon', which it was, particularly at the level of popular protests and street demonstrations. At its height, though, *Reformasi* achieved a cross-cultural breakthrough that created novel possibilities of multi-ethnic alliances.

Weeks before Anwar's sacking, Lim Guan Eng of the Democratic Action Party (DAP) was jailed for sedition. Guan Eng's trial and conviction arose in connection with the statutory rape of an underaged Malay girl. Rumours alleged that Rahim Tamby Chik, then UMNO Youth President and Chief Minister of Malacca, was involved. Rahim, however, was not prosecuted over the rumoured allegations but political pressure within and outside UMNO compelled him to relinquish his official posts. Many Malays were moved to temper their customary antagonism towards the 'Chinese chauvinist' DAP out of respect for Guan Eng's sacrifice of career and liberty to assist a girl 'who was not of his race or religion'.

The Anwar affair encouraged a further change in Malay attitudes towards DAP, long the major opposition party. At the same time, many NGOs with a largely non-Malay membership began to associate with the call for *Reformasi*. For them, Anwar's maltreatment represented a confluence of recent injustices (the imprisonment and other sufferings of Anwar and Guan Eng) and past scandals (of the 1980s).

The entry of PAS, DAP and Parti Rakyat Malaysia (PRM) into *Reformasi* began hesitantly, as might be expected of opposition parties who had once worked with the 'ABIM Anwar'. For instance, some PAS leaders saw Anwar's predicament as a vindication of their 'long-held distrust of the Anwar view that meaningful Islamization could be effected from within the BN'.[39] There were PAS figures, too, who devalued the need for 'reformation' on the grounds that 'PAS had been pushing both Islamic values *and* the demand for civil justice long before the Anwar crisis'.[40] The DAP also took its time to gauge *Reformasi*'s appeal before Lim Kit Siang recalled Anwar's personal empathy with the convicted Guan Eng in May 1998 and supported the Permatang Pauh Declaration.[41]

It quickly became clear, however, that *Reformasi*'s burgeoning dissent was real, if amorphous. In the early days of *Reformasi*, there was no visible political machinery or authoritative organizer. Anwar was in jail and several of his closest UMNO allies were detained under the Internal Security Act. Most of Anwar's other UMNO supporters of any party rank had switched sides or were paralysed into inaction. Yet thousands upon thousands of people protested, or went 'shopping for justice', to use Sabri Zain's memorable phrase, in response to informal invitations passed by word of mouth or via the Internet. Neither the political parties nor the NGOs could stay aloof and hope to influence the course of such a movement.

Wan Azizah Wan Ismail (Anwar's wife), Chandra Muzaffar and others attempted to provide an organizational structure by founding the Pergerakan Keadilan Sosial (ADIL, or Social Justice Movement).[42] The human rights NGO, Suara Rakyat Malaysia (SUARAM, or the Voice of the Malaysian People) took a different step by forming Gagasan Demokrasi Rakyat (GAGASAN, or The People's Democratic Coalition). Simultaneously, PAS coordinated the establishment of Majlis Gerakan Keadilan Rakyat (GERAK, or Council of the People's Movement for Justice). Both GAGASAN and GERAK were ad hoc groupings of opposition parties and NGOs trying not to trail behind *Reformasi*. They sought to direct *Reformasi* from the inchoate movement of protest it was to the political vehicle it could become. In a way, it was a matter of sensing, as Anwar's ally, Mohamad Ezam Mohd Noor put it, that 'the people, the reformasi movement, want[ed] to participate in the political process, rather than just voice their dissatisfaction in the streets'.[43] In performing this task, the more political GERAK swiftly overtook the more 'civil society' GAGASAN.

GERAK became a coalition that drew into its fold many types of dissidents: 'Anwaristas' (Anwar supporters and his key allies who abandoned UMNO); the Islamists from PAS, ABIM, and Jemaah Islah Malaysia (JIM); DAP's 'Malaysianists'; PRM's social democrats; NGO activists; representatives of women's organizations; concerned Christians; and students. It was a measure of *Reformasi*'s blurring of the ethnic divide that the new or reinvented leaders of dissent were figures identified with principles, and not the colours of their skins. They included Wan Azizah Wan Ismail, the leaders of the opposition parties, Anwar's team of lawyers, prominent NGO activists, and lawyers voluntarily helping arrested demonstrators.

Thus, GERAK gave *Reformasi* a form of institutional expression. This was particularly so when Wan Azizah led Parti Keadilan Nasional (Keadilan, or National Justice Party), founded one week before 'Black 14', into GERAK.

Initially, GERAK seemed experimental and reflective of the fluidity of *Reformasi* that, like social movements elsewhere, blended bits of the future with bites of the past. GERAK operated on the basis of regular consultation among its members but its own dialogues were often disagreements among partners. GERAK's fresh vision of broadbased multiethnic cooperation often had to contend with the old suspicions of formerly opposed parties (as well as the NGOs' own programmes). Its alliances were untested in an election but already its difficulties were considerable.

Some of GERAK's greatest difficulties were ideological ones. GERAK's parties typically appealed to specific constituencies. PAS's support came almost entirely from Malay voters. But non-Muslims and 'liberal-minded' Muslims were often hostile to its Islamic programme and its 'ultimate goal' of an Islamic state. DAP's 'Malaysian Malaysia' programme had always depended on non-Malay support but it had also long been dismissed by most Malays for its ill-disguised Chinese opposition to the New Economic Policy. PRM had variations of a radical Malay nationalist and socialist platform. Keadilan, most closely associated with Anwar, had enormous prestige but it was uncertain whether its untried multiethnic politics of 'national justice' and 'reform' could draw many Anwar supporters or much Malay support away from UMNO. Hence many, and not just regime or UMNO spokespersons, questioned whether GERAK's combination of PAS's Islam, DAP's multiculturalism, PRM's social democracy and Keadilan's 'national justice' was ideologically sustainable.

With a general election expected in 1999, GERAK had to resolve other issues. The two major parties in GERAK seemed to diverge in their electoral goals. PAS wanted a maximal goal of replacing the Barisan Nasional government, while DAP argued for denying the BN its customary two-thirds majority in parliament. PAS's confidence had been enhanced by three factors: its 1990 and 1995 electoral successes, its sense of a deepening Malay disaffection with UMNO, and the logical argument that GERAK could not pose as an alternative to the BN without being prepared to take power. DAP's caution stemmed from the rout it had suffered when trying to capture the Penang state government in 1995 and non-Malay unease over the consequences of a BN defeat and having PAS in power.

If GERAK was to present a unified opposition, it had to forge a power-sharing framework. The realities of an ethnically influenced demarcation of electoral constituencies gave PAS and DAP natural and non-overlapping targets. For PAS, these were the pronounced Malay-majority constituencies. For DAP, they were the urban constituencies with obvious non-Malay (essentially Chinese) majorities. The smallest party, PRM, would not contest many seats but it had previously contested urban middle-class constituencies with non-Malay majorities that could equally be DAP targets.[44] Keadilan's situation was more complex as it was new, undeveloped, predominantly Malay in membership, and grounded in an untried multiethnic *Reformasi*. Keadilan might contest a mix of Malay-majority and non-Malay majority constituencies that could lead to conflicts with PAS and DAP over seat allocation. Finally, some NGOs in GERAK were either interested in fielding their candidates, or could provide candidates for one or another party.

Against various domestic and foreign criticisms, GERAK overcame its internal difficulties in quite original ways. By August 1999, GERAK had reached an agreement on three critical matters: a common election manifesto, a 'one-on-one' strategy that would field only one opposition candidate in any contested constituency, and an undertaking to resolve issues of potential divisiveness by institutional procedures. This unprecedented level of cooperation and collective leadership among the opposition led to GERAK's being called 'Barisan Alternatif' (BA, or Alternative Front). The road from *Reformasi* to GERAK and eventually to the BA was paved with more internal problems than any summary account can capture. And yet, by November 1999, the BA had become sufficiently unified that it was prepared to offer itself as the alternative to the BN.

On 24 October, the BA released its joint manifesto, *Towards a Just Malaysia*.[45] In its political analysis, the joint manifesto linked the Anwar affair to the regime's post-July 1997 and particularly post-September 1998 economic policies. It questioned the entire system of administration of justice over Anwar's prosecution and conviction, the imprisonment of Lim Guan Eng and other controversial court cases, all of which, the manifesto argued, had turned the judiciary into the executive's political instrument. The BA's manifesto attacked the regime's intolerance of dissent and its use of police force against peaceful demonstrators. It also offered a wide-ranging programme of social and political reform that would investigate allegations of high-level corruption, reassess prevailing practices of privatization, and restore civil rights and liberties. While GERAK did not definitively address the differences between PAS's Islam and DAP's 'Malaysian Malaysia', the BA's manifesto affirmed the importance of a constitutional framework for dialogues between Muslims and non-Muslims.

In November, the BA went further and presented its *People's Budget* that clarified the BA's positions on several economic and financial matters, including capital controls, taxation, investment policies, and development priorities. Its cornerstone was a populist commitment to dismantling 'corruption, cronyism and nepotism', providing a safety net for neglected social groups, reversing the privatization of core social services, restoring professional integrity to planning and regulatory agencies, and terminating the regime's predilection for megaprojects.

The substance of the social, economic and political reforms and provisions envisaged by the BA's manifesto and budget was not entirely new. Most of the reforms had been encountered in the demands voiced by the opposition parties and NGOs during the crises and struggles of the 1980s. Nor was the idea of a 'second coalition' novel in and of itself. The idea had been tested in the 1990 general election via two opposition coalitions: Angkatan Perpaduan Ummah (combining Semangat 46 and PAS) and Gagasan Rakyat (combining Semangat 46, DAP, Parti Bersatu Sabah and other smaller parties).

The social and political significance of the two BA documents lay elsewhere. First, *Towards a Just Malaysia* in principle set aside the 'Malay dominance' parameters of BN politics and gave a glimpse of how far the BA was willing to go in building a 'rainbow coalition'. Second, Semangat 46's leading role in 1990 attested to the political assumption that any contending coalition had still to be built around a major wing of UMNO. But the UMNO elite in 1999, barring the departure of core Anwar lieutenants, was not split the way it was after 1987. To that degree, popular Malay support for the BA reflected a hitherto 'unthinkable' willingness, among Malay voters, to have a non-UMNO-led government. The BA's *People's Budget*, too, was not so much a detailed 'budget' as a 'vision' of what an alternative plan of economic development might be, should the BA come to power.[46] And to that extent, the emphases and directions of the *People's Budget* indicated the social base to which the BA hoped to appeal: the rural populace, urban poor, middle classes, professionals, small and medium-sized businesses, and the civil service. They constituted a broad social base that could respond non-antagonistically to the various platforms of BA's partners.

The tenth general election was held on 29 November 1999, about eight months ahead of its constitutional deadline. A total of 193 parliamentary seats were contested. Elections were concurrently held for all state legislative assemblies in Peninsular Malaysia but not in Sarawak, which had held its last state election in 1996, or Sabah where the BN had won the state election of 12–13 March 1999.

After fourteen months of post-Anwar turmoil, the BN's electoral objectives were straightforward: preserve its customary two-thirds majority in parliament, retain power in all states (except Kelantan), and abort the BA's emergence as a credible 'alternative coalition'. The BA aimed to win at least one third of the parliamentary seats, retain control of Kelantan, defeat the BN in other states, and introduce a vibrant opposition into Malaysian politics.

The basic tenor of the electioneering reflected the objectives of the principal antagonists. The BN argued that only its coalition could guarantee continued economic development, political stability, and, above all, untroubled interethnic relations. In an alarmist campaign that exploited ethnic fears, the BN told Malay voters that only UMNO could preserve 'Malay dominance' even as it warned non-Malay voters that only an UMNO-led coalition could safeguard them against 'ethnic violence' and an 'Islamic state'. On the other hand, the BA appealed for an end to the BN's monopoly of state power, and the institution of a process of political and social reform as a constitutional bulwark against the BN regime's increasing authoritarianism and corruption.

As in previous elections, the electoral contest took place on a 'non-level playing field'. The BN wielded unchallenged control over the electoral process, state machinery, public resources and the mass media. The mainstream media conducted its habitual publicity blitz for the BN, and either ran down or blacked out the opposition's campaign. The radio and television stations, all owned by the state or companies close to UMNO, became part of the BN's electoral machinery, while denying the opposition meaningful coverage or access to air time. The BA's media handicap was accentuated by the brevity of the campaign period. In eight days, BA's candidates had to contend with police restrictions on public rallies and the 'caretaker' government's refusal to allow the opposition to use public meeting places. Moreover, the BA suffered a crippling disadvantage when the Election Commission decided that the electoral rolls could not be fully updated in time for the 1999 election. Between April and May 1999, the Election Commission had conducted a voter registration exercise. This exercise drew in 681,000 eligible citizens, a number far exceeding the average 200,000 people who typically participated in a voter registration exercise. It was widely believed that the additional 481,000 registrants were predominantly young and/or opposition-minded people who had registered as first-time voters precisely to 'teach the BN a lesson'. On the grounds that it was unable to prepare fresh electoral rolls before January 2000, and against objections from all quarters except the BN, the Election Commission disenfranchised 681,000 new registrants.

Despite all this, had the election been conducted on the basis of proportional representation, *Reformasi*'s impact and BA's unified opposition would have transformed the political system into a meaningful 'two-coalition system'. The BA secured 40.3 per cent of the popular vote (out of a combined opposition share of 43.5 per cent) against the BN's 56.5 per cent. The BN's share of the popular vote entailed a nine per cent decline in support compared with its showing in 1995. But the first-past-the-post system, distorted by gerrymandering and patronage politics that privileged those commanding abundant resources, heavily favoured the BN in power terms: the BN took 148 parliamentary seats (almost 77 per cent of the total of 193 seats) while the BA only obtained 42 seats. (Parti Bersatu Sabah had three.)

Hence, the BN was returned to power. But this fact, if considered alone, would obscure UMNO's severe losses. In Kedah, the BN lost eight out of fifteen parliamentary seats, and UMNO only won five out of the thirteen seats it contested. The BN was again routed in Kelantan where the former S46 leader, Razaleigh Hamzah, scored the BN's sole victory amidst its thirteen defeats. In Trengganu, the BN suffered a notable defeat by losing all eight parliamentary contests. UMNO's parliamentary representation experienced a 23.4 per cent decline as it fell to 72 seats from 94 in 1995. At the state level, the BN won 281 out of a peninsular total of 394 seats. The former figure represented a seventeen per cent decline from the BN's 339 seats in 1995. Of the BN's 58 losses, UMNO alone accounted for 55 seats (coincidentally the total number of state assembly seats held by the opposition in 1995). In Kedah, the BA took one-third of the state assembly seats, the highest proportion ever won by the opposition. UMNO was virtually shut out again in Kelantan, winning two out of 43 seats. By securing 28 out of 32 seats in Trengganu, PAS wrested control of a state the party last won in 1959. The drama of UMNO's losses was highlighted by the defeat of one *menteri besar* (chief minister), four UMNO Cabinet ministers and five deputy ministers. The depth of UMNO's setback was exposed by the suspected failure of the 'party of the Malays' to gain 50 per cent of the popular Malay vote.

Still, the BA had failed to deny the BN its two-thirds majority in parliament. The extent of BA's relative failure could be gauged by comparing its component parties' individual performances with those of the opposition in previous elections. Keadilan won five seats. This was not a disgraceful result for a seven-month old party whose iconic leader was in jail. However, Keadilan's five seats were less than the eight seats won by the UMNO dissidents of S46 in 1990. Wan Azizah won in Anwar's constituency of Permatang Pauh but some of Keadilan's best-known *Reformasi* leaders – Chandra Muzaffar, Tian Chua and Zainur Zakaria – lost, albeit by slim margins. Again PRM did not win any seat. DAP won ten seats, one seat more than it did in 1995, yet only half what it had won in 1990. Worse, DAP's secretary-general and long serving opposition leader, Lim Kit Siang, was defeated as were its veteran parliamentarians, Chen Man Hin and Karpal Singh. Only PAS truly advanced. PAS won 27 parliamentary seats compared with its seven in 1990 and seven in 1995, retained control of Kelantan and regained the Trengganu state government after 37 years.

For many observers, the most important factor leading to BA's failure to secure at least one-third of the parliamentary seats appeared to be a non-Malay reluctance to vote for the BA, out of apprehension that a 'PAS-dominated' BA would damage 'non-Muslim interests'. Strong non-Malay support for the BN then offset the Malay voters' swing against UMNO. Such a scenario informed the BN's campaign which, backed by media and image consultants, propagandized that 'a vote for the BA is a vote for PAS'. Ironically, DAP gave its own variant of the same reasoning. DAP continually worried aloud that it was embarked on a 'great gamble' that could end in DAP's 'greatest disaster' if the party was 'wiped out' by non-Malay voters' disapproval of any coalition with PAS. The detailed election results defy any simplistic inference of a counteraction of a 'Malay swing to the BA' by a 'non-Malay swing to the BN'. Even so, an unforeseen but critical change in the electoral terrain had taken place. Between 1995 and 1999, UMNO's share of the popular vote declined from 36.5 per cent to 29.5 per cent. This seven per cent decline was itself substantial. More than that, as Maznah Mohamad observed, UMNO crucially lost 'the contest for Malay votes'. In 58 peninsular parliamentary constituencies having more than two-thirds Malay voters each, UMNO's share of the votes cast fell from 62 to 49 per cent,[47] with the fall ranging from six per cent to 32 per cent on a state-by-state basis. Here, within a symbolic rather than geographical 'Malay heartland', PAS and Keadilan together won 31 seats to UMNO's 27. Where the UMNO-PAS division was traditionally sharp, particularly in Kelantan and Trengganu, the anti-UMNO swing benefited PAS enormously.[48] Elsewhere (most of all in Johor, where UMNO won all its contests), UMNO's pronounced dominance over PAS cushioned the former against the Malay voters' swing.

With the non-Malay (and particularly Chinese) voters, however, the situation was different. The principal recipient of non-Malay opposition votes, DAP had a marginal gain in popular vote – from 12.1 per cent in 1995 to 12.5 per cent in 1999.[49] The BN won 51 per cent of the votes in 24 Chinese-majority parliamentary constituencies. Yet DAP defended its strong presence in non-Malay constituencies by winning five out of six constituencies with more than 80 per cent Chinese voters each. Even in Bukit Bendera, Penang, where Lim Kit Siang lost a parliamentary contest for the first time in 30 years, he almost completely overturned the majority that Chia Kwang Chye, the Gerakan incumbent, enjoyed in 1995. There was some increase in non-Malay support for the BN in certain contests that pitted Keadilan and PRM candidates against the BN,[50] even if there was no sudden non-Malay pro-BN swing of the order of the Malay anti-BN swing. Simply put, an earlier but enormous 1990-95 swing of non-Malay votes to the BN showed no reversion to the opposition in 1999. It was as if large sections of the non-Malay electorate, swayed by Vision 2020 and unruffled by *Reformasi*, declined to vote against the BN for fear of jeopardizing a tentative economic recovery.

Thus, it would seem that fourteen months of tumultuous dissent had challenged the hegemony of the Mahathirist regime only to force no more than small cracks in its bedrock of stability. But if the 1999 election did not produce a strong enough multiethnic opposition to institute a meaningful two-coalition system, the situation could not return to 'square one': the Anwar affair and the Malay voters' response had exposed the fragility of UMNO's claim to be the principal source of stability in the political system.

The End of UMNO's Hegemonic Stability

In 1996, UMNO's stability as a political party seemed all but 'ordained'. S46's submissive dissolution and the return of Razaleigh Hamzah and his allies to UMNO meant the party's successful reconsolidation on Mahathir's terms. Mahathir himself remained party president without challenge. Anwar was returned without contest as deputy president, and was considered to be Mahathir's 'anointed successor'. Nor did UMNO face a serious external challenge. DAP had suffered its worst electoral reverses in 1995. With the defection of its S46 ally to UMNO, PAS was placed in a precarious position since the post-1996 balance of power in Kelantan had changed from UMNO's wipeout in 1990 to a 25:18 division of state seats between PAS and UMNO. It appeared that UMNO's hegemony over the political system had become all but incontestable.

Shockingly – for surely there was no other way to put it – the Anwar affair erupted and threw Malay and Malaysian politics into turmoil. Whatever else 2 September 1998 signalled, it raised the spectre of intra-UMNO fighting once more, and threatened to bring UMNO's chronic factionalism to a head. The party's factionalism stretched all the way back to the 1950s when a major split over UMNO's programme and leadership caused a splinter group to reorganize itself as the Pan Malayan Islamic Party (PMIP), the English name by which PAS was formerly known. Thereafter, UMNO's in-fighting did not cease, as shown, summarily, by the detention of Aziz Ishak; the rebellion of Mahathir and Musa Hitam against Tunku Abdul Rahman's leadership; the prosecution of Harun Idris during the final days of the Tun Abdul Razak administration; and the 'communist witch-hunt' that broke out at the beginning of Hussein Onn's tenure. From the 1980s to the 1990s, UMNO's factionalism became rampant. Musa and Razaleigh fought two debilitating battles for the deputy presidency in 1981 and 1984. Team A and Team B split the party in 1987, and their confrontation was continued between UMNO Baru and S46 from 1988 to 1995. In 1993, the Anwar-led 'Wawasan Team' defeated

Ghafar Baba, Abdullah Badawi and Sanusi Junid. Three years later, support from the Anwar camp brought victory to Ahmad Zahid Hamidi in the Pemuda UMNO election, and helped Siti Zaharah to defeat Rafidah Aziz in Wanita UMNO. Thus, the Anwar affair was only the latest, if the most bizarre, episode in UMNO's history of factional fighting.

Two things should be said about this episode. First, the episode signalled UMNO's gathering implosion under its chronic factionalism even if it did not immediately split the party as happened with Team B's challenge to Mahathir's Team A in 1987. On the one hand, Mahathir had learnt from Musa's resignation in 1986 and his fight against Razaleigh in 1987 not to permit a dismissed Anwar from retaining his party base. This was crucial since Anwar was believed to have built up a very strong base after the 1998 divisional elections that would send voting delegates to the party election scheduled for 1999. From that perspective, it was insufficient for Mahathir to exercise his prerogative as prime minister to dismiss his deputy for being 'simply unsuitable' or on grounds of policy differences. That would have left Anwar set to fight Mahathir in 1999. Mahathir had to have Anwar removed from the party scene altogether. That was why the Supreme Council expelled Anwar for being unsuitable because of his alleged sexual misconduct. On the other hand, most of Anwar's 'boys and girls' remained in UMNO, but kept silent, whether cowed or disillusioned. Most importantly, the Anwar affair suggested that UMNO's factionalism was not only chronic but had become systemic. One might say the factionalism in UMNO had mutated into a system of intra-party management that was linked to patronage and rent-seeking in the heyday of the NEP, the Bumiputera Commercial and Industrial Community (BCIC) and Malaysia Inc. While UMNO's factionalism *qua* factionalism was manageable under conditions of high growth, when inequities in the 'division of spoils' among different factions were perhaps a matter of degree, its factionalism *qua* system could not function during times of economic squeeze. Consequently, the 'political culture in UMNO' had developed such that:

> Both the winning and losing side[s] realize that there will be attempts to finish off the loser's political career. The loser will be cursed, condemned and obstructed not only in their political activities but also to the extent of threatening their rice-bowl. This fate is not limited to those who contest, but also extends to their supporters....
>
> Not surprisingly, the contests are so intense and finally divisive. Hatred continues, animosity continues and purging continues. Under such conditions, contest within UMNO has truly become a matter of life and death.[51]

End of UMNO's Hegemonic Stability

That condemnation of UMNO's 'political culture', which was splitting the party, was not the less accurate for its being made by Musa Hitam, who was himself no stranger to UMNO's factional fighting, and who had even asked Mahathir to drop Razaleigh Hamzah from the Cabinet after UMNO's 1984 election.

Second, the Anwar affair and the Malay voters' backlash against Mahathir and UMNO marked the end of UMNO's self-proclaimed role of providing 'hegemonic stability', not just for the BN but the entire political system. Indeed, for about 25 years, since the BN was formed, the principal source of political crises was not DAP because of its supposed ethnic chauvinism, or PAS because of its alleged religious extremism. The chief source of political instability – dramatically shown by the ethnic tensions of 1987 and the *Reformasi* ferment of 1998 – was UMNO because the party's factionalism continually spilled into the political system at large. Consequently, UMNO's internal politics could no longer be conceived in the limited terms of policy differences, personality clashes, power struggles or leadership succession. Given the increasing economic and political stakes, the party's intensifying factionalism was very often all these at once. That was itself an indication that UMNO was fast approaching a state of systemic failure. As it were, 'the party of the Malays' was trapped. It could not recover the idealistic Malay nationalism that defined its historic mission. Nor could it cleanse itself of the relentless pursuit of political largesse that was built into its 'corporate mission' of fostering Malay capitalism.

In the wake of UMNO's losses and the shift in Malay electoral support to the opposition, John Funston noted, 'the initial reaction of most UMNO leaders and pro-government analysts was to acknowledge that UMNO needed to reform and to listen to the voice of the electorate'.[52] Predictably, Mahathir responded quite differently. He 'rejected this analysis, explaining the setback in terms of Malay ingratitude, lies – spread by Anwar, other BA leaders, the *ulama*, *Harakah* and the Internet – factionalism in UMNO caused by Anwar, and PAS's bribery in promising heaven to its supporters'.[53] Hence, in 2000, Mahathir showed that neither his regime nor UMNO would be conciliatory or reform-minded. Their predicament went beyond recovering lost Malay support. They had to retrieve their hegemony, if not with the consent of the majority of the Malay electorate, then by taking punitive action against their principal opponents.

Hence unfolded in 2000-01 the regime's series of repressive moves. All forms of state power – the law, police and bureaucratic regulation

– were used in a broad attempt to cripple Keadilan, contain PAS and control civil society. Several BA leaders who had been unsuccessful in the election, including Karpal Singh, Marina Yusof, Tian Chua, and Mohamad Ezam, were themselves charged with different kinds of offences – illegal assembly, sedition, and possession or leakage of 'official secrets'. The police routinely disrupted or prohibited BA *ceramahs* all over the country. Demonstrations to support Anwar, to oppose the Internal Security Act, and to commemorate 'Black 14' were met with regular police assaults. The Ministry of Home Affairs restricted the twice-weekly *Harakah* to a twice-monthly appearance, and prosecuted its editor, Zulkifli Sulong, and its printer, Chia Lim Thye, for sedition. The publishing licences of magazines such as *Detik*, *Wasilah*, and *Eksklusif* were not renewed. Even vendors selling *Harakah*, *Aliran Monthly*, and a host of single-issue 'magazines' (especially those published by Ahmad Lufti Othman), which the regime found objectionable, were harassed and intimidated. Zaharom Nain suggested that the campaign against the 'alternative media' was conducted as if the Ministry was engaged in a 'politics of vengeance' on behalf of the badly deserted mainstream media.[54] On the public university campuses, the administrations warned and threatened students, and in some cases were suspected of intervening in student elections; nonetheless 'opposition students', reputedly linked to PAS and other Islamic groups, swept the elections. The Malacca state government ludicrously forbade any official visit to Kelantan and Trengganu. The same government vengefully withdrew its deposits from certain banks whose staff evidently supported *Reformasi*, and blacklisted '*Reformasi* doctors, lawyers and contractors' who, it was claimed, had repaid government assistance with support for the opposition.

Perhaps no single measure was more indicative of UMNO's desperate determination to break the back of Malay opposition or halt its spread than the federal government's abrupt termination of Petronas's direct payments to the state government of Trengganu. For 22 years Petronas had made annual payments to every UMNO-led government of Trengganu arising out of Petronas's drilling operations off the coast of Trengganu. The payments were stipulated in contracts signed between Petronas and the state government in 1975 and 1987 and were universally regarded as 'oil royalties'. No one had ever disputed the legality of those payments or Petronas's contractual obligation to Trengganu. In 2000, however, the federal government unilaterally stopped the payment, amounting to about RM810 million for the year, that Petronas was due to make to the PAS-led government. The federal government claimed that its previous payments had been voluntary and constituted special contributions to help develop Trengganu because of the poverty of the state. Accordingly no 'royalty' was implied and Petronas was under no contractual obligation to continue to pay Trengganu. However, the federal government, led by 'the most gentle party of all – very kind, very responsive', as Abdullah Badawi described UMNO,[55] would instead channel 'goodwill money' (*wang ehsan*) from Petronas to Trengganu through the various federal departments and agencies. This treatment of Trengganu conformed to a longstanding federal government practice of starving opposition state governments of development funds. Sabah under the Parti Bersatu Sabah, and Kelantan under PAS had been so treated before. But the federal government's 'fiscal assault' on Trengganu in 2000 went beyond the denial of funds to one state government. It was meant to deny PAS the capability of demonstrating what 'Islamic development', amply funded, might mean in Trengganu, of course, but potentially in Kelantan as well. Compelled to 'build Islam' in one impoverished state before, PAS could only 'extend Islam' to another impoverished state.

Perhaps no single development more amply exposed the regime's extensive loss of credibility than cynical reaction to the Al Ma'unah incident. The Al Ma'unah was an unknown group (of 'Islamic extremists') until some of its members seized a hoard of arms and ammunition from two army camps in July 2000. After a gun battle with security personnel, the Al Ma'unah group killed two hostages taken from security forces, but were captured after losing one of their own members. As the court trials of the captured Al Ma'unah members proceeded, there was, almost incredibly, considerable scepticism over the veracity of official and media accounts of what had happened and who was involved. What the mainstream media called Al Ma'unah's 'arms heist', cynical opinion in the alternative media castigated as *sandiwara*, a drama that, in the most conspiratorial version of events, was staged by the regime. Neither BA parties or leaders, and especially figures from PAS (who stood to lose the most if somehow the latter were connected to 'Islamic extremism') ridiculed the proceedings of the Al Ma'unah trial. Rather it was the regime that went to great lengths to dispel suspicions that the Al Ma'unah incident was an elaborate *sandiwara*. At one point, the Ministry of Defence actually staged a much publicized 'reenactment' of the incident to show that such a heist could indeed have taken place and that the Al Ma'unah assailants could have borne away the seized military hardware in the mode of transport they used.

In short, UMNO and the Mahathir regime kept raising the stakes of confrontation: the continued prosecution of Anwar, other court actions against unelected opposition figures, police assaults on BA's street protesters, universities' imposition of 'discipline' upon dissenting students, state governments' blacklisting of 'dissident businesses', further restrictions on *Harakah*, harassment of alternative media, disruptions of *ceramah*, and the termination of oil royalty payments to Trengganu. All these made up in effect a political war on many fronts that the regime conducted with most of the powers of state available to it.

And, still, Malay anti-regime sentiment resisted a 'turning over'. The 'opposition students' swept the campus elections. On the streets, the BA was still able to mount big protests. In the Malay heartland, PAS *ceramah* continued to attract huge and appreciative crowds. The Malay-dominated civil service's loyalty to UMNO remained suspect. If anything, the stance of Malay opposition stiffened in a jocular and derisive way: UMNO was 'irrelevant', Mahathir was 'Pharoah', and the regime's actions were mostly *sandiwara*.

Casting about for a solution to the persistence of 'Malay disunity', Mahathir tried playing a card that UMNO habitually dusted off its shelves when the party was in trouble: the contrivance of a 'Chinese threat' to 'Malay rights'. The selected target of UMNO's latest recourse to interethnic politics was the ad hoc Chinese Organizations' Election Appeals Committee (Suqiu). The '17-Point Appeal' composed by Suqiu, and endorsed by over 2,000 Chinese organizations and societies, had been accepted by the Cabinet before the November 1999 election. Mahathir admitted as much and more by saying that the BN 'had no choice' but to agree to Suqiu's 'appeal' in order to win the support of Chinese voters. But in mid-2000, when Suqiu called for the implementation of some of its appeals, Mahathir attacked Suqiu for encroaching upon Malay 'special rights' and 'privileges'. Newspapers such as *Utusan Malaysia* and *Berita Harian* played up Suqiu's 'demands' and provocatively warned non-Malays against violating constitutional agreements and taking advantage of 'Malay weaknesses'. In his 2000 National Day message, Mahathir likened Suqiu to the communists and other extremists, including Al Ma'unah. Support for Mahathir's anti-Suqiu stance came from fringe Malay groups as well as a desperate Pemuda UMNO that threatened to burn down the Selangor Chinese Assembly Hall if Suqiu did not retract its demands. Eventually Suqiu backed down, 'to avoid violence', in accordance with a deal that was brokered by Gerakan politicians. The Suqiu appeals were no longer an issue. Under such circumstances, however, not even

End of UMNO's Hegemonic Stability

Suqiu's apparent capitulation did anything to rally 'Malay unity'. Suqiu was publicly and quite staunchly backed by BA's 'Malay leaders', who saw nothing 'racist', 'extremist' or 'anti-Malay' in Suqiu's '17-Point Appeal'. Indeed, PRM's Rustam Sani openly expressed his disappointment with Suqiu for capitulating to Pemuda UMNO's threats when Malay dissident support for Suqiu had refused to yield.

In January 2001, Mahathir tried yet another tactic refurbished from the days of the Team A-Team B split. He invited the leaders of PAS and Keadilan to join UMNO in holding 'Malay unity' talks. Keadilan rejected UMNO's invitation outright. For Wan Azizah, 'Malay disunity' was not the issue:

> 'Malay support has merely shifted to the opposition. ...The main issue today is a crisis of confidence in the leadership and other issues like the misuse of power, corruption, police brutality, weak economic management and a subservient judiciary.'[56]

The leaders of PAS did not immediately spurn Mahathir's call but they hinted at preconditions for meeting with UMNO that made impossible any real talk. Ironically Mahathir complained that, 'To get the Chinese votes, PAS wants to make out that UMNO is anti-Chinese and that is why PAS wants to talk about national unity and UMNO wants to talk about Malay unity'.[57] Indeed, Mahathir told the UMNO General Assembly held in May 2000: 'If in the past UMNO succeeded in uniting the Malays, can it not do the same now? Actually, we do not know. Maybe yes and maybe no. But whether this is possible or not, we must try.'[58]

Clearly, the 'Malay unity' talks could not proceed without Keadilan and PAS's participation. Under the circumstances, there was no real likelihood that 'Malay unity' talks could serve as an antidote to the condition of 'Malay disunity'. The problems of the deep split in the Malay community and the profound change in Malay attitudes towards Mahathir, UMNO and the regime could not be disembodied from the crisis of September 1998. The schism that arose with Anwar's persecution could not be approached, let alone bridged, as if no one in particular was to blame. Consequently dissident Malay opinion dismissed Mahathir's call for unity as a transparently opportunistic attempt to moderate the mass Malay anger at UMNO as if that anger could be mollified by an elitist exercise in statesmanship: 'I asked him [PAS President Fadzil Noor] if we could discuss the four provisions ... he said no ... if he had said yes, everything would have been settled yesterday ... I would have only taken five minutes.'[59] To no one's great surprise, therefore, the proposed 'Malay unity' talks did not take place. The proposal itself may even be said to have come to an inglorious end in February 2001 when the Malay Action Front, a fringe group initially supportive of Mahathir and strenuous in its defence of 'Malay rights', declared that it was time for Mahathir to 'clean up' his government and restore credibility'.[60]

It has become one of UMNO's stock political myths that 'disunity' was something the Malay community could not afford because it implied a weakness that would be exploited by others. The issue of 'Malay disunity', assumed to be profoundly disturbing to the Malay community, had come up before, notably in 1969 and 1987. Whatever the dissimilarities between those two earlier occasions, their commonality of 'Malay disunity' arising against the background of intensifying interethnic tensions was critical.

In 1969, as some analysts have recalled, UMNO had suffered a substantial decline in Malay support although UMNO's representation in parliament was only reduced by seven seats (from 59 in 1964). But crucially, then, according to an estimate by K. J. Ratnam and R. S. Milne, the Pan Malaysian Islamic Party (PMIP, or PAS by its old name) received 52.3 per cent of the valid Malay votes to UMNO's 47.7 per cent.[61] How UMNO would have managed that problem of 'Malay disunity' in 1969, had there not been a 'May 13', is, of course, not answerable now. In the aftermath of violence, however, the advent of the NEP, politically grounded in the Alliance's supersession by the 'grand coalition' of Barisan Nasional, revealed a keystone of Tun Abdul Razak's reconstitution of the political system: 'Malay unity' would be restored within an ambit of 'national unity'. In a relatively short period, that strategy encompassed PMIP's co-optation into the BN before the general election of 1974.

The origin of the problem of 'Malay disunity' in 1987 lay in UMNO's internecine battle between Team A and Team B which reached its peak at the same time that Malay-Chinese tensions were manipulated to their height as well. In the 1990 election, UMNO overcame S46, importantly by warning Malay voters that the future of Malay political power might be undermined by non-Malays acting in coalition with S46. Only subsequently was 'Malay unity' laid aside as a political problem in the triumphalism of Vision 2020. Set against the conditions of 1969 and 1987, the singular peculiarity of the post-1999 election scenario for UMNO lay in the absence of a credible 'non-Malay threat'. If 'Malay disunity' was a real thing, it was a 'Malay thing' so that repression and resistance were left to spiral, as it were, on an almost exclusively Malay socio-political terrain.

That may broadly help to explain why neither Mahathir nor UMNO would not 'listen to the voice of the electorate' or to 'reform'.

End of UMNO's Hegemonic Stability

They, arguably, could not afford to do so. Had they genuinely desired to be conciliatory towards the disaffected majority of the Malay community, UMNO would have had to reach a broad accommodation with Keadilan and PAS under which Anwar would be speedily released from prison. Instead, Anwar's second trial resumed in 2000 and ended in August with Anwar's conviction and his imprisonment for another nine years. Were UMNO truly reform-minded, Mahathir would have had to resign, and with him a number of the party leaders whose personal credibility *Reformasi* had severely attacked. However, UMNO's entire leadership had acquiesced in Anwar's downfall, leaving no one of any rank to hold individual leaders to account over the 'Anwar factor' that had inflicted such damage on UMNO. A maverick such as Shahrir Samad, reportedly no friend of Anwar's and respected enough to be elected to the Supreme Council, might express 'contrarian views' but Shahrir's 'independent voice' was ineffectual.[62] When the BN lost a state assembly by-election in Lunas, Kedah, a BN stronghold for over 40 years, Shahrir blamed the defeat on 'the character of our leader, Dr Mahathir'.[63] But Mahathir had earlier said of Shahrir's opinion that 'It is not something to which I pay attention. It is something I throw into the rubbish bin'.[64]

Other murmurings about the party's need for change turned out only to be low-level pleas for changes in leadership 'style'. Unlike in 1969 (after May 13), or in 1987 (with UMNO split into Team A and Team B), there was not a groundswell of party dissent aimed at replacing the incumbent leadership. In the absence of open dissent, there was the grim reminder of Anwar's fate to deter anyone in UMNO from uncompromisingly shouting '*Undur Mahathir*' in the way that Mahathir had demanded Tunku Abdul Rahman's exit 30 years earlier. It was no small comment on what remained of UMNO's boast of practising democracy within the party that 'Pharoah' himself was 'the last Malay rebel'.[65]

It was left to an old hand, and still very much a party man, like Musa Hitam, to articulate a brooding unease at the party's threatened 'irrelevance'. Musa warned that the election campaign of 1999 provided convincing evidence that UMNO had to rejuvenate itself:

> My experience was extremely peculiar, one that I had never experienced in my entire life. In Malay-majority areas, BN leaders and workers looked weary and exhausted as well as pressured.
>
> This was because in a very open, fearless and unhesitant manner, so many Malays – young, old, labourers, the learned, the rich, the poor – worked hard and earnestly for the opposition parties, no matter whether it was PAS, DAP, Parti Rakyat or Keadilan. Only in Chinese-majority areas

were the BN and UMNO leaders and workers relaxed. 'There's no problem here, Tan Sri', they told me jovially.[66]

The substance of Musa's dispirited observation had already been captured in one of Zunar's post-election cartoons in which a character remarked that the difference between a Malay and a Chinese was, the Chinese supported UMNO! For UMNO, Musa had in mind an elitist course of 'rejuvenation' based on a voluntary change in the attitudes of the party leaders. In particular, Musa urged the party to address rank-and-file disenchantment with the leadership by liberalizing competition for the top posts at the party election of 2000. Musa's plea was made in vain. UMNO's leadership did exactly the opposite by virtually foreclosing any challenge to Abdullah Badawi, not to say Mahathir. As it turned out, the apex of the party hierarchy that emerged from the 2000 election was that of 1996 – minus Anwar! Moreover, UMNO's leadership amended party rules so as to replace the hitherto triennial party election with a party election to be held 'within twelve months of a general election'. The ostensible reason for this amendment was to curtail any divisive jockeying for power. Its effect was to enable the incumbent leadership to control party elections even more firmly.

There was conceivably a less elitist way for UMNO to 'rejuvenate' by drawing in new members and stemming the flow of support to PAS and Keadilan. That way would in principle draw upon UMNO's past 'ability to co-opt different strategic Malay constituencies'. But its practical prospects of succeeding were dim, as Maznah Mohamad correctly assessed. Having 'first depended on Malay teachers and religious leaders ... actively embraced Malay doctors and lawyers ... brought in radical Islamists ... [and taken] on board Malay businessmen', UMNO could turn to no fresh constituency. Maznah's point was indirectly substantiated by the establishment in 2000 of Puteri UMNO, a women's equivalent of Pemuda UMNO that would recruit Malay women under the age of 40. It was possible that young Malay women who were uneasy about the implications of stricter and more conservative Islamization for their status and liberties might support UMNO especially given Mahathir's own liberal policies towards women. Indeed some popular female singers and starlets had actively lent their image to pro-BN advertisements on television in the run-up to the election. Puteri UMNO's establishment fulfilled an immediate but negative purpose of denying PAS the support of younger Malay women.[67] Unlike previous waves of co-optation of new strategic constituencies, the creation of a 'princesses' wing' – which even prompted unease among the existing Wanita UMNO – did not spur UMNO 'to evolve as dynamically as it once did'.[68] To that extent, it was no indication of any tendency towards rejuvenation, reform or reinvention.

Notes

[1] In fact, ABIM, Jemaah Islah Malaysia (JIM), the National Muslim Students Association of Malaysia (PKPIM) and the Malaysian Academy of Islamic Science had formed a 'reformation movement' with 'the declared intention of arousing public awareness of the "injustices" done to Datuk Seri Anwar Ibrahim' as early as 6 September. See 'Four groups launch "reformation movement"', *New Straits Times*, 7 September 1998.

[2] For an eyewitness account of the arrest that was not reported in the local media, see Matthew Moore, 'The Day That Rocked Malaysia', *The Sydney Morning Herald*, 22 September 1998.

[3] Suh and Shameen (1998: 41).

[4] 'Malaysia: Trial of Anwar Ibrahim: a defining moment for human rights in Malaysia', Amnesty International Press Statement, 1 November 1998.

[5] 'Police officer: Investigation must be carried out without fear or favour', *New Straits Times*, 4 September 1998.

[6] *Ibid.*

[7] *Ibid.*

[8] 'IGP: Anwar interfered with investigations', *New Straits Times*, 6 September 1998.

[9] 'Anwar sacked for "moral misconduct"', *New Straits Times*, 9 September 1998.

[10] 'We were sodomised', *New Sunday Times*, 20 September 1998.

[11] 'Anwar has no support', *Asiaweek*, 18 September 1998, p. 51.

[12] 'Blowing hot and cold', *Asiaweek*, 2 October 1998, p. 30.

[13] 'Dr M: The truth will finally prevail', *New Sunday Times*, 13 September 1998.

[14] Joceline Tan, '"Reformasi" a camouflage for the man of many contradictions?', *New Sunday Times*, 20 September 1998.

[15] Philip Khoo (1999: 6).

[16] *Ibid.* For a scholarly discussion of this cultural code as a 'social contract', see Cheah (1998).

[17] Philip Khoo (1999: 6).

[18] Musa Hitam (2000: 9).

[19] Wan Azizah Wan Ismail, quoted in Suh and Shameen (1998: 49).

[20] The obverse of being consumed by shame was the adoration shown to Wan Azizah and even more so Nurul Izzah, Anwar's eldest daughter, whom many adulated as 'Reformasi Princess'.

21 Sabri (2000: 129).
22 *Ibid.*
23 For a review of Amir Muhammad's column, Sabri Zain's diary and Shahnon Aḥmad's novel, see Khoo (2002a).
24 See especially Zunar (2000).
25 Sabri (2000: 158).
26 A post-modernist reading of *Reformasi* is offered by Farish (1999).
27 It is not feasible here to give an adequate citation of the extensive coverage of Anwar trials. BBC had a useful series of reports on the trials, 'arsenic poisoning' episode and popular protests between September 1998 and November 1999; see 'A crisis unfolds: Timeline' (http://news.bbc.co.uk/hi/english/special_report/1998/10/98/malaysia_crisis/newsid_204000/204632.stm).
28 *Malayan Law Journal* (1999: 33).
29 Philip Khoo (1999: 4).
30 For the full judgement, see *Malayan Law Journal* (1999).
31 Suh, Ranawana and Oorjitham (1999: 24).
32 Sabri (2000: 122-29).
33 Philip Khoo (1999) provides a thoughtful commentary on the political ramifications of the 'Anwar affair', verdict of the first trial, sentence on Anwar, and the growing dissent, particularly among Malays.
34 *Malayan Law Journal* (1999: 33).
35 Of course, by the logic of law, having secured convictions of sodomy against Munawar Anees and Sukma Darmawan, the Attorney-General could hardly refrain from charging Anwar.
36 Case (2003).
37 CNN, 10 September 1999, cited in Sabri (2000).
38 For a prominent *Reformasi* activist's sceptical view of Murad's declaration, see Petra Kamarudin (2000: 76-79).
39 Hilley (2001: 200).
40 *Ibid.*, p. 201. Nik Abdul Aziz Nik Mat, the Menteri Besar of Kelantan was reported to have said it was 'better for those seeking reforms to join PAS ... rather than set up their own movements' ("Those who want change should join Pas", *New Straits Times*, 7 September 1998).
41 *New Straits Times*, 17 September 1998.
42 See http://www.geocities.com/SouthBeach/Palms/3277/adil/istihar_adil.html for ADIL's Declaration.
43 Mohamad Ezam Mohd Nor, upon his return from exile in March 1999 ('New and More Moderate', *Asiaweek*, 2 April 1999, p. 29).
44 Kua (1996).
45 *Towards a Just Malaysia* was available at http://www.malaysia.net/dap/ba-ind.htm.
46 There was no official English translation of BA's budget strategy, Belanjawan Rakyat 2000: Demi pemulihan, pembangunan dan keadilan (The

People's Budget 2000: Towards recovery, development and justice) (http://www..malaysia.net/dapmnet/bljw.html).
47 Maznah (2003).
48 Halim (2000).
49 DAP probably had more Malay support in 1999 than ever before although the extent of the support is indeterminate.
50 The contest in the state assembly constituency of Machang Bubuk, Penang, was a case in point, where increased Chinese support helped the Gerakan incumbent, Toh Kin Woon, to overcome a loss in Malay support. See Toh (2003).
51 Musa (2000: 10).
52 Funston (2000: 56).
53 *Ibid.*, pp. 56-57.
54 Zaharom (2000: 4).
55 'UMNO is known to change', *Asiaweek*, 10 December 1999, p. 32.
56 Wan Azizah, quoted in 'Mahathir Reaches Out', *Far Eastern Economic Review*, 1 February 2001, p. 29.
57 Mahathir, quoted in 'Dr M: Fadzil refused to discuss Malay rights', *The Sun*, 21 March 2001.
58 Mahathir (2000e).
59 Mahathir, quoted in 'Dr M: Fadzil refused to discuss Malay rights', *The Sun*, 21 March 2001.
60 'Asiaweek Newsmap', *Asiaweek*, 16 February 2001, p. 18.
61 Ratnam and Milne (1970: 219).
62 See Elegant (2000).
63 Zakiah Koya, 'Dr M to blame for Lunas defeat: UMNO veteran', *Malaysiakini*, 30 November 2000.
64 'Laporan Suhakam jejas peranan polis', *Utusan Malaysia*, 24 August 2001.
65 Maznah (2000: 6).
66 Musa (2000: 8).
67 Maznah (2002).
68 Maznah (2000: 6).

6
The Cultural Imperative of Coalition Building

> Use whatever means you can to instill hatred against those who are kind to you. Poison-pen letters, the press, Internet, all these can be used. Call them with (*sic*) disparaging labels because in this way we can incite greater hatred against certain individuals. Label them as 'Mahazalim, Mahafiraun'. Do we like tyrants, pharaohs? Of course not. So just hate those who are labelled 'Mahafiraun' or 'Mahazalim'. There is no greater satisfaction than the feelings of hate. Therefore the politics of development is replaced by the politics of hatred. Hate him and vote for me!
>
> Mahathir Mohamad, Speech at the UMNO General Assembly,
> Kuala Lumpur, 11 May 2000

> Great masses of people suddenly awaken to political life. They become aware that things are not quite what they ought to be and that they can be changed. They are carried away by new experience and ready to storm heavens. And they naively believe that *everybody* has undergone the same transformation – a rare case of human vanity being prepared to forego the distinction of being ahead of the others.
>
> Rosa Leviné-Meyer, cited in Joseph Schwartz (2000)

Historians might look back upon the 1999 election as an untidy contest that produced an inconclusive outcome. This was particularly true for the parties that constituted the Barisan Alternatif (BA). *Reformasi*'s profound social meanings, GERAK's cross-cultural breakthrough, and the BA's ambitious experimentation marked a confluence of political economy and culture that reverberated far beyond the BA's electoral performance. Yet, it was not UMNO alone that had to confront an uncertain post-election scenario.

PAS, the most successful of the BA parties, had accurately assessed the Malay electorate to be ripe for the taking and played the maximal hand of leading the BA to victory over the Barisan Nasional (BN). However, PAS's advance precisely demarcated the boundary of its influence:

PAS was unable to match UMNO outside the Malay heartland. The BA's other major party, DAP, was not wrong to be concerned over non-Malay reservations about DAP's joining PAS in an 'alternative government'. Yet DAP's 'catastrophic loss', that supposedly left non-Malays in the worst possible situation, reflected as much DAP's failure to recover its past as its inability to chart the future of opposition politics. As the 'true child of *Reformasi*', Keadilan had taken *Reformasi* to a limited success that sustained it as a threat to UMNO. But Keadilan's failure to gain a much higher representation in Parliament, thereby forcing an electoral breakthrough, meant that the injustices wrought upon Anwar would not be sufficiently redressed by a direct political triumph.

In short, the political system was in a state of flux and each of the parties was in a fix. If all parties had to adapt to unfamiliar topography, the BA's parties had to demonstrate specifically that *Reformasi* could sustain its momentum and that the BA would maintain its integrity.

DAP and the Pendulum of Minority Politics

In the 1999 election, if the damage sustained by UMNO was brought about by a Malay revolt, DAP's difficulty lay in the relative passivity of the Chinese electorate. The election results showed that Chinese voters were probably not less 'disunited' than Malay voters. As a crude indication, the BN's 'Chinese-based parties' (MCA and Gerakan) won fifteen out of 24 Chinese-majority parliamentary constituencies but only took 51 per cent of the popular vote. Within a symbolic 'Chinese heartland' comprising six very large urban constituencies with more than 80 per cent Chinese voters each, DAP won five seats and 53 per cent of the popular vote.[1] Although these results are insufficient for a conclusive analysis of the Chinese's voting patterns, they confirmed the persistence of a basic division of the Chinese community of political parties, associations and voters into two large camps.

One camp consisted of MCA and Gerakan supporters who were partial to a 'politics of negotiation' within the BN while the other consisted of oppositionists rallying around DAP who favoured exerting a 'politics of pressure' on the regime.[2] While the parties ostensibly differed in ideological tenets, the definitive issue for most Chinese voters was how best to protect the economic, cultural and educational interests of the 'Chinese community'. Thus, the degrees of electoral support for the political antagonists varied from election to election, depending on prevailing socio-economic conditions, current policies, political controversies and voter perceptions of how hostile or accommodating the UMNO-led regime was to 'Chinese interests'. This formed a key variable in what was popularly regarded to be a 'pendulum effect' that reflected the Chinese voters' tendency to provide stronger support for the BN in one general election, only to swing to DAP in the next election, and so on. Many observers used this idea of a pendulum effect to explain Chinese voting patterns during the era of NEP politics, suggesting that Chinese voters would cast for 'negotiation' as the more effective way of protecting Chinese interests at one election, but switch to 'pressure' in a subsequent election out of disillusionment with the regime. The politicians facing this oscillating pattern of Chinese voting behaviour were apt to label it either positively as 'tactical' and 'pragmatic' or negatively as 'opportunistic' and 'unreliable', depending on how their fortunes were affected. For example, when Chinese voters, having swung to the BN in 1982, shifted massively to DAP in 1986, Mahathir denounced the latter swing as proof that the 'urban [read: Chinese] voters were not very bound to any party'.[3]

'Negotiation' and 'pressure' were not unbridgeable but formed the two ends of a spectrum. For many Chinese analysts, politicians and voters, the goal of 'Chinese politics' was to find an ideal position along that spectrum, or fine-tune an optimal balance between the two kinds of politics. However, one should not reify this so-called pendulum. Here, it is invoked to allude to DAP's quandary in the 1999 election. Towards the latter half of the NEP period, during the 1986 and 1990 elections, the pendulum appeared to have stayed its arc in DAP's favour, as can be seen from Table 6.1. (DAP's apparent decline between these two elections may be attributed to its tactical withdrawal from Sabah in favour of its Gagasan Rakyat ally, PBS.)

Between 1986 and 1990, the urban Chinese voters' resistance to the regime sustained DAP as the leading opposition party. However, the post-NEP elections of 1995 and 1999 showed a reverse pro-BN

Table 6.1 DAP's Parliamentary Performance, General Elections, 1974-99

	1974	*1978*	*1982*	*1986*	*1990*	*1995*	*1999*
Seats	9	16	9	24	20	9	10
% vote	18.3	19.1	19.5	21.1	16.5	12.1	12.5

Source: Suruhanjaya Pilihan Raya (various years).

Cultural Imperative of Coalition Building

oscillation that reflected a corrosion of resistance induced by two socio-political developments.

First, there was the defeat of Gagasan Rakyat's attempt to introduce a two-coalition system in 1990 that represented a bold move to supplant the BN in power. In Penang, especially, Gagasan Rakyat's formation as a 'second coalition' was greeted with excitement and hope and the DAP came to within three seats of capturing the state government. Despite broad appreciation for the accomplishments of the Lim Chong Eu-led BN government, the majority of the Chinese electorate in Penang was ready to replace Gerakan with DAP. The dissatisfaction of the Chinese voter then was visited upon MCA that lost every contest in Penang. But while UMNO lost every seat in Kelantan, Semangat 46 in Penang delivered a morale deflating naught! When Gagasan Rakyat failed to dent the BN's position seriously in parliament, or in Penang, say, the Chinese voters' resistance to the BN declined.

Second, the 1990s brought material prosperity and the regime's offers of financial assistance to Chinese schools and MCA-led educational projects, both of which gave reason to the Chinese voters to barter a seemingly profitless recalcitrance for social, economic and cultural gains. By the time of the 1995 election, a socio-political transition favourable to the BN had been in place. DAP's leaders did not overlook the transition but underestimated or opted to defy its significance.[4] DAP withdrew from Gagasan Rakyat and tried to win Penang on its own. Perhaps DAP leaders hoped that the Penang non-Malay electorate that had enthusiastically supported the party's 1986 'Tanjung' and 1990 'Tanjung 2' campaigns would back a 'Tanjung 3' effort. But the DAP's campaign, even if it had been better packaged and conducted, was a plan to win a local battle in the midst of a lost national war. 'Tanjung 3' ended in a debacle that completed DAP's rout across the nation – the consequence of continuing to bet on a bolted ethnic horse.

To recover the half-defiant, half-expectant resistance of the 1980s within a few years of the 1995 defeat, DAP had to meet several conditions. One was a major party reorganization and mobilization. That DAP did not have or could not summon. DAP's cadre structure made the party heavily reliant on its leaders' courage and self-sacrifice to inspire voters. It was not for nothing that DAP leaders had been frequently prosecuted or detained for all manner of alleged offences. As the prosecution and conviction of DAP's parliamentarians, Wee Choo Keong and Lim Guan Eng, showed, DAP's leaders still exhibited both types of personal qualities. Even after several key leaders had withdrawn from DAP, the party undertook no reforms after the 1995 elections.⁵ Worse, in early 1999, DAP was wracked by one of its sporadic intra-party fights when Wee Choo Keong, Teoh Teik Huat and others mounted their 'Kick Out Kit Siang' campaign. A second condition was related to DAP's limited membership which made the party's outreach highly dependent on its close networking with the traditional centres of Chinese dissent – the educational movement, the guilds and the associations. DAP, however, had not maintained its alliances while both MCA and Gerakan had extended and consolidated their control over that network. Arguably, the third condition was decisive. To overcome its own weaknesses as well as the strengths of the BN's political machine, DAP needed the Chinese voters' recalcitrance to thrive in any election. Then, regardless of what DAP leaders could or could not do for their constituencies, they would be returned through protest votes. This was the case with the 1986 and 1990 elections when DAP was buoyed by the Chinese electorate's 'dare to struggle, dare to win' spirit. A decade later, there was no comparable wave of dissidence. The Chinese electorate's response to the imprisonment of Lim Guan Eng was a distant sympathy expressed in isolated actions whereas the imprisonment of Anwar Ibrahim inspired a widespread solidarity fueled by an inappeasable anger.

In 1998-99, while Malay sentiment counted heavily against UMNO, *Reformasi* sentiment did not count sufficiently with the Chinese electorate. Non-Malay backing for *Reformasi* was indirect and was limited to the interventions of individual figures (the most prominent of whom was Tian Chua), DAP's membership in the BA, the entry of young non-Malay activists into Keadilan and PRM, and the support of many NGOs for GERAK, GAGASAN and the BA. While these were significant political developments, they did not reach deeply into the Chinese or non-Malay electorate at large. Wan Azizah alluded to this limitation when she commented on interethnic involvement in GERAK and GAGASAN: 'the Malays mostly got *belasah* (whacked); the Indians [were] mostly the lawyers [for arrested protesters]; and the Chinese [were] the co-ordinators'.⁶ Where *Reformasi* reached the level of the Chinese voters, it renewed the 1980s' discourses of democracy and civil society but it could not interject the reverberations of the Malay cultural revolt.

The specific circumstances of July 1997, September 1998, and the principal antagonists were additionally crucial. The 1985-86 recession was severe partly because it exacerbated a slowdown that had begun in 1982. In contrast, while the 1997-98 crisis was sharp and sudden, it had not bitten deeply enough to generate widespread insecurity or impoverishment. High-flying corporate fortunes were devastated in the securities market and much money was lost because of foreign exchange plunges. The crisis, however, had not created massive unemployment before the economic shield of capital controls and currency peg appeared to bail out not just cronies but also to save business in general.

The Chinese business community, like other domestic business communities, was initially alarmed at Mahathir's anti-market rhetoric and stances but was gradually reassured by the capital controls and a tentative export-led recovery in late 1999. Politically, the Chinese community, for whom nothing could be more threatening than the anti-Chinese violence in Indonesia, found double solace before *Reformasi* began: they were not only safe in Malaysia; their home even served as a sanctuary for many Chinese who had fled the violence of May 1998 in Indonesia.

Besides, Anwar was not Razaleigh Hamzah in vital aspects. While leading S46, Razaleigh was free to organize as a potential national leader. Anwar, however, was imprisoned and written off as a political loser. When electoral politics was fought against the backdrop of the NEP, it was Razaleigh, not Mahathir, who was rumoured to be the true friend of Chinese business. Anwar and his austerity package of December 1998 could not cut Razaleigh's figure vis-à-vis Mahathir and his policies of 'rescue, recapitalization and reflation'.

These reasons, which are unrelated to any belief in Anwar's guilt, explained the Chinese reluctance to take up Anwar's cause.[7]

The convergence of all these social, cultural and economic trends and developments pointed to a political milieu in which the Chinese electorate was no longer the locus of staunch anti-regime sentiment. While some of the larger Chinese-majority constituencies kept faith with DAP, these were islets of dissidence. There was little to move the Chinese electorate at large from its 1995 moment of 'negotiation' to a fresh crest of 'pressure'. In such a milieu, what befell Suqiu's initiative offered a telling lesson.

Suqiu's original 'demands' were nominally consistent with the reforms envisaged by BA's *Joint Manifesto*. However, an accommodation brokered by MCA and Gerakan within the 'BN framework' diluted Suqiu's 'demands' into 'appeals' that the BN could accept before the election, only for UMNO to reject thereafter. Thus, even if there was a distinction between the 'politics of pressure' and the 'politics of negotiation', it was a distinction without a difference. Balancing between both kinds of politics was practicable, indeed comprehensible, only when 'Chinese-based parties', 'Chinese leaders' and 'Chinese voters' had implicitly accepted the relegation of 'Chinese politics' to no more than 'minority politics'. It might still be the politics of the largest minority but all the same its ideological summons soared no higher than a discourse of development projects, public works and community services, as Francis Loh has amply demonstrated. Consequently, 'like the non-Malay BN leaders, much of the non-Malay public appears to have turned away from "old fashioned" controversial issues like justice, transparency, accountability, and democracy itself'.[8]

To its credit, DAP attempted to buck the trend in 'Chinese politics' when *Reformasi* and the BA's challenge to the BN turned on precisely these 'controversial issues'. In principle and tactics, an alliance between *Reformasi* and DAP would have been synergistic. DAP needed a major cause to revitalize its appeal, and *Reformasi* was at hand to provide several causes close to DAP's heart – corruption of the regime, abuse of the judicial process, and assaults on civil liberties. *Reformasi* needed vehicles and advocates, and DAP offered an expansion in experienced organization and mobilization. DAP's 'Chinese image' could lend an ethnic balance to the Malay revolt that could in turn garner Malay support for the party. The parallel plights of Anwar and Guan Eng symbolized *Reformasi*'s emergent multiethnic political consciousness. Even so, DAP realistically campaigned 'not to topple [BN] from power' but to effect 'a paradigm shift in Malaysian politics by breaking the BN's political hegemony and its uninterrupted two-thirds parliamentary majority'.[9] DAP was not wrong to work with Keadilan, PRM and especially PAS in the BA, although the cooperation did not help DAP regain its past pre-eminence among opposition parties. Neither was DAP's performance a 'catastrophe', even if the defeats of Lim Kit Siang, Karpal Singh and Chen Man Hin were harsh setbacks. Although the DAP's leaders thought that they had suffered a massive defeat, the party had in fact obtained an additional parliamentary seat, half a per cent rise in popular vote and a few more state assembly seats. These were marginal gains that caused Kit Siang to lament, rightly, that the Chinese electorate had neglected to seize the extraordinary moment of *Reformasi* to force a historic breakthrough in the political system. It was a tacit concession that the Chinese voters were prepared only to keep a semblance of 'pressure' while opting for 'negotiation'. If DAP's performance stayed outside the BA's 'big picture' aspirations, it stayed within the parameters of 'minority politics'. The result appeared to be an ominous Chinese rejection of DAP only when it was set against the BA's high expectations and PAS's signal triumphs.

Cultural Imperative of Coalition Building

Therein lay the problem for the opposition: the support of the Chinese electorate for the BA was thin. In several urban, ethnically mixed constituencies, notably in Kuala Lumpur, Selangor and Penang, well respected Keadilan and PRM candidates such as Chandra Muzaffar, Syed Husin Ali and Zainur Zakaria lost, despite the Malay swing against UMNO. Non-Malay and especially Chinese support was critical in enabling UMNO to defeat PAS in constituencies having small Malay majorities. It was more than likely that large segments of the Chinese electorate were swayed by the BN's alarm that the BA's 'alternative government' would be a PAS-imposed 'Islamic state'.

Again context is critical. Non-Muslim apprehension towards PAS goes back a long way. Soon after Merdeka, non-Malays tended to regard PMIP as a party of extreme Malay nationalism. In the 1969 electoral revolt against the Alliance, however, the depth of non-Malay (and for that matter, Malay) oppositionist sentiment was not affected by an electoral pact – albeit not a coalition – reached between DAP, Gerakan (then in opposition), PMIP and the People's Progressive Party (PPP). After the late 1970s – following PAS's break with UMNO (and the BN), the Islamic resurgence in the country, and the global ramifications of the Iranian revolution – non-Muslims began to be concerned about PAS's being a party of so-called Islamic fundamentalism. In tactical deference to this concern, two opposition coalitions were formed in 1990 – a 'multiethnic' coalition of S46, DAP, PBS, PRM, and a parallel 'Muslim' coalition of S46 and PAS. The BN's 'Chinese-based parties' denounced DAP for entering an alliance with PAS that was no less 'unholy' for being 'indirect'. Yet the majority of Chinese voters then were determined to support DAP in a venture that would have offered an 'alternative government' that might be dominated by 'S46's Malay-centric tendencies and PAS's Islamization policy'.[10] For that matter, there was hardly an election during which the BN's 'Chinese-based parties' did not purport to uncover an 'unholy alliance' of DAP and PAS so that 'until 1998 both PAS and Democratic Action Party leaders avoided working and being seen together on the same platform so that the electorate as well as their own supporters would not be confused'.[11] Perhaps UMNO's vulnerability vis-à-vis PAS (and Keadilan) in 1999 provoked more Chinese anxiety than in 1990 when voters could choose, as it were, between two UMNO factions. But where the 'PAS factor' weighed upon Chinese voters, it did not create a new and overwhelming rationale so much as added to the many reasons they already had for preserving their 1995 level of support for the BN.

So little changed in the immediate circumstances because so much had changed in the recent past. The socio-political situation was as inimical to DAP's customary claim on the loyalty of the Chinese electorate as it was to UMNO's quest for 'Malay unity'. Whatever soul searching DAP conducted behind closed doors in 2000 did not bring the party any closer to rejuvenation than UMNO had attempted for itself. DAP had broadened its cooperation with opposition parties and NGOs, for example, by yielding some seats it used to contest to other candidates – Chandra Muzaffar (of Keadilan) in Bayan Baru, Zaitun Kassim (of Women's Candidacy Initiative) in Selayang and Jeyakumar Devaraj (of Parti Sosialis Malaysia) in Sungei Siput. Building upon Lim Guan Eng's standing in the Malay community, DAP's coalition in the BA further lessened previous Malay antagonism towards the party. These two developments did not help DAP appeal to any new 'strategic constituency'. DAP also did not use the urgency of defeat to reorganize its leadership. As the DAP had been too reliant on a group of recognized veterans, it could not quite replace a leadership that had led the party to consecutive electoral setbacks. There were also limits on how radically DAP could rethink its programme. On the one hand, a DAP leader with an assured standing in the BA such as Lim Kit Siang could make substantial contributions to advancing the BA's venture in multiethnic and multireligious cooperation in order 'to check the dangers of a re-polarization of race and religion'.[12] On the other hand, DAP was burdened with its own 'grassroots feedback' that the 'PAS factor' had tarnished DAP's credibility with the Chinese electorate. DAP dealt with the tensions between these two positions by falling back upon the political commitments that once made DAP the largest opposition party. This meant, first, that DAP would champion 'Chinese causes' as and when they arose. In 2000, other than UMNO's harassment of Suqiu, there were two such causes, namely the Chinese educational movement's opposition to the regime's 'Vision Schools', and some students and parents' objection to the relocation of SRJK Damansara. DAP, as usual, attacked the complicity of the BN's 'Chinese-based parties' in undermining the independent status of Chinese education. What was unusual was the staunch support that the BA's 'Malay-based' parties, including PAS, gave to the 'Chinese community' in the Suqiu, Vision Schools and SRJK Damansara episodes. Second, DAP continued its strenuous defence of civil liberties and human rights in a climate of intensifying repression. Again, DAP's positions were firmly matched by those of PAS, Keadilan and PRM in a bold and broad 'Malay front' of protest against draconian laws and police repression. These were benefits conferred by *Reformasi*.

However, a former plank of the DAP's platform – its defence of 'non-Muslim concerns' against the regime and PAS's different Islamization policies – presented difficulties. In this regard, Lim Kit Siang's exposition of DAP's stance during the 3rd Australian-Malaysian Conference, held in Canberra, 2000, was illuminating. 'For the BA to succeed', in Kit Siang's view:

> it must take the initiative in laying to rest the two spectres which the BN used to frighten Malaysian voters in the 1999 election: that on one hand, the Democratic Action Party is anti-Malay and anti-Islam and wants to see the destruction of Islam and that on the other, PAS is extremist and fanatical and wants to end the religious, cultural and political rights and freedoms of non-Muslims in Malaysia.[13]

Such a balanced statement of the BA's real obstacles would not have been controversial within the BA. But Kit Siang's idea of sharing the burden of exorcising those two 'spectres', unaccompanied by any suggestion for dealing with the 'spectre of DAP', might begin to unsettle PAS:

> the BA must project in particular that the 'political Islam' represented by PAS is an Islam of tolerance and justice which is fully compatible with democracy, which upholds open and accountable government and cultural pluralism, and is compatible with a flowering of human rights and democracy.[14]

Nor could the following implicit criticism of the BA's consultative inadequacy have offered much comfort after BA leaders had committed so much effort towards building common ground from diverse ideological commitments:

> the Democratic Action Party in particular, and the BA in general, learned to their cost that it was not adequate for the opposition parties in the BA to reach a common accord on a wide spectrum of subjects ... while controversial issues, such as that of an Islamic state, were avoided or deferred. For indeed the question of an Islamic state does not lend itself to rational discussion and resolution in a multi-ethnic, multi-religious society like Malaysia, even less when elections approach and fears and emotions are manipulated.[15]

What was most puzzling was why, if 'the question of an Islamic state does not lend itself to rational discussion and resolution', Kit Siang was nonetheless insistent that:

> the issue of an Islamic state must be addressed and resolved by the BA itself, once and for all. Once resolved, greater trust and cooperation can

develop among the BA component parties. The resolution of this issue can also be the basis to regain lost ground and to win new support.[16]

By and large, the puzzle was answered: in order to 'regain lost ground and to win new support', in Kit Siang's opinion, 'the component parties of the BA must acknowledge that many non-Malays did fear that the Democratic Action Party's co-operation with PAS ... would lead to the formation of an Islamic state'.[17]

Whatever else Kit Siang's line of reasoning implied, it illustrated DAP's post-1999 predicament, which was the typical predicament of parties and politicians who could *not* afford to castigate their natural constituencies for letting them down, and thus habitually found it politic to lay the blame for their defeats at someone else's door. For instance, when Mahathir lost his Kota Star Selatan seat to PMIP's Haji Yusof Rawa in 1969, Mahathir did not attribute his defeat to Malay disaffection with UMNO but instead blamed it on Chinese defection from the Alliance. Thirty years later, DAP leaders were led to thinking aloud that the Chinese voter's 'fear of PAS' had made DAP 'the biggest loser in the BA'.[18] However accurate it might have been, such an assessment informed DAP's developing stance of 'reconsidering' its membership in the BA as DAP increasingly criticized the PAS governments in Kelantan and Trengganu for not projecting 'an Islam of tolerance and justice which is fully compatible with democracy'.

Finally, it is a laudable principle that the members of a political coalition should consult and share. However, partnership in practice, including the basic need of accommodating ideological and other differences, is always conditioned by considerations of power. Fundamentally numbers count: how many seats does each party have, shall it have, or can it win? With ten seats in Parliament, the DAP still enjoyed a core of support but, so to speak, the DAP could no longer count on 'free admission' into the big urban constituencies that used to elect and re-elect DAP leaders, regardless of what they did or did not do. With only ten seats, the DAP had to relinquish the leadership of the opposition to the PAS and would have had to even if there had been no BA. From that perspective, the post-1999 DAP was more or less like the post-1990 S46 which could not determine the future of Gagasan Rakyat Malaysia after S46 emerged from the 1990 election with considerably fewer seats than either the DAP or the PBS. In defeat, S46 took a Malay turn while the DAP went its own way as the leader of the opposition in Parliament. This time around, unable to develop the BA's promise of a new politics of opposition or to expect the pendulum of minority politics to restore its former pre-eminence among opposition parties, the DAP chose to 'go it alone' to serve the causes of the 'Chinese community', 'the non-Muslims' and civil society. Perhaps the DAP leaders thought to reinvent the party thus. Perhaps theirs was a neat, even nostalgic, way of freezing complex social changes and political realignments in the mould of pre-Vision 2020, not to say pre-*Reformasi*, ethnic politics. But was that the path of reinvention? Or was it only a way of staking the party's future on its past?

The Rise and Rise of PAS?

At first glance, PAS was not beset with the dilemmas which their respective defeats had brought upon UMNO and DAP. In victory, after all, PAS clearly showed the advantages of having a developed organization, unified leadership and motivated membership. The party's programmatic goals and the principal constituencies to which it appealed also seemed to be unambiguous. The two governments PAS led in Kelantan and Trengganu were secure, because, barring unforeseen upheavals, UMNO would not be able to overturn PAS's massive winning margins in those two states in the next election. However, the quality of PAS's success, when judged by the limits of its electoral gains, scope of influence and depth of appeal, revealed the difficulties PAS encountered when trying to move from being a regional opposition party to being the dominant partner of a second coalition that could wrest power from the BN.

Before Anwar's fall, in fact, PAS's position in its Kelantan base had been weakened by UMNO's recapture of eight state seats in 1995, and S46's split with PAS followed by S46's dissolution as a party in 1996. Only one of S46's eleven state assemblymen joined PAS while the others rejoined UMNO, which gave PAS 25 state seats in Kelantan against the remaining eighteen controlled by UMNO. PAS's majority in the Kelantan state assembly still betokened a stable government until the next election while Menteri Besar Nik Abdul Aziz Nik Mat's administration remained popular. However, those familiar with PAS's 1962 loss of the Trengganu state government through defections to UMNO, its 1978 loss of Kelantan after a party split and the end of its troubled alliance with UMNO in the BN, as well as the 1994 toppling of PBS in Sabah would have realized that PAS's control over Kelantan no longer wore the unshakeable solidity of 1990 when the PAS-S46 combination took every state seat. Moreover, despite frequent speculation since the late 1970s that the Islamic resurgence would expand

Table 6.2 Parliamentary Seats (Proportion of Popular Vote) of Principal/Predominantly Malay Opposition Parties, General Elections, 1978-99

	1978	1982	1986	1990	1995	1999
PAS	5 (15.5)	5 (14.4)	1 (15.5)	7 (6.6)	7 (7.3)	27 (17.4)
S46	–	–	–	8 (14.4)	6 (10.1)	–
Keadilan	–	–	–	–	–	5 (11.5)
Total	5 (15.5)	5 (14.4)	1 (15.5)	15 (21.0)	13 (17.4)	32 (28.9)

Source: Suruhanjaya Pilihan Raya (various years).

PAS's influence throughout the 'Malay heartland' (including Trengganu and Kedah, two other states where PAS had had an electoral presence), PAS's nationwide performance had not demonstrated an appreciable expansion in electoral terms. Between the two elections of 1990 and 1995, PAS gained slightly in popular vote at the parliamentary level, yet won exactly seven seats in each election (Table 6.2).

In the pre-September 1998 period, finally, PAS's programmatic and ideological appeal had not seen significant growth. Many Malaysians in and out of Kelantan admired the Nik Aziz-headed government of Kelantan for its religiosity, honesty, a lack of ostentation, and close ties with the local populace. But Kelantan remained an economic backwater burdened with the highest incidence of poverty (19.2 per cent in 1997) in the country. The high incidence of poverty could just as well be blamed upon UMNO, which ruled Kelantan on its own between 1978 and 1990, and the federal government that starved the Kelantan state government of development funding thereafter. Even so, Kelantan's economic situation would hardly have commended PAS's 'model of development' to many others outside the state, no matter how sincerely some Kelantanese believe in the virtues of simple living 'stressing values of social collectivism, civil justice and redistribution through Islamic practices',[19] or accept 'a lower standard of material existence ... not incompatible with the existing capacity of the people'.[20] PAS also consistently encountered wide and staunch Muslim as well as non-Muslim opposition each time the party (and its allies among the *ulama*) sought to institutionalize or enforce a much stricter public compliance with Islamic law and moral codes, including PAS's move in 1993 to enact *hudud* laws in Kelantan.

The triumphalist and developmentalist pre-crisis milieu was not hospitable to the combination of Kelantan's economic disadvantage and PAS's religious determination. PAS's programme and its 'brand of Islam' were mostly regarded to be conservative, inflexible, even obscurantist – significantly, the opposite of the liberal, modernist, even futuristic vision of Islamization promoted by Mahathir, then with Anwar's assistance. Yet, where PAS retained a traditionally strong presence (notably in Kelantan and Trengganu), an exceptional intersection of social developments, cultural changes, ideological trends, and political conflicts made politics turn on a rather even UMNO-PAS divide uncoloured by interethnic differences.[21] Hence just a small but definite voters' swing could decisively affect electoral outcomes in those two states. This was particularly so when internal strife in one party caused a swing that prompted the defection of many members and sympathizers on the eve of an election. In 1977, PAS's infighting cost the party its control of the Kelantan government the following year. UMNO's split in 1987-88 brought its downfall in 1990. And Anwar's persecution provoked an anti-UMNO swing that devastated UMNO's chances of recapturing Kelantan and ceded Trengganu to PAS.

Suddenly, according to both alarmed anti-PAS and exuberant pro-PAS assessments, PAS was launched from an uncertain tenure in Kelantan onto a path of seemingly inexorable rise across the Malay heartland and maybe beyond. The stock view of this political turn held that since a PAS-led opposition now faced an UMNO-dominated regime, the thrust of future politics lay in the direction of an intense intra-Malay struggle between UMNO's 'secularism' and PAS's 'theocracy'. Just ten days after the 1999 election, for example, Ajay Singh of *Asiaweek* wrote of a 'new Malay dilemma' – the possibility that the political system was now more endangered by religious extremism than interethnic divisiveness.[22] Perhaps Ajay Singh represented the relief many foreign observers felt at Mahathir's return to power to thwart this new dilemma.[23]

The implications of PAS's post-election position were not so dire. PAS had gained 20 parliamentary seats, defended Kelantan, taken over Trengganu and expanded into Kedah entirely at UMNO's expense. These were impressive results by the standards of previous PAS performances (Table 6.2). But PAS's 27 seats only constituted 14 per cent of Parliament's total of 193 seats. PAS's share of the popular vote was

17.4 per cent, coincidentally the combined PAS-S46 share in 1995 (although PAS's share would surely have been higher had Keadilan not existed). When UMNO, suffering its worst setback, still held 72 seats in Parliament, PAS was not any closer to governing the country than DAP was when DAP won 24 parliamentary seats (out of 177) and 21.1 per cent of the popular vote in the 1986 election. Equally important, PAS's victories were almost entirely attained in the symbolic Malay heartland of 58 constituencies having more than two-thirds Malay voters each. Beyond that heartland lay constituencies with smaller Malay majorities, so-called ethnically mixed areas, which were dominated by UMNO and remained virtually impenetrable to PAS. PAS's sweep of the Trengganu parliamentary seats was impressive, and in winning control of the Trengganu government, PAS ended Kelantan's isolation as an opposition state government. Yet the overall significance of PAS's performance had to be qualified. Historically, the triumph in Trengganu may be regarded to be PAS's long awaited repeat of its victory there in the first post-Merdeka general election. Three years after that, in 1962, defections from PAS handed Trengganu to UMNO. A split in PAS led to UMNO's control of Kelantan for twelve years before PAS-S46 recaptured the state in 1990. Thus, a dispassionate assessment of PAS's results might view the 1999 results as marking PAS's recovery after almost 40 years of declining influence, although it was exactly a recovery that demarcated the limits of PAS's advance.

Indeed, PAS was further restricted by the reduction of the resources at its command. The major economic policies that PAS might derive from its basic Islamic programme have never been clearly spelt out. PAS had not revealed what 'Islamic development' might mean for a national economy integrated with global capitalism. In Kelantan, the party had practised forms of economic populism that would benefit the poor, landless, and underprivileged, relying sometimes on age-old Islamic instruments of charity, welfare and redistribution. For Trengganu, PAS's 1999 General Election Manifesto had planned to 'make [petroleum] royalty revenue the catalyst of state economic production' and to 'generate economic growth and expansion based on natural resources such as petroleum and gas'.[24] A section of the Manifesto devoted to 'petroleum and gas' pledged to:

13.1 Strive to obtain a fairer share of royalty from the Federal Government with a minimum receipt of 20%.
13.2 Ensure that the development of the petroleum and gas industry, which will create related industrial growth, shall expand and continue.

Cultural Imperative of Coalition Building

13.3 Ensure the involvement of local labour at all strata and levels of service.

13.4 Ensure that Petronas will provide larger contributions to the people of Trengganu in the field of higher education.

13.4 Make it a requirement that the State Government shall own equity in all investments based on petroleum and gas from Trengganu.[25]

What Menteri Besar Abdul Hadi Awang and his government could have accomplished with the petroleum revenues was never tested. The federal government hollowed PAS's electoral pledges by stopping Petronas from making direct payments to the state government. Instead the federal government redefined as 'goodwill money' (*wang ehsan*) the revenues that had been regarded as royalties for 23 years, and hence diverted about RM850 million annually to federal agencies operating in Trengganu. Hadi Awang condemned the federal government's action as being '*haram* [forbidden] from the point of religion, from the point of democracy, from the point of universal human morals'.[26] The Trengganu government's lawyer, Tommy Thomas, submitted before the High Court that, 'These actions of the federal government and its agents and servants were oppressive, arbitrary or unconstitutional'.[27] But the damage was done, and it could not be undone by PAS in the foreseeable future. Bereft of substantial financing and facing federal government hostility that discouraged 'foreign investment', no opposition-led government in a state like Trengganu could develop a 'modern' economy, to use a simple term. Its subsequent failure would be propagandized as proof of PAS's doctrinaire refusal or administrative inability to implement 'pragmatic', 'investment-friendly', 'growth-facilitating', or 'market-augmenting' policies, or whatever the preferred words may be. Later, when Hadi Awang said that Trengganu could not repay its loans to the federal government because of its loss of petroleum income, Deputy Prime Minister Abdullah Ahmad Badawi sanctimoniously supplied the rationale for the federal government's tactic:

> If we want to take over a company because we think that it is not being managed as well as it should, and that we are more clever, then we should prove it.
>
> How can we take over a company and not pay for it and then whine, 'Oh, this is not ours' or 'That, we did not do'.
>
> If that is the case, then we may as well not eradicate poverty or develop the state and leave it to the Federal Government to do everything.[28]

Meanwhile the triumvirate of federal government, Petronas and UMNO would decide the types and pace of development to be funded by the 'goodwill money'. Sauce for the goose being sauce for the gander, Trengganu under PAS would be compelled to fall back upon remedial, piecemeal and resource-scarce programmes to assist the disadvantaged sections of its populace; the scenario had been encountered in Kelantan before. By and by, Trengganu, with its 17.3 per cent incidence of poverty (in 1997) after 25 years of UMNO rule, would become Kelantan's soul mate in showcasing 'impoverishment under Islamic government'.

Of course, the party faithful was free to make a virtue of living simply, of living Islamic principles, as it were, in a dignified defiance of punitive power. It was also understandable that the defiance was expressed in a spirited Islamic idiom that set aside mundane calculations of material interests. After all, the Malay opposition rallying around PAS in 1998-99 had drawn heavily from a moral repugnance and cultural revolt that redefined the ethical boundaries of political conduct. Combining religiosity with political ideology, PAS had committed itself to 'practise Islam as *Ad-din*',[29] as a way of life requiring an integration of religion with economics, politics and socio-cultural life, thus distinguishing it from 'UMNO's Islam', the latter seen as a 'vehicle of modernization' to 'propel the Malays into mainstream global (capitalist) development'.[30] It was crucial for PAS to show how it could accomplish its ideological mission of 'making the development of the human being the core of development'[31] while grappling with the actual tasks and material difficulties of managing economic development. But financial deprivation, if not economic sabotage, left PAS with hardly a 'pragmatic' option to demonstrate the superiority of 'Islamic government'. Instead, there was the 'dogmatic' recourse of injecting a stricter observance of religious piety, moral fervour, and exemplary conduct in personal and public life.

Before the election, PAS had declared its intent to 'prohibit all forms of gambling and vices and limit licences to premises selling liquor and intoxicating drinks' and to 'prevent and eradicate social ills'.[32] Afterwards, the local authorities in Trengganu closed '*karaoke* lounges', reduced the number of establishments permitted to sell liquor, restricted the operations of 'unisex hair salons', and considered new ways to minimize the mingling of the sexes in public places. These ways of handling 'matters which are forbidden by Islam but have not been fully eradicated'[33] were prompted by ideological conviction, but PAS's lack of developmental alternatives cast them in starker tones. If 'fundamentalism' prevented PAS from 'facing up to modernity' – a typical criticism made of PAS – UMNO's *realpolitik* denied PAS the resources needed for a frontal and earnest engagement with contemporary facets of modernity. So to speak, there would be no 'modern development' to balance PAS's social conservatism – the way that high growth came to offset UMNO's ethnic discrimination under the NEP. PAS often protested that its welfare programmes, administrative changes and non-discriminatory practices protected the interests of women and non-Muslims 'under Islam'. Not for the first time, however, instances of the moral policing of seemingly petty matters lent themselves to shaping public discourse.

One could argue that PAS's actions were not misguided when judged by the conventions of electoral politics: where in power, more so when newly returned to power, a party implemented its programme. Political practice, though, showed PAS's programme bifurcating. *Being in opposition at the national level*, PAS, together with its BA partners, defended civil liberties, human rights, democracy and the rule of law. PAS leaders, members and supporters placed themselves at the forefront of demonstrations against unjust laws, unfair rulings, unpopular policies, and unacceptable harassment. PAS spurned Mahathir's call for 'Malay unity' talks, protested the use of draconian legislation such as the Internal Security Act, resisted police harassment, and supported the 'Chinese community' at the time of the Damansara school controversy. That is to say, PAS maintained a course of political liberalism that rejected ethnic politics, stood with the national human rights movement, and showed a new appreciation of 'minority rights'. *Being in government at the state level*, PAS on its own enforced measures of social conservatism that encroached upon individual liberties and intruded into the sphere of private life and personal choices. PAS's moral policing unsettled non-Muslims who feared an 'Islamic state', 'liberal-minded' Muslims who feared it no less, and women who opposed illiberal attitudes towards their social status and freedom. Besides, PAS took the Trengganu government closer to being an 'administration based on the Qur'an and *Sunnah*' by proposing the Syariah Criminal Offences (*Hudud* and *Qisas*) Bill.[34] Thus Hadi Awang replicated the Kelantan government's enactment of the Syariah Criminal Code (11) Enactment of 1993, and PAS tried to 'build Islam in two states'.

How should PAS's programmatic bifurcation be interpreted? One way was to focus on the tactics PAS adopted to deal with the realities of politics and calculations of power in two different sets of circumstances. In the national setting, PAS alone was no match for the BN.

The party's hopes of extending its influence rested upon its ability to continue to lead the BA's broad based campaign – over civil liberties, along constitutional lines, and around the rule of law, of secular law, that *Reformasi* had inspired. In the state settings, the devastated UMNO was no match for PAS whose governments could implement their programmes, albeit against the opposition of the federal government. Here, PAS's priority was to build stable and durable administrative platforms that would support living models of the society envisioned by 'PAS-Islam' in contradistinction to Mahathir's 'Vision Islam'.[35] Another way was to interpret the bifurcation in terms of the differences in 'political consciousness', for lack of a better word, displayed by PAS's sources of support in Kelantan and Trengganu, and beyond these two states. For Trengganu and Kelantan's predominantly Muslim population, Islam had long informed the discourse of UMNO-PAS rivalry and PAS was esteemed by its supporters for 'upholding and protecting every aspect of the religion and takes pride in being a religious party'.[36] There was accordingly a higher empathy for PAS's intent to 'propagate the integration of the religion with the economy, politics and socio-cultural life to create an alternative Islamic civilization'.[37] Outside Kelantan and Trengganu, PAS could not, at least not yet, take for granted the pre-eminence of its Islamic idiom of opposition within the ranks of the Malay opposition. It was true that the Islamic resurgence had reached a generation of young, urban, and middle-class or professional Malays whose

> zeal to Islamize Malaysia as a response to globalisation pushed them into direct coalition with the older and more traditional Islamists in PAS. They invigorated the latter with fresh blood as well as new skills and technology. …PAS is now fused with religiously inclined young professionals who are knowledgeable in both current world affairs as well as the new technology in all fields including … IT.[38]

Yet, this social group had its large pro-UMNO or 'liberal Muslim' counterpart for whom PAS policies were anathema. If members of this second group of young Malays abruptly broke with their customary pro-UMNO voting patterns, their actions were prompted by *Reformasi*'s cultural revolt, rather than embracing of PAS-Islam. However captivating PAS's slogan – *dulu UMNO, sekarang PAS* (formerly UMNO, now PAS) – might be, a resolution of UMNO's primary difficulties might swing the *dulu UMNO* voters against PAS in much the same way as had happened to S46.

Finally, one could approach PAS's programmatic bifurcation by way of the 'non-Muslim factor' in PAS's calculations. Within Kelantan

Cultural Imperative of Coalition Building   153

and Trengganu the electoral significance of the small non-Muslim population was low and interethnic political differences were a rarity. Judged by UMNO's past policies, or by PAS's hostility to 'pre-Islamic' Malay cultural practices (notably in Kelantan), the PAS government abided by their professed non-discriminatory stance towards non-Muslim religious and cultural practices. Even in their moral policing, PAS made allowances for non-Muslim non-conformity with certain Islamic injunctions.[39] The non-Muslim factor was significant at the national level. Neither during the 1980s, when non-Malay dissidence peaked, nor in 1998-99 was PAS able to moderate non-Muslim suspicion of the party's 'ultimate' goal. That suspicion was summed up in the implacable non-Muslim opposition to any proposal of an 'Islamic state', in effect a major impediment to PAS's advance in the ethnically mixed constituencies. The major exceptions to this non-Muslim sentiment were activists and members of DAP, PRM, Keadilan and the NGOs who intermittently cooperated with PAS in campaigns for civil liberties and human rights until the BA's formation institutionalized their cooperation. Slim as this category of non-Muslims already was, its willingness to engage with PAS had always presupposed a common commitment to secular constitutional government.

In a subtle understanding of PAS's challenge to the hegemony of Mahathirism, John Hilley noted that PAS's strategic gain at the 1998-99 conjuncture was a promising 'cultivation of a new "moral politics"' in which 'its [Islamic] principles were being fused with broader secular concerns about justice, transparency and good governance'.[40] A popular receptivity towards this 'new moral politics' had helped PAS to attain 'a major expansion of its *national-popular* base'. But the chief utility of this 'moral politics' was to 'illustrate the contextual space within which the arguments and ideas for [PAS's] project were now located'. Hence, PAS's practical goal of leading a new 'opposition alignment' – 'a proto-project involving wider ethnic support and intellectual streams' – 'still had to find direction' on the basis of 'meaningful accommodations with the other parties and the wider *reformasi*'. Therefore, one might add that, in the flush of electoral success, PAS had to adapt, if not reinvent, itself to broaden its appeal and truly to advance. PAS might argue that objections to *hudud*, *qisas* and other replacements of civil law with 'divine law' arose from the unexamined fears of non-Muslims who did not understand Islam, or of Muslims who did not fully practise the religion. But, politically, as Raja Petra Kamarudin bluntly expressed it: 'PAS has to decide what its political platform is. Is it to Islamise the nation or to form the next federal government. It cannot be both....'[41] From that perspective, PAS's programmatic bifurcation offered neither novel directions nor 'meaningful accommodations'. Insofar as PAS persisted with its 'Islamic state' project, the party had failed to comprehend that its temporal feat at the 1999 election was brought about by the Malay revolt over Anwar's persecution, rather than a clamour for a theocratic state.

Keadilan Between Vision and Fulfilment

Among the parties of the opposition, Parti Keadilan Nasional was the true child of *Reformasi*. Although it had an institutional antecedent of sorts in ADIL, Keadilan was born not just of the sustained public reaction to Anwar's travails, but also of the urgent need by Anwar's closest associates and their supporters to join the electoral battle against the BN. Not quite eight months old as a party when the 1999 election was held, Keadilan won five parliamentary seats. This was not an inspiring performance, given *Reformasi* expectations, especially since several of its best known leaders – Chandra Muzaffar, Tian Chua and Zainur Zakaria – were defeated. But the low number of seats belied Keadilan's 11.5 per cent of the popular vote, which was almost as large a proportion as DAP's, and which could be taken as a reliable indication of the depth of Malay anti-UMNO sentiment. With time and favourable circumstances, Keadilan's leadership might have found ways to entrench 'Anwar's party' as a leading party of an unabated *Reformasi*. Several factors, however, caused Keadilan to lead an agonized existence in which survival rather than advance became the party's highest priority.

One critical factor, which greatly hampered Keadilan, was the regime's repression against the party's leadership. While the regime could not risk taking heavy-handed action against Wan Azizah herself, it subjected other party leaders – including Azmin Ali, N. Gobalakrishnan, Lokman Adam, Marina Yusof, Mohamad Ezam Mohd Nor, and Tian Chua – to police harassment, arrest, and prosecution on charges that included 'illegal assembly', 'sedition' and violation of the Official Secrets Act. Despite their persistent maltreatment by the regime, the Keadilan leaders energetically pursued the *Reformasi*'s street-level tactics of protests and demonstrations, mostly within the greater Kuala Lumpur area. That was partly because Keadilan could not but keep alive the 'issue of Anwar' as Anwar was convicted at the end of his second trial in 2000 and was sentenced to a further nine years' imprisonment. Partly it was because Keadilan had no physical base, unlike PAS, which in Kelantan and Trengganu, and to a lesser degree in Kedah, continued to hold almost nightly *ceramah*, often ignoring police warnings or resisting police disruptions. As the political turmoil continued into 2000, the Keadilan leaders constantly faced the threat of detention without trial under the Internal Security Act.

Keadilan faced other internal difficulties that might be traced to the very formation of the party. Formally launched on 4 April 1999, only ten days before 'Black 14', Keadilan's leadership was hastily assembled from three main groups of people. One group was made up of Wan Azizah and others who were personally close to Anwar, such as Chandra Muzaffar who in the 1990s had renewed his former 'civil society ties' with Anwar. A second group included Anwar's former allies in UMNO who had not turned against him. Prominent among them were Azmin Ali, Mohamad Ezam, Ruslan Kasim, and Saifudin Nasution. Third, there were NGO activists and other public figures who became 'Anwaristas' of different shades: they included Zainur Zakaria, a member of Anwar's team of lawyers from the first trial; Tian Chua, a human rights activist from Suara Rakyat Malaysia; Mohd Anuar Tahir, one of the leaders of Angkatan Belia Islam Malaysia; and Marina Yusof, a veteran of past dissenting factions in UMNO. Other than the ex-UMNO politicians, the Keadilan leaders were respected figures who possessed no direct political experience, including Wan Azizah, who became a symbol of *Reformasi* in her own right. Moreover, Keadilan's combination of quite dissimilar figures represented an ideologically non-unified leadership which, in the harried circumstances of 1999, was hard pressed for time and opportunity to resolve difficulties that were bound to emerge as 'different agendas' contested for priority and emphasis.

Keadilan's membership, too, was recruited unsystematically. Keadilan's leadership strove hard to present a multiethnic front and an inclusive message meant to attract a multiethnic membership. When Keadilan was launched as a political party, Raja Petra Kamarudin wrote optimistically that Keadilan drew:

> very strong support from the intellectuals, intelligentsia, professionals, yuppies, arts community, executives, and so on – a group that, in the past, was apolitical and never even bothered to register as voters or came out to vote in the General Elections.[42]

More than that, Keadilan's supporters, by 'being multi-racial and multi-religious', supplied the 'missing link' to the BA whose other parties 'only served a certain segment of the population'.[43] A year later, Raja Petra could barely contain his disappointment at the gap between sincere intention and limiting reality:

> Parti Keadilan Nasional was born with great expectations just over a year ago.... Now, at last, there is a party that is genuinely multi-racial and multi-religious. But, then, when they looked closer, keADILan became, more and more, like a Malay/Muslim party in appearance. Where were the non-Malays and non-Muslims? What they saw was a mere handful of non-Malays/non-Muslims who could not legitimately claim to represent the other races and other religions.[44]

Some young non-Malays responded to *Reformasi*, and in search of a multiethnic political party, they chose to join Keadilan, instead of DAP. But non-Malays did not enter Keadilan in sufficiently large numbers to confer a truly multiethnic character upon the party. Consequently, Keadilan's members were young, energetic and full of initiative but overwhelmingly Malay. Once again, except for those who had crossed over from UMNO, Keadilan's members tended to be unaccustomed to party politics. Most members' pre-Keadilan organizational affiliations, if any, lay with Islamic NGOs such as ABIM, and Jemaah Islah Malaysia (JIM).

The ideological convergence for Keadilan's diverse membership was probably captured by *Reformasi*'s most popular slogans of 1998-99: *Justice for Anwar!* and *Undur Mahathir!*. Indeed the Keadilan leadership had practically no time to develop a distinct or visibly coherent party programme beyond a moralistic interpretation of the goals of *Reformasi* as they were enunciated in Anwar's Permatang Pauh Declaration. Until the BA developed its *Joint Manifesto* and its *People's Budget*, Keadilan's own programmatic orientation was ambivalent, as if the party could not avoid being pulled along two different (though not necessarily conflicting) directions. 'Justice for Anwar' was unavoidably Keadilan's strongest cause to the extent that the opposition, its NGO allies, and their supporters accepted that there would have been no *Reformasi* without Anwar. Yet, they and others also realized that *Reformasi*, as the harbinger of deeper social change and political reform, could only advance in practice if it went 'beyond Anwar'.

While leadership, membership and direction were Keadilan's main but ambivalent strengths, they also brought organizational stresses and ideological differences, especially when Keadilan had to negotiate its position within the BA and to prepare for the election. In Malaysian political history, some opposition parties were able to construct viable organizational structures and efficient electoral machines 'at the last minute' because they did so around large breakaway factions or even whole and experienced parties. For example, the core of S46 in 1990 was UMNO's Team B from 1987. When Parti Bersatu Sabah emerged in 1984, it was constituted from a big splinter of the ruling Parti Berjaya. In 1969, Gerakan Rakyat Malaysia was built around the United Democratic Party, social democrat remnants from the Labour Party and politically active trade unionists. Keadilan had none of these advantages. The reputedly large contingent of 'Anwar's boys and girls' in UMNO did not defect in as large a number as had been expected. Or many defectors, like Kamarudin Jaafar, a close Anwar ally in ABIM and UMNO, chose to join PAS rather than Keadilan. Other than the ABIM leaders perhaps, the NGO activists who joined Keadilan's leadership had no mass membership upon which to draw new entrants into Keadilan. While numbers are not everything in politics, Keadilan soon found out that party structures and networks could not be quickly constructed out of spirit alone.

Paradoxically, Keadilan's greatest advantage as well as its most crippling disadvantage was Anwar's imprisonment. Keadilan was sustained by public anger over Anwar's fate, Malay sentiment predominantly, which definitely did not subside with his conviction at the end of his second trial and his imprisonment for a further nine years. In a show of sympathy with Anwar's family, *Reformasi* supporters practically revered Wan Azizah while the BA honoured her. Anwar's incarceration, however, left Keadilan's chief asset – its young and courageous membership – with no strategic and experienced leadership. Other Keadilan leaders were energetic and ran enormous personal risks in mobilizing supporters for demonstrations and protests. Had Anwar been free, he might have welded the qualities of leadership and membership into a formidable party structure and organization. With his personal stature, extensive experience in ABIM and UMNO, and the enormous sympathy for his predicament, he might have unified the disparate elements, differing agendas and even divergent loyalties among Keadilan's leadership and membership. But Anwar was in jail, rendered practically incommunicado, and permitted to emerge only in court – and not even there, when his second trial was adjourned before the election. Anwar served as a rallying point, for Keadilan certainly, and for the BA who named him the coalition's leader in the event of the coalition's success in the election. Beyond that, Keadilan's leaders had to cooperate with one another in tentative ways, almost just as GERAK and the BA had to discover ways for a diverse opposition to cooperate in the circumstances of 1998-99.

Up to the end of 1999, Keadilan's organizational stresses were probably camouflaged by the spirit of *Reformasi* supporters who thronged protests, demonstrations and marches and by the BA's efforts at building an 'alternative coalition'. After the election, however, certain disputes broke out that suggested that Keadilan was finding it difficult to consolidate itself as a party with long-term prospects. The first dispute to come to public light was a disagreement between Chandra Muzaffar, the deputy president, and Marina Yusof, one of the vice-presidents. This disagreement had been festering since January 2000 but degenerated into a public confrontation in June. Then, Marina and Chandra took turns to trade accusations of bad faith and questionable conduct via *malaysiakini*, but not before Marina resigned as a vice-president for reasons of 'health and business' and left the party.[45] Next was a controversy related to the BA's nomination of a candidate to contest the Teluk Kemang by-election, scheduled for June 2000. It would seem that DAP had a prior claim on the candidacy since the party had contested the Teluk Kemang constituency before. But it was rumoured that Keadilan had insisted on its being given the seat to contest and that Chandra had given the BA an 'ultimatum' on this matter. In any event, Chandra denied having issued the ultimatum but Keadilan was given the seat to contest over DAP protests. Keadilan's Ruslan Kasim lost in Teluk Kemang, although he reduced the BN's 1999 majority by 40 per cent.

Strangest of all was a dispute that developed in an entirely unprecedented manner. Ahead of the Teluk Kemang by-election, the webmasters of five popular *Reformasi* websites suddenly 'blacked out' their sites for several days. This 'alternative information strike' turned out to be the webmasters' way of conducting a 'campaign of reflection' on the future of *Reformasi*. While many of the websites' regular visitors agonized over the black-out, and the reasons behind it, there were suggestions that the webmasters had meant to chastise Chandra, and Keadilan's secretary-general, Anuar Tahir, for 'not adhering to Anwar Ibrahim's instructions'. None of the webmasters ever offered to clarify just what 'Anwar's instructions' were. But they were reportedly referring to Chandra and Anuar Tahir's opposition to a proposal to merge Keadilan with Parti Rakyat Malaysia. The proposed merger, based on hopes of combining Keadilan's greater outreach with PRM's established and coherent leadership, was an idea that had significant but not yet decisive support within each party.

It may be suggested that Keadilan owed its existence to the idealism it derived from *Reformasi*'s push for political change, for its vision of a future that could break with an unbearable past, and for its opposition of fresh meanings of democracy, reform and social justice to authoritarian leadership and manipulative politics. These may seem to be mere 'intangibles' when measured by the standards of hardnosed politics, but they constituted the political equivalent of (commercial) 'goodwill' that would always be crucial for a new party like Keadilan. But a creative deployment of political goodwill required an authoritative leadership, an effective organization, and a coherent programme. For Keadilan, there was the added difficulty of tending to those tasks within a coalitional framework that remained largely experimental.

Whatever their specific details, the Chandra-Marina split, the rift with DAP on seat allocation and the webmasters' intervention pointed to severe organizational weaknesses that Keadilan never satisfactorily overcame. If, in fact, 'Anwar's instructions' played a major role in these disputes, the party's structural stresses were more extensive than suspected. Indispensable as Anwar was to Keadilan, it had to be an odd idea that Anwar *in prison* could run a political party to the extent of being a source of instructions, written or otherwise, on strategy, tactics, and the practical details of agenda-setting, problem-solving, and even negotiating with other parties.

Throughout 2000 and 2001, *Reformasi* protests, demonstrations and marches continued under BA auspices, often led by the most intrepid of the Keadilan leaders. These expressions of protest displayed sheer will and resolution that had not been encountered for at least a generation in Malaysian history. Then, Keadilan's difficulties were still submerged in these waves of popular dissent. But without strong organization and clear direction, no political party can withstand the decapitation of its leadership – which was what befell Keadilan before it could consolidate itself.

The Cultural Imperative of Coalition Building

Three dates and their respective importance are worth recalling. April 1995 signified the end of an era of NEP politics and an ideological shift away from an earlier pattern of bitter interethnic contestation. July 1997 marked the end of a Mahathirist programme of capitalist rationalization when Malaysia Inc. chose to use its 'economic shield' in preference to reforming itself out of the East Asian crisis. September 1998 sealed the end of UMNO's privileged position as the source of hegemonic stability when the Anwar affair spilled UMNO's factionalism into the political system. These three ideological, economic and political transitions framed a conjuncture at which the bases of

Mahathirist politics had been eroded. As a result, the political issues of the day could be posed in unanticipated ways, some of which were not formulated by political parties but thrown up by civil society's dissent. This historical conjuncture awaited only agency, or human intervention, to forge a novel reorganization of the political system. The agency came by way of a progression from *Reformasi*'s inchoate protests to GERAK's experimental networking and eventually to BA's 'rainbow coalition'.

There was nothing inevitable about the *Reformasi*-GERAK-BA sequence. Before 2 September 1998, and even months later, no one could have predicted such a rapid and almost choreographed movement from spontaneous dissent to tentative cooperation and then to organized opposition. Nor was there anything inexorable about it. There were always several possibilities that the progression would be aborted. They ranged from the remote chance of Mahathir's voluntary exit from politics to the more probable failure of PAS and DAP to reach an accord. But the progress, for the progression can be called that, too, happened partly because 'all along … there were incidents and accusations, there were hints and allegations'[46] that catalysed it. It might be said, therefore, that both progression and progress encapsulated the tensions and contradictions of Malaysian society that were exposed by Anwar's fall, reflected in *Reformasi*, mediated through the BA and temporarily checked by the November 1999 election. Indeed, had PAS, DAP, Keadilan, PRM and the NGOs who supported the opposition not established the BA in time for the election of November 1999, Malaysian politics would have had to invent some other form of a 'second coalition' for three fundamental reasons.

The first is a pragmatic reason. No opposition party has been able, singly, to challenge UMNO, let alone the fourteen-member BN. In the 1986 election, DAP enjoyed huge success while PAS was shut out by UMNO. Four years later the opposition's hopes were realized by DAP, PBS and PAS, but S46 failed to deliver. As a consequence of what one might call an asynchronism of opposition performance, even established parties such as PAS and DAP had to 'hang together' if they did not want to 'hang separately'. Thus a putative second coalition, always ready to ally itself with UMNO dissidents, had suggested itself since the late 1980s. It was indicative of UMNO's fractious state that Mahathir twice obliged those who harboured hopes of building that second coalition by forcing out two key UMNO figures in ten years: Razaleigh in 1988, and Anwar in 1998.

Cultural Imperative of Coalition Building

The second reason had to do with the political impasse of 1999. Years of the BN's domination of the legislature and executive aggrandizement had so weakened key public institutions that the political system had seemingly become subjected to one-party rule. Hence, while 'any coalition that is formidable enough to fight Barisan Nasional has to be broad-based', as Mohamad Ezam stressed,[47] it was not critical that the BA remained ideologically heterogeneous, as its detractors claimed. It was sufficient that BA's multiethnic, multi-religious and NGO-supported four-party coalition represented the only practical chance of erecting a bulwark against the further erosion of constitutional government. Or, to recall Sabri Zain's diligent and unforgettable record of his own experience of coalition:

> The four of us posed for the camera and, as the flash dazzled my eyes for a moment, it suddenly dawned on me. Here were four people, from four different political parties – Keadilan, PRM, DAP and PAS. We were held arm in arm, not giving a damn about our political or ideological differences, but just united in celebrating the birth of yet another force for justice, and joined by a common desire for change in our country.[48]

There is a third reason that may be termed a cultural imperative of coalition building. In the immediacy of political developments, partisans and observers were liable to overlook the confluence of contemporary events with half-remembered history. *Reformasi* grew into GERAK because of civil society's discovery of a confluence of recent injustice (Anwar's maltreatment, Guan Eng's incarceration, and the assaults on *Reformasi* demonstrators) with the half-forgotten resistance of the 1980s (the dissent linked to the financial scandals and political crises of the period). By extension, GERAK's transformation into the BA connected current developments to an impressive history of coalition building in Malaysian politics.

A full history of Malaysian political coalitions would have to consider the following: Putera-AMCJA, as well as the Alliance during the last decade of colonial rule; the Socialist Front of the Labour Party and Parti Rakyat Malaya soon after Merdeka; the Malaysian Solidarity Convention prior to Singapore's secession; Barisan Nasional in the first years of NEP; and Gagasan Rakyat Malaysia and Angkatan Perpaduan Ummah after the UMNO split in 1987-88. Even without being subjected to any thorough assessment, this record of coalition building was clearly a chequered one of relative failure in some cases (Putera-AMCJA, Malaysian Solidarity Convention, Gagasan and APU) and comparative success in others (Alliance, Socialist Front, and the BN).

Against the historical record of these previous coalitions, it may be too early to make a definitive evaluation of the BA's impact on the political system. Tentatively, we might be able to say this much: until mid-2001, the BA stayed intact as the conduit for *Reformasi*'s continued ferment that defied repression and rejected UMNO's efforts to divert dissent to interethnic quarrel. While the BA could not bring about serious reform of the political system, it compelled the regime to establish in 2000 the Suruhanjaya Hak Asasi Manusia Nasional (Suhakam), or a National Human Rights Commission, even if only a cobbled one. This was no mean feat and for some time, it appeared as if the BA could consolidate itself as the alternative front that would draw on a deepening Malay dissidence to force through a more pluralistic politics.

On 28 October 2000, for example, over two thousand people from the BA parties and some NGOs demonstrated outside the Kamunting detention camp to commemorate the fourteenth anniversary of the mass arrests of 27 October 1987, and to protest '40 years of the Internal Security Act'. It was the biggest anti-ISA demonstration in recent times, and the first time that Malay protestors against the ISA outnumbered non-Malay protestors by a wide margin. After this, came the massive Kesas Highway rally of 5 November. Keadilan had called for '100,000' persons' to rally in Shah Alam in defence of civil liberties and the right to peaceful assembly. The police predictably refused to give a permit for the rally and instead arrested several of its suspected organizers. Still thousands and thousands of people – mostly Malay and 'too many to count' according to the tactful reporting of some Chinese-language newspapers – participated in the rally. The police diverted the marchers to the Kesas Highway where the protestors were met with water cannon, tear gas, mace sprays, arrests, and beatings. After such incidents, UMNO politicians, who used to say that Chinese Malaysians could 'go back to China' and Indian Malaysians could 'go back to India' whereas the Malays had nowhere else to go, were telling 'BA and Free Anwar Campaign Malays' that 'if they didn't like Malaysia, they should leave'! The remark, a reflection of UMNO's desperation, would have been as unthinkable before the BA's formation as the idea of a government that was not led by UMNO.

Then, on 29 November, a by-election was called in Lunas, Kedah (after the BN's incumbent representative, Joe Fernandez of the Malaysian Indian Congress, was murdered in a case that remains unsolved). At the time of the by-election, the BN had held Lunas for 40 years and now had exactly a two-thirds majority in the Kedah legislative

Cultural Imperative of Coalition Building

assembly. The BA's choice of Saifuddin Nasution – who led the Pemuda UMNO's disruption of the Asia-Pacific Conference on East Timor II in Kuala Lumpur in 1996 – as a Keadilan candidate caused serious intra-BA disputes. The DAP, which had expected to field a candidate, almost boycotted the BA's electoral campaign. The Lunas by-election raised such rancorous issues as 'Malay special rights' and the status of Chinese education that would have cleanly pitted pro-government 'Malay votes' against pro-opposition 'Chinese votes' had the by-election been held in the 1980s. Astonishingly, an ethnically mixed electoral revolt against the BN narrowly handed Lunas to the BA. It was the only by-election won by the opposition in the year following November 1999.

The opposition exulted in its unexpected victory. Yet the Lunas result marked the height of the BA's progress. In April 2001, a plan for another mammoth protest in conjunction with 'Black 14', the date of Anwar's first conviction, was thwarted by the ISA arrests of seven Keadilan leaders – namely, Abdul Ghani Harun, Badrul Amin Bahron, N. Gobalakrishnan, Lokman Adam, Mohamad Ezam, Saari Sungib and Tian Chua – and three activists, that is, Hishamuddin Rais (a student leader of the 1970s, journalist and film director), Raja Petra Kamarudin (director of the Free Anwar Campaign) and Badaruddin Ismail (of Suara Rakyat Malaysia). The threat of large-scale arrests, after the manner of 27 October 1987, loomed. Suspected members of a so-called Kumpulan Militan Malaysia (KMM, or Malaysian Militant Group), allegedly an underground movement of Muslim extremists bent on a violent overthrow of the government, were likewise arrested under the ISA. The regime ignored domestic and international protests and legal suits against its latest use of detention without trial against the opposition.

The strain of coping with this wave of repression brought tensions in the BA to a head. Keadilan was already crippled by the incarceration of its most determined and capable organizers. The remaining Keadilan leaders could only respond with ineffectual protests. The detentions of the 'KMM suspects' (including the son of Nik Aziz, the Menteri Besar of Kelantan) drew allegations of Islamic militancy closer to PAS. Not only was this a tactic to deflect criticisms of the regime's use of the ISA, it probably made it less likely for PAS to soften its Islamic programme, particularly in Trengganu. In turn, the DAP 're-considered' its place in the BA on grounds that PAS's commitment to an 'Islamic state' contravened the BA's *Joint Manifesto* and could not assuage non-Muslim fears. Then came 'September 11'. Its global repercussions redefined Malaysian politics significantly. From being defensive about its use of the ISA, the Mahathir regime now extolled the legislation as a proven instrument of national security. From being (symbolically) rebuffed by the Clinton administration over the Anwar trials, Mahathir now 'won praise from President Bush' for his 'cooperation in the war on terror'. The USA-led invasion of Afghanistan in October 2001 made it impossible for PAS not to express its solidarity with the Taliban regime, which made it convenient for PAS's opponents to 'Talibanize' the PAS. As there was no practical chance of resuming any formal DAP-PAS collaboration, the BA was no more, despite the claims of PAS, Keadilan and PRM to the contrary.

For some time to come, the manifestations of Malaysia's plural society – seen as an ethnic division of labour at one historical point, as social engineering at another, and as an Islamic resurgence at a third – will continue to present any coalition of its political parties with genuine problems of ideological heterogeneity, political representation, and power sharing. Even so, and in spite of past interethnic clashes, Malaysian society may have been saved from the spectre of ethnic balkanization by the experience of coalition building. As an experience inspired by a collective intuition that diversity in a plural society must be more than a virtue, coalition building must go further and recognize that diversity is a necessity that invents social and political experiments.

Notes

1. For an analysis of these results, see Ng (2003).
2. *Ibid.*
3. Khoo (1995: 238).
4. Kua (1996: 39).
5. *Ibid.*
6. Quoted in 'Fighting for a Cause', *Aliran Monthly*, Vol. 18, No. 10 (November 1998): 6.
7. A typical 'coffeeshop' version would have it that 'Anwar has been victimized by Mahathir, but one would be a fool to support Anwar'.
8. Loh (2001: 201).
9. Lim (2003: 158).
10. Kua (1996: 28).
11. Lim (2003: 158).
12. *Ibid.*, p. 167.
13. *Ibid.*
14. *Ibid.*
15. *Ibid.*, pp. 167-68.

Cultural Imperative of Coalition Building 165

16 *Ibid.*, p. 168.
17 *Ibid.*, p. 167.
18 *Ibid.*, p. 162.
19 Hilley (2001: 194).
20 Halim (2000: 3).
21 *Ibid.*
22 Singh (1999: 34).
23 For an examination of the pre-election international and regional media's discreet support for Mahathir, see Khoo (1999b).
24 Translated from PAS, *Manifesto Pilihanraya Umum 1999 Negeri Trengganu Darul Iman* (http://www.parti-pas.org/Trengganu/manifesto99.htm), Subsections 7.2 and 7.3 respectively.
25 *Ibid.*, Section 13.
26 'Wang Ehsan: Tindakan Kerajaan Pusat yang haram – MB Trengganu', *harakahdaily.net*, 7 February 2002.
27 'Oil royalty: Petronas acted (sic) double standards', *harakahdaily.net*, 20 February 2002.
28 'Prove you can run Trengganu, DPM tells PAS', *The Star*, 17 December 2002.
29 Translated from PAS, *Manifesto Pilihanraya Umum 1999 Negeri Trengganu Darul Iman* (http://www.parti-pas.org/Trengganu/manifesto99.htm), Subsection 1.3.
30 Halim (2000: 5).
31 Translated from PAS, *Manifesto Pilihanraya Umum 1999 Negeri Trengganu Darul Iman* (http://www.parti-pas.org/Trengganu/manifesto99.htm), Subsection 1.8.
32 *Ibid.*, Subsections 1.6 and 1.7.
33 *Ibid.*, 'Foreword'.
34 For a summary of the central legal implications of *hudud* and *qisas*, see 'Q and A on the Hudud and Qisas Enactment', *Aliran Monthly*, Vol. 22, No. 6, 2002, pp. 25-29. The Trengganu bill was passed in July 2002.
35 The terms, 'PAS-Islam' and 'Vision Islam' are from Hilley (2001).
36 Halim (2000: 5).
37 *Ibid.*, p. 4.
38 *Ibid.*, p. 6.
39 Funston, (2000: 38) observed thus: 'Formal BA statements reiterated a commitment to the constitutional guarantee of Islam as the religion of the state, and promoting Islam as a way of life (*ad-deen*), along with freedom of worship for all. They made no mention of an Islamic state, and indeed Nik Aziz pointed out that this was not even in the PAS constitution – it had been removed many years ago and replaced with a commitment to establishing an Islamic society. Separate PAS manifestos for Kelantan and Trengganu did promise to ban gambling and limit the sale of alcohol, but party spokesmen went to great lengths to emphasize

that non-Muslims had not been unfairly treated under PAS in Kelantan, with freedom of worship guaranteed and non-Muslims even allowed to continue such practices as rearing pigs. Islam was, however, the one area where differences between coalition members became apparent, with DAP leaders publicly dissociating themselves from PAS statements in favour of *hudud* and the death penalty for apostates.

40 Hilley (2001: 222).
41 Petra (2000: 225).
42 *Ibid.*, p. 159.
43 *Ibid.*, pp. 159-60.
44 *Ibid.*, p. 223.
45 It appeared that the rest of the Keadilan leadership tried to rise above this incident. Wan Azizah described it as a 'personal matter' while the party's general assembly elected without any fuss a new vice-president, Zainur Zakaria. Vice-president Tian Chua was reported to have said that some quarters were trying to undermine Marina's position, but subsequently said only that the party's Supreme Council had not taken a stand on the issue.
46 Paul Simon (1986), 'You can call me Al', *Graceland*, Warner Bros. Records.
47 Ezam's point was made just before Keadilan was founded. See 'New and Moderate', *Asiaweek*, 2 April 1999, p. 29.
48 Sabri (2000: 110).

7
The Coming of the Second Dilemma

But now I reverse my stand. I no longer believe what I wrote in *The Malay Dilemma*. ...The Malays are not inferior to others ... in fact we are now a model to many other races. They come here to see how we managed to change our situation and develop our country.

Mahathir Mohamad, quoted in 'PM: I reverse my stand',
Business Times, 12 May 1997

So what is the new Malay dilemma? Their old dilemma was whether they should distort the picture a little in order to help themselves. The new dilemma is whether they should or should not do away with the crutches that they have got used to, which in fact they have become proud of.

Mahathir Mohamad, Speech at the Harvard Club of
Malaysia Dinner, Kuala Lumpur, 29 July 29 2002

On 22 June 2002, some way into his closing speech to the UMNO General Assembly, an event shown 'live' on television, Mahathir abruptly announced his intention to resign as the party's president and from all his positions in the Barisan Nasional. The delegates attending the Assembly reacted with disbelief. There had neither been any hint of Mahathir's move nor any indication that he had consulted senior members of his party, coalition or government over the matter. There was some commotion as several UMNO leaders, notably Rafidah Aziz and Hishamuddin Hussein, rushed to the podium to interrupt a tearful Mahathir and then to usher him to a private conference with party seniors and elders who reportedly beseeched Mahathir to retract his decision. Whatever details of his retirement and plans for a political succession Mahathir might have meant to offer – for he had been speaking from prepared text – were not revealed. Instead, Abdullah Badawi emerged from the closed meeting to reassure the Assembly that Mahathir had agreed not to depart office. Mahathir did not reappear before the Assembly. He left quietly for a scheduled holiday in Europe. At a press conference held three days later, UMNO Secretary-General Khalil Yaakob officially unveiled a compromise arrangement reached between Mahathir and the party leadership: Mahathir would stay in office until October 2003. After that Abdullah Badawi would succeed him. In a matter of months (albeit no shorter than one and a quarter years), therefore, a 22-year 'Mahathir era' would be drawing to a close.

Or would it? We may leave other finer and mostly melodramatic points of Mahathir's announcement of resignation to a future historian's proper chronicle of the episode. Suffice it here to note, first, it was uncharacteristic of Mahathir to 'set a timetable' for his retirement, let alone accept one imposed by others, which was how many observers perceived the compromise retirement schedule. Mahathir had pointedly refused to set a retirement schedule in the past to avoid his becoming a lame duck premier. Second, the sixteen-month transition from Mahathir to Abdullah Badawi was unusually long in Malaysia's experience of succession at the prime minister's level. The only comparable duration of such leadership change was the interregnum from May 1969 to September 1970 (coincidentally sixteen months, also) when Tunku Abdul Rahman remained as nominal head of government, while effective political and administrative power had been transferred to the Tun Abdul Razak-led National Operations Council in the aftermath of 'May 13'. Third, although Mahathir had been pressured by *Reformasi* and the Malay revolt against UMNO to say that the November 1999 general election would be his last, there were many who doubted that this prime minister, who had outlasted three deputies and stayed in power more than twenty years, would behave otherwise than 'die with his boots on'. Indeed, at the UMNO General Assembly of 2000, Mahathir had indirectly but adamantly rejected suggestions he should resign over UMNO's electoral losses when he said, 'I have not decided when I will retire. Normally, I will keep it a secret since there are calls for me to be the Prime Minister for three, four more terms, that is 25 years....'[1] At the subsequent UMNO General Assembly, Mahathir told a journalist that, 'If you listen to the debate today, there seems to be quite some support for me. Because of that, I have to find the right time to step down.'[2] And, fourth, Mahathir's timing of his announcement was puzzling, considering the circumstances. The state of the economy, though nowhere as robust as in the mid-1990s, had improved since 1997-98, thereby making it easier for Mahathir to relinquish control. But the aftermath of 11 September 2001 was a more difficult matter. The global repercussions of the attack on the World Trade

Center and the Pentagon had helped Mahathir seize the initiative in UMNO's battle against PAS, and, by extension, the rest of the opposition. The post-September 11 international situation, however, had brought uncertainties and complications, the appropriate responses to which seemed to require Mahathir's staying hand.

For these reasons and possibly others as well, Mahathir's unfinished declaration at the 2002 Assembly led to much sceptical speculation in Malaysia that the resignation was Mahathir's latest *sandiwara*!

Limits to Personalized Hegemony

Whatever else one might think of the melodrama of 22 June, UMNO's patent shock at Mahathir's intended departure, the drawn-out transition plan, and the suspicions of another *sandiwara* surely suggested a certain timidity on the part of Mahathir's supporters and opponents alike. One repeatedly heard or read reports that indicated great incredulity or at least urged caution: October 2003 was a long way off and Mahathir had not actually departed. Many were unable to contemplate seriously 'Malaysia without Mahathir', even after 22 June.[3]

This phenomenon should come as no surprise: after 50 years in politics and 21 years in power, Mahathir's ability to survive controversies and crises was legendary. His will to power was intimidating. Hence, it was a rare person – whether within Mahathir's party, outside his circles, or even beyond Malaysia[4] – who had not reconciled himself or herself to Mahathir's indefinite extension of his tenure, except 'if for some reason I should drop dead or become disabled', in Mahathir's own words.[5] While Mahathir was 'still around', it could seem as though the many crises of Mahathirist politics were somehow inconsequential, indeed as if Razaleigh Hamzah's challenge did not take place, UMNO was never split, Anwar Ibrahim was untouched, and *Reformasi* was mere cyber-invention.

Now *this* is hegemony.

Mahathir could personalize hegemony because he was a tireless and thorough ideologue who had no equal among his contemporaries in formulating a 'vision'. Out of an assemblage of arguments, ideas and policies, Mahathir had fashioned a powerful and coherent 'national vision' with two enduring qualities. One: while there were alternative visions of development, say, none had been able to compete with Mahathir's in posing fundamental questions, articulating and moulding a broad range of popular expectations, and finding policy forms to manage those expectations. This was as true of the NEP, the formulation of which borrowed from *The Malay Dilemma*, as it was of Vision 2020 whose proclamation directly expressed the grandest of Mahathirist ambitions. Two: the vision itself was sufficiently protean so that it could adapt to crises and 'respond to challenge', the latter phrase being a favourite cliché in the Mahathirist vocabulary. For example, just when the goals of Vision 2020 appeared to have been popularly received one decade after their enunciation, but might be in need of amendment after the setbacks of 1997-98, Mahathir was already hinting that:

> Our targets have changed and changed radically. The Vision 2020 that we imagined in 1991 is not the same as the Vision 2020 we picture today. Perhaps it will change again in the 20 years before the arrival of 2020. The Malaysian people at all levels must be conscious of this truth in order to handle targets that are constantly changing.[6]

The strength of Mahathirist ideology did not derive from a system of finished ideas, even though Mahathir's writings, speeches and policies covered an extensive range of subjects. In fact, *Paradoxes of Mahathirism* employed the term 'Mahathirism' in order to explore the tension-ridden ideology of a rising multiethnic ruling class that was consolidating itself under Mahathir's leadership and the rubric of Malaysia Inc. What the ideologue and prime minister could forcefully project, however, was a worldview that, fraught as it was with contradictions, captured the core concerns, varying problems and even the potential of Malaysian society over almost 50 years. Mahathir habitually perceived and sought to grapple with the emergent problems of a rapidly changing world through his own, basically unaltered, untinted lenses. He was not being coy when he maintained often enough that while others, including former foes, had modified or abandoned their views to join or support him, he remained 'the same Mahathir'. To others, though, he appeared to change his positions continually to suit the times. To that degree, the Mahathirist vision was compelling because Mahathir's thinking seemed capable of renewing itself. Whenever an important issue emerged, Mahathir would not hesitate to respond by painting a 'big picture'. Often the 'big picture' did not supply settled meanings. Rather, as shown by the examples of the 'futurism' of the Multimedia Super Corridor or the 'new imperialism' of the global money market, Mahathir's 'big picture' conveyed a strong polemical point, a dynamic 'feel', or a refreshing 'take', thus making it plausible for

Mahathir to assert that he was pragmatic, flexible and not worshipful of any sacred cow.

'Mahathirism' has sometimes been used as a loose cipher for Mahathir's supposedly unique ability to diagnose the social problems of the day, to foresee challenges ahead of anyone else and to prescribe solutions in advance of his time. We can glimpse this presumed quality of Mahathir's in the transformation of the status of his first and most important book, *The Malay Dilemma*, from being the outlandish writing of an embittered UMNO outcast to the eminent thought of a victorious prime minister. (No doubt, Mahathir's possession of the administrative power to lift the ban on his book after he became prime minister helped to effect a change in its reception.) Likewise, Mahathir's ability to project this ability can be gauged from the shift in 'international attitudes' towards his capital controls of September 1998 – from a hard rejection to a grudging acceptance. In these and other instances, Mahathir showed that he had the courage of his convictions to treat his varied and staunch opposition with contempt. In 1986, he dared to 'hold the NEP in abeyance' despite its predictably divisive impact on UMNO, while in 1998 he adopted capital controls in defiance of the economic orthodoxy of the international money market. On another occasion, Mahathir was alone among Muslim politicians to object publicly to proposed legislation punishing apostasy in Islam.

Even on the eve of his departure from active politics, Mahathir would not desist from pointing 'the way forward', to use another phrase he liked, and, if needs be, by stirring up fresh debates and provoking greater dissent. Mahathir's move to overhaul current policies on language, education and the NEP's affirmative action, many of these being policies he had helped shape and implement, has already created controversy. Some might consider such a course of policy reversal to be tactless, even ungracious, of an outgoing prime minister who really should not be saddling his successor with additional burdens. But it was comprehensibly Mahathir. Although Mahathir had said he would not accept any role in government once he departed, he would not be a lame duck during his remaining time in office. Abdullah Badawi has promised to be a loyal 'No. 2' until Mahathir left, while other aspirants to UMNO's top posts were in no position to demur. In any case, while Mahathir's opinions and positions were sometimes bitterly contested, he had held so much power for so long that, on the domestic scene at least, his ideas and policies generally prevailed.

However, it was more than a matter of Mahathir's having things 'My Way'. With an unswerving faith in his own judgements, Mahathir believed himself to have been vindicated repeatedly by events and history. While Mahathir occasionally spoke as if he disdained popularity or courted adversity, that rarely rang true for Mahathir knew only too well the worth of popularity in mass politics. 'After our dismal performance in the 1999 general election,' he advised UMNO:

> We cannot alienate ourselves from those whom we think do not support us or disagree with us. We need to know if they support us or not and if they understand their stand. If they do not understand, then it is our responsibility to explain the real situation. Hopefully with the explanation given, they will accept them (*sic*) and will stop opposing us.[7]

Ultimately Mahathir expected to do no less than to demonstrate that he had and could diligently put to work the distinguishing quality, the one true sign, of a leader, that is, 'the ability to provide guidance ... something *superior* to what your people can do by themselves'.[8] It was little wonder then, amidst personal reasons or tactical motivations, and despite the heavy demands of high office, that Mahathir troubled to write and speak so much. He needed to communicate 'initiatives and ideas that are not common'.[9] Once, when Mahathir was asked 'whether true leadership consists of being the embodiment of the hopes, dreams and aspirations of your people', he replied, 'Well, lots of people think they are such an embodiment; I don't really know whether my aspirations are the same.'[10] His and the people's aspirations were not quite the same, judging by Mahathir's innumerable criticisms of Malay and Malaysian traits that he sought to improve by exhortations and injunctions. The candour of his reply suggested not so much an individual boast as an elitist refusal to pander to popular sentiments. Between Mahathir and those he led was a divide that had to be managed by the deeply personalized hegemony of Mahathirism.

However, one would be taking Mahathir's disclaimer too much at face value if one thought that Mahathir did not express popular aspirations in different ways. He did so, but in an unusual manner. Mahathirism was an ideology of many parts: nationalism, capitalism, Islam, populism and authoritarianism. There were contradictions in each and tensions among these parts, as *Paradoxes of Mahathirism* has tried to explain. But over the years, the co-existence of these different ideological components of Mahathirism gained Mahathir a wide, effective and, surprisingly, balanced appeal among the populace (and even foreign audiences). There were Mahathir devotees, of course, for whom Mahathir could do no wrong. But it was not necessary to like everything about Mahathir to back him. If some disapproved of

Mahathir's nationalism, they could find solace in his commitment to capitalism. If some considered his shrill nationalist refrains to be 'out of sync' with globalization, they might admire instead his futurist dedication to technology. Some frowned on his nurture of capitalist developmentalism and yet they could not deny the nationalist impulses behind it. There were those who hated his politics – meaning the Anwar affair, for example – but took Mahathir's imposition of capital controls to be a brave refusal to surrender to the bullying of the Washington consensus. Others opposed his authoritarian ways but rallied around him as a liberal and moderate counterpoint to obscurantist or less tolerant interpretations of Islam. Mahathir's political instincts were anti-democratic and his methods were authoritarian in moments of stress; still, no other Malaysian leader had taken so much trouble and pride in trying to engage, influence and change a people by exhortation, motivation and example. One can continue with observing people half-disliking Mahathir but finding enough in him to support. Still, Mahathir did not set out to compartmentalize himself in these ways. But the many parts to Mahathir's ideology, together with the different political personae he assumed, constituted a medium that, in a process which may be likened to the reverse of refraction, recombined society's diverse expectations and tensions into a powerful 'vision'. If this is not an inappropriate representation, then Mahathir's personalized hegemony might have lain in his ability to appear wondrously whole, while others fragmented him according to their partialities, dreams and fears, and thereby accepted him.

To be sure, this peculiar dynamic of ideological appeal was not derived from Mahathir's person or his personal ability alone. The dynamic was mediated by a monopoly on the resources and regulation of mass communication that promoted only 'positive' images of Mahathir. Simultaneously, his barely contested exercise of state power conferred a larger-than-life stature upon him. Enjoying these kinds of advantages, and buoyed by the conjunction of regional triumphalism and domestic progress, Mahathir's personalized hegemony seemed permanent. The sporadic and scattered criticisms of Mahathir that were made by opposition or dissident quarters scarcely dented his appeal. But when East Asia 'melted', Anwar 'fell', and the Malays 'disunited', masses of people rejected Mahathir 'whole'. They would not see him as an embodiment of distinct pluses and minuses that one could judiciously assess and separately select. In Mahathir they saw the personification of all that was wrong about a Mahathir-led UMNO and a BN-dominated political system. Personalized hegemony had reached its limit. *Undur Mahathir!* Although it seemed improbable then, *Reformasi* hastened Mahathir's 'voluntary' departure.

Of UMNO's present cohort of aspirants to the premiership, none possesses the hegemonic quality that once marked Mahathir's leadership. Without this quality, the likes of Abdullah Ahmad Badawi, Najib Tun Razak, Muhammad Muhammad Taib, Muhyiddin Yassin, Rafidah Aziz, and Hishamuddin Hussein may institute makeshift alterations to existing policies that bear the imprint of Vision 2020. However, they would not be able to offer a grand vision, that is, a vision that dominates by comprehensively addressing the major expectations and issues of the time. Ironically, the one person who could have asserted a reasonable claim along that line is Anwar Ibrahim. Had Anwar succeeded Mahathir after the July 1997 crisis unfolded, he might have blended ideas about an 'Asian Renaissance', ABIM-type Islam, caring civil society and a reformed political economy into a coherent vision that was identifiably his. No one knows now if such an attempt could have succeeded. All one recalls is, Anwar's political trajectory wove together more diverse strands of ideology, commitment, and appeal than was ever shown by the senior UMNO leaders who abetted his removal and acquiesced in his continued incarceration. With Mahathir's departure ends a 50-year trend whereby Malaysian society laboured under overarching visions – Merdeka with its promise of nation building, the NEP with its goal of social restructuring, and Vision 2020 with its ambition of 'First World' prosperity. In the absence of a comforting vision and not the disruption of specific policies benefiting particular interests, lie the uncertainties of a transition from Mahathirism.

Ambitions, Ideals and Discord

Naturally Mahathir's initiatives and ideas bore the marks and touches of his individual thought, idiosyncratic formulation, as well as contingent responses to political and other crises. However, no matter how 'superior' or 'not common' they might have been, Mahathir's ideas could scarcely have acquired and retained hegemonic force were they *his* alone. Marx has famously said, and no one has put it more concisely, that the ruling ideas of any epoch were the ideas of the ruling class. In a more limited way, so it was with 'Mahathir's ideas': they dominated a period over which Mahathir first exercised some influence as an ideologue and then superintended as prime minister. Through much of the 'Mahathir era', not least when Mahathir seemed vigorously to address the hopes and dreams of *bangsa, agama, negara* (race, religion, country), Mahathirism represented the general and most advanced expression of the collectivity of ruling class interests and aspirations.

No Malaysian leader has tendered more 'vision' than Mahathir. None has enjoyed greater support or invited fiercer derision – whether within society or his party, or even among foreigners. Of course, there was a simple reason for this. Having stayed much longer in office than his predecessors, Mahathir has had ample time and opportunity to record both success and failure and to win over or alienate more people. Many observers have indirectly explained the unevenness of public stances towards Mahathir in terms of his assertive, not to say confrontational, temperament. While Mahathir has dismissed the idea that he was confrontational, it has some truth, considering his unyielding positions and combative stances on most issues. Beyond these obvious explanations, however, lay something deeper. The shifts and swings in political and popular attitudes towards Mahathir reflected (though never perfectly) the fluctuating fortunes and the restive tensions of the nationalist-capitalist project that Mahathir had advocated and pursued with matchless determination.

For over 30 years, after the NEP began, officialese, Barisan Nasional propaganda and popular understanding presented the substance of this project as 'development'. Yet this project could alternately be regarded as a nationalist project driven by capitalist impulses or a capitalist project imbued with nationalist imperatives. In either case, successive regimes undertook or extended the project to contain the class and ethnic contradictions of Malaysian society and also to respond to the pressures of an accelerating globalization. The project has worn different names and labels reflecting its diverse successes and stresses since commencing officially as the NEP's restructuring to social-engineer the creation of a Bumiputera Commercial and Industrial Community (BCIC). After 1981, the project was deepened by a programme of modernization, privatization and late industrialization that was implemented within the framework of Malaysia Inc. Its pace was retarded by economic recession which compelled the Mahathir regime to 'hold the NEP in abeyance', and by UMNO's internal crises of the late 1980s. Subsequent economic recovery and high growth took the project to its apogee in the mid-1990s when it was captained by the *Melayu Baru*'s corps of entrepreneurs. It was clad with Vision 2020's progression towards 'developed country status', linked by 'Asian values' to the 'East Asian miracle', and symbolically globalized via the Multimedia Super Corridor. But July 1997 dangerously undermined the project's continued viability. The ailing project was then rescued and revived by the capital controls of September 1998, only to be immediately convulsed by Anwar's persecution and *Reformasi*'s revolt. After November 1999, Mahathir, his regime and UMNO have tried to tame the revolt and restore the primacy of their project.

Seen from the perspective of these 'ups and downs', the desperate post-1997 politics emanated from the desperate condition of the project when its 1990s' triumphalism yielded to much foreboding. It is unnecessary to revisit the international money market's role in causing that state of affairs. Still, if the past successes of the nationalist-capitalist project offered scant assurances about its future, it was because its state-sponsored creation of a Malay capitalist class was wracked by contradictions that neither Mahathir nor Mahathirism had satisfactorily resolved. For quite some time, the NEP-induced social conflicts had followed foreseeable patterns of interethnic competition. But as Halim Salleh astutely noted, a major contribution to 'social acquiescence' came from the NEP's efficacy as a 'tool to domesticate and Malaysianize the non-Malays' in exchange for an expansion of the Chinese share of the economy.[11] There were opportunities as well for different segments of domestic Chinese capital to adapt to restructuring, form joint ventures with influential Malays, and thereby profit from the high rates of state-led growth. Ironically, for those who only saw the NEP as an interethnic zero-sum game over targets and quotas, the protagonists in the dramatic rise of the BCIC proved to be less easily 'domesticated'.

By 1981, when Mahathir became prime minister, the dynamics of Malay politics, the achievement of the NEP's targets, and the overall efficacy of the state's economic policies were dependent on the functional integrity of a Malay 'party-bureaucracy-class' axis. UMNO, as the dominant party in government, had to supply the political power to impose the NEP's agenda. The increasingly Malay-dominated bureaucracy had to provide the administrative and technocratic capacity for implementing the NEP programmes. An incipient class of Malay capitalists had to show good performances and results to vindicate their receipt of state assistance and nurture. However, the NEP's plentiful opportunities for rent-seeking practices and 'instant wealth' spawned influential coalitions and alignments of rival centres of power among the ranks of party, bureaucracy and class. Then the intra-Malay tensions, initially camouflaged by interethnic disagreements, surfaced with a vengeance. The 'party of the Malays' supplied the political power vis-à-vis all other parties in and out of government, but UMNO built itself an enormous business empire into the bargain.

The 'Malay bureaucracy' rapidly expanded to implement and manage the NEP but its technocrats and administrators came to control and manage vast economic resources and public enterprises in the name of 'Malay trusteeship'. On the other hand, individual capitalists soon emerged or consolidated within the BCIC who became impatient with the constraints of 'Malay trusteeship'. Over time, as the coalitions formed of party figures, senior bureaucrats and influential capitalists contended for power, access to resources, and opportunities for private accumulation of wealth, their agendas could less and less be amicably subsumed under the NEP. All based their claims on restructuring. Each pursued its disparate interests. Flashpoints of competition and conflict were created which turned the party-bureaucracy class nexus into an axis of discord.[12] Arguably the earliest conflict between party and bureaucracy took place when the NEP's repudiation of *laissez faire* capitalism shifted power to Tun Razak's coterie of 'young Turks' from UMNO's 'old guard' who were not thought to possess 'the 'vision and technocratic skills to carry through the restructuring of society'.[13] After Razak died in January 1976, the UMNO 'old guard' struck back at Razak's protégés by instigating a witch-hunt for 'communists' within UMNO. By the time of Anwar's fall, the clearest political manifestation of this trend of intra-Malay conflict was the factionalism that haunted UMNO.

When the first decade of the NEP bounty reached a limit in the slow growth of 1982-84 and the recession of 1985-86, and, later, when the high growth of the 1990s ended in July 1997, the Malay party, bureaucracy and class suffered declining fortunes in turn. The first to lose ground were the bureaucrats who controlled the proliferating public enterprises and 'off budget agencies' of the 1970s and early 1980s. In the name of civil service reforms, privatization, and structural adjustment, Mahathir, with Musa Hitam initially, and then with Daim Zainuddin, disciplined the bureaucracy and its unprofitable public enterprises. To this day, the bureaucracy has not recovered its early NEP pre-eminence. It is a junior partner of Malaysia Inc. who remains burdened with criticisms of inefficiency. The big Malay businesses, and especially the UMNO-connected conglomerates, prospered under Malaysia Inc. but their captains and helmsmen were the next to suffer. July 1997 sent most of them into insolvency while their rescue by the measures of September 1998 and after have stigmatized them as cronies or worse. Finally, came UMNO's turn. The party dominated the government, monopolized policy-making and created a sprawling business empire. Consequently, whenever an economic recession threatened all rival BCIC coalitions, UMNO could not escape being the principal arena of intra-Malay conflict. The 1985-86 recession preceded UMNO's split. The 1997-98 crisis precipitated Anwar's expulsion. In short, the deepest and most unstable faultline of Mahathirist politics was an intra-Malay divide that was not directly related to UMNO's programmatic or doctrinal differences with PAS. Post-1997 politics was just the harshest confirmation that this divide among the Malay elites, rooted in the NEP and Mahathirist political economy, would persist as long as the party-bureaucracy-class axis served as the virtual clearinghouse for state contracts and projects, and as a rapid transit to fabulous wealth for those who rode it successfully.

Mahathir, with his intimate ties to all three 'partners' in the axis, could not have remained aloof from this axis of discord even if he had wanted to. At his clearest and most powerful, Mahathir could not secure the integrity of this Malay party-bureaucracy-class axis for other reasons of political economy. After July 1997, the voices of the international money market and the Washington consensus prescribed radical pro-market reforms as the antidote to crony capitalism, patronage, rent-seeking, the lack of transparency and the absence of 'good governance' in East Asia. There is no need to overlook criticisms of East Asian regimes that harmed popular welfare and not just foreign investors' profit-maximising expectations. The real issue, however, was not whether 'East Asia Inc.', as it were, had gathered together capitalism's bastards who could only be legitimized by neo-liberal free-market adoption. In Malaysia, the post-colonial record of socio-economic achievement could not be credited to any 'free market'. If there had been a colonial 'free market', it did not prevent the state then from conducting its plunder, producing its own cronies, and remaining far less responsive to social restructuring either of an ethnic or class nature. The true *riddle* of the NEP and Mahathirist political economy, to use Peter Searle's formulation, was whether the state's 'incubation' of 'indigenous entrepreneurs' could produce 'real capitalists' who would foreswear their 'unorthodox origins'.[14]

Searle offered a typology (resembling a 'stages of development of capitalists' model) that depicted Malay capitalism as 'a complex amalgam of state, party and private capital' having a variety of human forms: figurehead capitalists, executive-professional directors, executive-trustee directors, functional capitalists, bureaucrats-turned-businessmen, state managers-turned-owners, politicians-turned-businessmen, UMNO's proxy capitalists-turned businessmen, UMNO's proxy capitalists-turned-corporate captains, rentiers, transitional entrepreneurs and private capitalists. Was it plausible that some of them would emerge from 'the cocoon of state/UMNO-supported patronage networks and rent-seeking activity' as 'real capitalists' bearing the credentials of independence, dynamism and resilience alien to habitual rent-seekers? With pre-July 1997 optimism, Searle imagined so. With so much at stake, Mahathir had to believe so. Even then, Mahathir, surely, would have known that in social engineering, incubation was no guarantee of birth, let alone many, many births without defects. With his realism, Mahathir did not expect most, let alone all, of the entries in Searle's typology to bear the standard of his own *Melayu Baru* aspirations. One could see that from Mahathir's constant criticisms of unproductive Malay rent-seeking practices – 'Ali Baba' arrangements, unwillingness to learn or manage business in determined ways, frequent sale of projects followed by demands for more contracts, *ad nauseam*. However, that was not enough to disown the East Asian developmental state's formula of having 'strong coordination between government and business', as Mahathir in fact lectured the Japanese on how 'going western' would not solve the problems of a recessionary Japanese economy.[15] As long as corruption in the system did not lead to sheer predation, as it did in other countries, Mahathir could maintain that 'development is our monument'.

Meanwhile, Mahathir's deepest hopes lay in picking global winners, of South Korean or Japanese stature, for international competition. There the problems were more daunting. After 22 years of Mahathirist policies, the economy may roughly be divided into three sections. One privileged section is made up of manufacturing multinational corporations (MNCs) that dominate the export-oriented industrial sector. They have been offered or demanded and received all kinds of incentives that are never stigmatized as market-distorting 'subsidies' by economic experts or the media. For the MNCs, global competitiveness is decisive. Another large section comprises small and medium-scale enterprises (SMEs). Most of the SMEs are oriented towards the domestic market although some have become successful subcontractors to the foreign MNCs. Malay-owned SMEs, still dependent on state patronage and protection, make up a politically significant component of this section. A larger component is more resilient and not reliant on the state, but, being largely Chinese-owned, it is politically much less influential. The third section comprises Malay, non-Malay, and 'interethnic' conglomerates. These are corporate entities congregating in banking, resource exploitation, plantations, construction, real estate, gaming, tourism, transport, utilities and services, and selected import-substituting industries. They dominate these domestic sectors where state patronage, protection and regulation make the difference between success and failure. Mahathir had radically departed from early NEP policies by spurning the bureaucracy in favour of creating such conglomerates after the South Korean experience of 'picking winners' to spearhead a global drive. Mahathir had hoped that these conglomerates would mature into world-class corporations. For a brief period, during the heyday of the 'East Asian miracle', the conglomerates looked as if they would mature as some of them ventured to be the foreign investors for economies less developed than Malaysia's. Since then, Malaysia Inc.'s corporate imitations of the Japanese *zaibatsu* and the South Korean *chaebol* have not proven their ability or willingness to free themselves from a chronic dependence on state assistance. Thus, the conglomerate sector, once the site of intense contention under the NEP, remains insecure. This may be variously deduced from the state's selective renationalization of the Malaysian Airlines System, Indah Water Konsortium, PUTRA and STAR (when these large privatized projects failed); the decline in the stature if not fortunes of such figures as Tajudin Ramli and Halim Saad, and the puzzling resignation of Daim Zainuddin as Finance Minister in 2001; and Mahathir's brief attack on the 'rich' in UMNO in 2001 which did not herald a sweeping separation of business and politics within the ruling party but pointed to the persistence of 'money politics'. One might now predict that the 1997-98 Mahathir-Anwar skirmishes over the most effective solutions to the threatened collapse of prominent Malay corporations will reverberate in the future and haunt the conglomerates whose vulnerability to the 'challenges of globalization' is palpable.

But if Mahathir had not picked the right winners, he still had to secure a 'rightful place' for the conglomerates in the division of power between the state, foreign capital and domestic capital. Such a tripartite balance of power had underpinned political economy since independence. It was Mahathir's intuitive and obdurate defence of a hard won foothold for Malay capital, and, arguably, more than that for the new Malaysian capital, that led him to erect the 'economic shield' of capital controls and reflation. Behind that shield, Danaharta, Danamodal and the Corporate Debt Restructuring Committee tended to the specific problems of ailing companies and the banking system. Following the disaster in Indonesia which discredited IMF intervention, after the international mainstream media's indiscreet 'pro-reform' push was implicated in Anwar's fall, and faced with fears of PAS's rise to power, the money market finally appreciated Mahathir's effort to maintain the basis of stability in Malaysian political economy. Hence the market's rapprochement with Mahathir's post-September 1998 capital controls and reflationary measures in time for the November 1999 election.

In that sense, late Mahathirism triumphed to the extent that it was able to keep that tripartite balance of power intact after the post-1997-98 economic and political turmoil. But just as Malaysia Inc. no longer contained an impetus towards capitalist rationalization and reform, so late Mahathirism had no further vision to offer beyond that.

Rumours of an Islamic State

There were other dissenting visions, not restricted to political economy, that had dramatically come to light in *Reformasi*, the Malay voting patterns of 1999 and PAS's electoral gains. In manifold, creative and spontaneous forms, various populist and democratic notions of government, which were opposed to elitist and statist discourses, had emerged in *Reformasi*. Despite the BA's electoral limitations, these visions continued to have a life of their own in civil society, most of all via alternative media and internet publications, of which the most enduring and successful were PAS's *harakahdaily* and the independent online newspaper, *malaysiakini*. Depending on one's view of what *Reformasi* represented, one may or may not now pronounce *Reformasi* 'lost' or 'dead'.[16] But there was no denying that *Reformasi*'s powerful burst of popular consciousness and the demands it made for moral and cultural dimensions to governance had rudely overturned elitist expectations of the obedience of civil society and the regime's assumption of Malay fealty. Or, as Mahathir had to admit to UMNO, 'people whom we used to direct and [who would] follow the directive are now not adhering to our directive'.[17] That obedience to the regime had to be administratively restored by an order to all civil servants and university students to sign the *Akujanji* – a 'promise of loyalty' to the 'government of the day' – was a sure sign of 'a new politics for UMNO where we can no longer ask people and hope they will carry out the task for us'.[18]

Thus, there was another intra-Malay divide apart from the axis of discord. In this divide, along with *Reformasi*'s ideal of a 'vibrant and pluralistic democratic culture', there was 'PAS-Islam' which contested not just Mahathir's 'Vision-Islam' but UMNO's continued rule. It was to the problems of this intra-Malay divide, as captured by UMNO-PAS rivalry, that Mahathir referred when he spoke at the Harvard Club of Malaysia Dinner in Kuala Lumpur on 29 July 2002. Invited to speak on the 'Malay dilemma', he took the opportunity to remind his audience not to overlook another kind of dilemma:

> The dilemma that the Malays and the people of Malaysia face is whether we should, in the name of democracy, allow the country to be destroyed or we ensure that people are not subjected to manipulations to the point where they will use democracy to destroy democracy.[19]

Many times before, Mahathir had issued such general warning against the 'excesses' of democracy. This time his point was unmistakably directed at PAS and at the prospect of PAS's coming to power. The prospect is typically raised as a future scenario of a political system based on an 'Islamic state' that is politically governed by PAS, shaped by a leadership of the *ulama*, and administered under 'divine law'. And this scenario, prompted by the scare of UMNO's decline in November 1999, has been accentuated by the shock of 11 September 2001.

On the face of things, the prospects for such a scenario are simply dim. An 'Islamic state' hoisted by a democratically elected PAS-dominated federal government will not come to pass in the foreseeable future. Considered in any evaluation of politics as politics, and not as a reflexive reaction to premature prophecies of religious extremism, PAS's rise in 1999 has already indicated the limits of its advance. Moreover, PAS does not possess the resources to overcome an extensive range of problems and obstacles. Its effective electoral base is narrow and confined. Its best electoral performance still left it far behind UMNO, despite the latter's wounded state. PAS's electoral gains, after an almost unrelieved history of setbacks between 1959 and 1990, were made possible by the unique window of political opportunity in 1998-99 that has since been drawing to a close with the regime's repression and the BA's demise. PAS's claim to command a majority of Malay-Muslim voters – a claim based on a split *ummah* – can be politically convincing to a multireligious electorate in one of two ways. One way is for PAS to win a decisive majority of Malay-Muslim supporters in subsequent elections such that UMNO's claim to being the 'party of the Malays' is completely discredited. But PAS itself faces staunch opposition from the segments of the Malay-Muslim population that PAS and its religious allies sometimes denounce as 'secularists'. The other way is for PAS to secure a meaningful non-Malay or non-Muslim alliance through a viable 'second coalition'. Here

PAS's hopes of doing so were seriously dashed by DAP's abandonment of the BA. That alone confirmed, after 'September 11' if not before, that PAS would confront a solid non-Muslim rejection in a polity where 'minority politics' is not at all marginal to the outcome of UMNO-PAS electoral competition. In power terms, UMNO remains dominant and is only too willing to exercise its immense control of the state to forestall any extension of PAS's influence. Despite UMNO's inability to force a quick return of alienated Malay-Muslim voters to UMNO (up to 2001), PAS has been forced on to defensive terrain, as was indicated by the loss of the parliamentary seat of Pendang – and the very narrow retention of the state assembly seat of Anak Bukit – in the by-elections held after the death of former PAS president, Fadzil Noor. The regime has revealed its determination to undermine PAS's position by a variety of measures, including the denial of resources, mobilization of wider ideological opposition to the *ulama*, and repression against PAS leaders and allies. In the Election Commission's latest exercise of creating new or re-delineating existing electoral constituencies, Kelantan and Trengganu are the only states left without any additional parliamentary seat. Before the next general election, PAS's strategic priority has become the maintenance of its present position rather than advance.

And yet, there are ways by which, *not* PAS, but UMNO-BN could undermine constitutional government to the point that popular support abandons the shell of a secular system for the promise of an 'Islamic state'. Hadi Awang, the man widely regarded as PAS's most radical leader, stated before the 1999 election that PAS had peacefully accepted defeat in nine general elections. Hadi Awang then asked whether UMNO would know how to accept a single defeat! The question was not rhetorical. In the full range of its electoral experience since 1959, PAS had controlled Kelantan and Trengganu, reached accommodations with UMNO after 1969, made errors during its BN days, forced to retreat in its 1980s' radical phase, recovered in the 1990s, and only retrieved its past fortune in 1999. In his balanced review of the potential and real convergences between Islam and democracy, Syed Ahmad Hussein considered PAS's electoral commitment and advocacy of its Islamic programme within the ambit of democratic practices to be unmatched by 'Islamic parties' elsewhere in the world.[20] A non-partisan analyst would say that PAS's record of lawful participation in democratic politics was all the more remarkable for PAS's having had to suffer the disadvantages and harassments to which all Malaysian opposition parties are subjected.

Yet the same analyst would note that the suspicion dies hard that PAS in power would seize the first opportunity to use 'democracy to destroy democracy'. Such is the extent of the fear of an 'Islamic state' among non-Muslims and 'non-PAS Muslims' that, conversely, it is readily assumed – or else merely accepted – that UMNO 'plays by the rules'. At least half the Malay-Muslim electorate, though, regarded the events of 1998-2000 as evidence that the regime has scant respect for the principles and practice of constitutional government. Two cases illustrate the point more forcefully than any theological or jurisprudential disquisition. One: it was axiomatic among many Muslims that Anwar Ibrahim would never have been convicted in a *syariah* court. Anwar's two convictions and total prison sentence of fifteen years have not persuaded many that he was the perpetrator of an obstruction of justice, and acts of sodomy. On the contrary, Anwar's legal defeats, including the dismissal of every one of his appeals to date, leave him regarded as the victim of the worst miscarriage of justice committed under the regime's rule *by* law, by *secular* law. Two: the federal government and Petronas abjured the laws of contract by denying the Hadi Awang government the oil revenues that were paid to BN-led Terenggau governments for 25 years. In a single instance, UMNO gave the lie to any claim the regime and its supporters might make of the superiority of constitutional government embedded in the rule of law, of *man-made* law, as PAS would retort.

There was a time, during the early Mahathir regime, when Mahathir responded to the 'call of Islam' with the confidence that marked his reformist drive. He boldly fashioned 'Vision Islam' as a relatively coherent 'moderate', 'modernist' and 'secular' ideological and practical alternative to 'PAS Islam', or the appeal of certain 'deviationist' groups such as Al Arqam. Then Mahathir attempted to integrate Islamic values with Malay nationalist impulses and an East Asian work ethic, to advance and yet control the trend of greater religiosity in public life. While PAS and other Islamic groups expressed their scepticism towards the validity of Vision Islam, Mahathir's cooptation of Anwar Ibrahim (and his ABIM allies who entered UMNO, too) resulted in substantial support for the regime's policies and institutions of Islamization. With Anwar's fall and PAS's support of Anwar's cause, all that is left of Mahathir's Islam, for dissident Islamic opinion, is an instrumentalist, not to say, 'secularist' deployment of selective 'Islamic values'. On 29 September 2001, Mahathir claimed that Malaysia was an Islamic state. Mahathir's claim had no persuasive resonance; it merely evoked an equivocal support from the BN's non-Malay parties, a strong opposition from the DAP, and a scornful dismissal by PAS. Nine months later, at the 2002 UMNO General Assembly, Mahathir explained that

> When we stated that Malaysia is a Muslim nation, the reason was because we want the matter not to be made a political issue, which can split the Muslims in Malaysia. We stated this because all the conditions for a Muslim state according to the teachings of Islam are found in Malaysia.[21]

Mahathir's usage of 'Muslim nation', 'Muslim state' and 'Islamic state', as if these are interchangeable terms within 'the debate on the Islamic nation',[22] merely confirmed that in crisis, 'Vision Islam', like other elements of late Mahathirism, had lost its discursive clarity, to say nothing of shedding its ideological power.

In what other ways might 'political' Islam be persuasive, by default as it were? Although it is hazardous to predict, three factors, themselves contingent on certain developments, are worthy of consideration. First, there is the vulnerability of the *Melayu Baru* who have for more than a decade been proclaimed to be the NEP's success story and hence paraded as Mahathirist role models. Well might Mahathir now denounce 'the creation of the devil' that portrays 'the new Malays as drunkards, womanizers and gamblers', whereas, for him, 'the new Malays are those who hold strongly to Islam and practise noble values such as discipline'.[23] There remains an unbridgeable gulf between the extravagance of the *Melayu Baru* elite – which was flaunted before the July 1997 crisis, and flayed during *Reformasi* – and PAS's mode of simple living. The regime forced economic and financial austerity upon Kelantan and Trengganu, but for over a decade PAS supporters in Kelantan have worn austerity as a symbol of resistance. For much longer than a decade, PAS supporters have complained of systematic discrimination in the allocation of economic and social benefits by the regime, the state bureaucracy, and UMNO. And unrealistic though it may be as an answer to the problems of contemporary political economy, the simple living that approximates 'Islam as a way of life' may be attractive, in times of economic hardship, as a morally preferable, religiously ennobled, and politically equitable way of dealing with privations. Second, if or when the Malay party-bureaucracy-class axis experiences further fractures, the splits will channel dissent along the line of the most well organized opposition – PAS and no one else at present. In 1998-99, the disaffected UMNO supporters who joined PAS out of hardnosed political calculations were correct: not Keadilan or PRM but PAS would inflict the greatest damage on UMNO. No doubt such developments can be temporarily checked by draconian measures but habitual and intensified repression would take politics into a much more dangerous spiral.

There is, finally, an almost imponderable factor. One might think of it as the internationalization of PAS's predicament. It is related to the condition of the global *ummah* under the USA's war of terror against radical Muslims, against recalcitrant Muslim states, and *against Islam* to all intents and purposes. In spite of its internal divisiveness and internecine wars, the 'world of Islam' is unlike any other relatively distinctive international community found in recent times. The global *ummah* inhabits a horrifying topography of suffering, ravage and angst. Every conceivable form of political upheaval has been found: the Palestinian *intifada*s, the siege of Sarajevo, the secessionist campaigns in Jammu and Kashmir, and Chechnya, the state terror in Algeria, the invasions of Afghanistan, sectarian violence in Maluku, pogroms in India, and, most recently, the war on Iraq. Overall, unending cycles of war, massacres and martyrdom have engulfed Muslims supporting or opposing organizations such as Hamas, Hezbollah, Islamic Jihad, Taliban, Groupe Islamique Armée, and Al Qaedah. Karen Armstrong convincingly suggests that the Muslim *ummah* characteristically responded to crises and threats not by advancing theological innovations but by searching for political solutions that would build a just 'Islamic state'.[24] Should the socio-political conditions of the global *ummah* deteriorate – almost a foregone conclusion for the critical centres of Palestine, Chechnya, Kashmir, Iraq, and in much of the rest of the Middle East – is there reason to believe that their repercussions will not encourage more people within the Malaysian segment of the *ummah* to interpret the world in stark Islamic terms that precludes a compromise with 'secularism'? In the 1970s, political developments outside Malaysia but in the world of Islam, including the revolution in Iran, had partly inspired the present PAS leaders to redirect the party's programme from its earlier Malay nationalist stance to a stricter Islamic orientation. Among those PAS leaders were Hadi Awang and Nik Aziz who studied in Saudi Arabia and India respectively. So it happened, too, with an NEP generation of foreign-educated, western-trained and technology-empowered Malay-Muslim professionals and technocrats, not to say other students studying or sojourning in non-western or Muslim countries. So it will happen again with many who belong to the younger generation, and whose formative political experiences are Anwar's fall and *Reformasi* within the country, and, outside Malaysia, September 11 and the wars against Afghanistan and Iraq. The less political of them help to form the membership and provide the leadership of a range of Islamic non-governmental organizations. The more political among them have been drawn to PAS's politico-juridical programme, organization and quest for electoral influence if not success. As to the most extreme of them, little is known, properly speaking, since the arrests of purported Islamic militants under the Internal Security Act are, by their nature, secretive, alarmist and frequently self-serving. Some ISA detainees were alleged to have had links to Afghanistan-based 'extremists' but in the 1980s, the Malaysian government gave aid to the same 'freedom fighters' resisting the Soviet occupation of Afghanistan.

One year before 'September 11', given its residual unease with Mahathir, UMNO's loss of legitimacy among Malay voters, and Anwar's imprisonment, *The Asian Wall Street Journal* could suggest that

> PAS will need to develop a more inclusive ideology and approach if it is to provide leadership for the combined opposition and broaden its base. While PAS cannot be expected to jeopardise its fidelity to Islam, it must move away from the goal of an Islamic state, which disturbs many Malays as well as others.[25]

After 'September 11', not the least of PAS's worries must be the 'new imperialist' hostility of foreign powers towards 'political', 'radical' or 'fundamentalist' Islam. Inasmuch as any of these labels of 'terror' fits – or can be used to fit – PAS's Islam in contradistinction to UMNO's 'moderation', it is improbable that the USA, primarily, would idly watch a PAS accession to power via constitutional means. It would be a myopic PAS leadership that has not noticed how quickly post-'September 11' USA lost its diplomatic interest in Anwar's fate as the Mahathir regime, to use the international media's disingenuous phrase, 'won praise from President Bush' for the regime's 'cooperation' in the 'global war on terror' to the extent of agreeing to establish a regional anti-terrorist centre in Malaysia.

It is one thing for Mahathir, with a measure of political realism and informed diplomacy, to oppose the USA-led wars against Afghanistan and Iraq, and to call for the substantial redress of the 'root causes' of political extremism among the global *ummah*: 'The only thing that will stop their terrorism is the removal of the cause or causes of their struggle.'[26] It is something else to expect Mahathir to address the 'root causes' of homegrown Islamic dissent: 'The enmity towards UMNO by some Malays is due to the influence of PAS causing extreme hatred, hatred which was sown from childhood, until it becomes part of the culture of these people.'[27] Neither Mahathir nor UMNO has come close to answering, with rationality and self-criticism, the central question, 'Why do they hate us?', any more than the USA's rulers could in the wake of 'September 11'. Listening only to Mahathir's side of the argument in his Harvard Club speech, one may forget that across the world the standard way of 'using democracy to destroy democracy' is for an elected government to turn authoritarian and crush lawful dissent ruthlessly. The recognition and the defiance of the tendency towards authoritarianism supplied the hidden text of *Reformasi*'s cyber-references to *Mahazalim*, and of the BA's significance generally. Focusing on PAS's ascent, one may be tempted to share a view of Mahathir as a strong leader whose stern hand was necessary to maintain the stability of the political system. Certainly someone will note that Mahathir has not been a brutal ruler by 'Third World standards', or, to avoid double standards, when judged against the conduct of the *Mahafirauns* of the 'First World' who impose imperial rule with unspeakable violence.

Mahathir has been a conservative law-and-order politician who so treasured stability, while pursuing his historic mission, that he was wont to consider any challenge to his leadership or regime as foreshadowing anarchy. The irony was, Mahathir caused, catalyzed or was party to the principal episodes of instability that had developed in UMNO, the Malay community and Malaysian society since he came to power.

Mahathir's Final Dilemma

The reasons for that were complex, but two points suggest themselves. First, the past 22 years were not a period of Mahathir-guaranteed calm. They were a time of far-reaching socio-economic transformation punctuated by political instability. To appreciate the point, one has just to recall that under Mahathir's premiership there were UMNO's eruptions; the constitutional crises pitting the executive and legislature against the royalty; the executive's assault on the judiciary; the major incidences of detentions under the Internal Security Act; and *Reformasi*. Second, one might look back upon these cases of 'instability' – mild by the scale of violent upheaval elsewhere – as crises of Mahathirist politics. The politics was grounded in the NEP's profound restructuring of Malay society that accelerated during the Mahathir era. In that light, and except for the interethnic tensions preceding the mass arrests of 27 October 1987, the definitive crises involved 'Malay politics'.

For that reason, Mahathir has been unsurprisingly engrossed with the problems of the Malay community, arguably far more than he had been during the halcyon days before July 1997. But, here, nothing is more surprising than that Mahathir's re-examination of post-1997 political economy, and of the Malay revolt of the past few years, has led him to end his career practically where he had begun: by resurrecting the 'Malay dilemma' – only this time, he speaks and warns of a 'second Malay dilemma'.[28]

What could Mahathir have meant? To begin with, he evidently thought that the Malays were already regressing, and as usual, he thought it his duty to reprimand them because too many among them seemed ignorant of the fact:

> Maybe we think that Malaysia will definitely be forever independent and the Malays will definitely be in power and the country will be wealthy. Maybe we believe that we can enter the new century and millennium with our country's condition unchanged, with us being independent and sovereign.
>
> But the former colonizers have already planned to re-colonize us. This time a different method will be used to occupy our country. This method is known as globalization and a borderless world.[29]

Mahathir had not lately joined the popular worldwide anti-globalization movement. Rather his attitude to the 'borderless world' had lost its pre-1997 sense of a balance between global opportunity and threat that was implicit in the conceptualization of the Multimedia Super Corridor. But, as usual, when Mahathir wanted to fend off an external menace he would target the internal weaknesses that one had still to overcome. In one of his favourite 'big pictures', Mahathir remarked that:

> The Malays have only emerged over [44] years as a race with a modern civilization. In that time, a dignified and respected race has been forged and raised. But it hasn't matured yet, hasn't reached its possible peak. Unfortunately there are already signs that this young and fragile civilization will decline rapidly.[30]

It was a peculiar error to conflate political independence and 'modern civilization', but Mahathir intended to jolt any Malay who might have complacently overlooked that 44 years of independence were a mere blip 'compared with the period of 450 years when this country was colonized by several foreign powers'.[31] Fundamentally what irritated Mahathir was a seeming Malay penchant for illusions about the lasting security of their political power: 'If we talk about Malay supremacy, and we love to talk about it, have we become "masters" merely because we are no longer colonized? Even if we are called "master", a master who lives like a beggar is no master.'[32] Or, in one of those self-flagellating questions that irked a lot of Malays, Mahathir asked, 'If we talk on (sic) Malay supremacy but polish other people's shoes, what is the point?'[33] His point was:

> We cannot truly become masters just because we want to be masters. If we wish to be masters, we must possess definite abilities. We must be knowledgeable, competent, successful in life's competition, and own appropriate assets of wealth. For this an effort must be made.[34]

But after 30 years of the NEP, NDP and Vision 2020, what effort was required and of whom was it required? For Mahathir, the ultimate effort was to *learn* – (useful) knowledge, the ways of business, lessons of history, importance of discipline, substance of Islam, mastery of English, and, above all, the reasons for 'our failures'. To take an example that reminded Mahathir of a painful past, if shops were not to mean 'the ubiquitous Chinese shops', then the Malays had to enter and learn the difficult business of retailing, which required them to adjust their culture to their customers, and not limit themselves and their market to Malays alone.[35] Malay entrepreneurs, too, should start small and expand slowly, 'make an assessment of themselves and ensure that they have the financial means, know-how and efficient management skills before venturing into big businesses' as 'otherwise they will not only face a lot of problems running their business but they will eventually be forced to close down their businesses'.[36] The Malays also had to appreciate that 'cultural differences between the Chinese and the Malays' made the latter eager 'to get rich quick' by selling their 'shares, licences, permits, timber concessions and whatnot' while 'other people must bear the cost of buying the concessions, [but] they can still profit and succeed'.[37]

Mahathir reserved his sternest reprimand for two groups of people – Malay students, and Malay-Muslims who focused on the 'forms', not the 'substance', of Islam. Having benefited from the government's educational policies and programmes of assistance, the Malays seemed not to notice that

> Chinese culture greatly stresses a demand for knowledge to the point that they [Chinese students] and their parents earnestly focus on the learning of knowledge by their children. Many of them sacrifice a big portion of their income to support their children's education. There are Malay parents who do the same but not many.[38]

Neither did the Malays seem overly concerned that 'the performance of Malay students at the universities is not that good',[39] for which excuses were unacceptable:

> If we say that the education system is at fault and we need to correct it, it is the same system followed by the Chinese, so how can the Chinese students do so well?
>
> If we say the teachers are no good, they are the same ones who teach Chinese students. The medium of instruction, too, is in Bahasa Malaysia, so why can't we Malays excel?[40]

Exempting from criticism the 'more responsible' Malay female students who 'do not loiter around',[41] Mahathir was certain the Malay (male) university students 'did not dedicate all their time and effort to learning knowledge'.[42] Hence, he asked, 'When will male Malay students realise their responsibility towards their race, religion and country? Do they think society must support them all the time?'[43] In mock ignorance, Mahathir inquired:

> Where have the *bumiputera* male students gone to? Are they not interested in education? Or are their qualifications (to enter university) too low?
>
> Do the guys think the women will work to support them? Do they think that in the future if they do not have money, they can marry an educated woman and depend on her financially?
>
> Is this the kind of men we will have in the next generation?[44]

Evidently, what invited such harsh comment was not just the lack of learning among Malay male students, but that too many Malay male students had 'involve[d] themselves in other activities,'[45] meaning presumably that a critical segment of the future generation had rallied to the present opposition.

Mahathir had no patience either with those who thought that 'Islam was for wearing' rather than 'for practising'. His own attitude towards any preoccupation with 'form' rather than the 'substance' of Islamic teaching was defined a long time back:

> I can still remember when I was small there was a heated debate on whether or not electric lights can be installed in mosques. It is *haram* to use electric lights. Corpses must be carried by people and not by vehicles with engines because engines are for the infidels, said the people of Kedah.[46]

Likewise he was dismissive of those who were inclined to imitate elements of an Arab culture they believed to be superior because of its associations with the origins of Islam: 'Muslims are asked to foster brotherhood', observed Mahathir, but 'in the Arab world ... they are often at war with each other'.⁴⁷ In his exasperation with Malay or Muslim neglect of discipline, Mahathir abandoned his usual reluctance to criticize other (non-western) societies and exclaimed:

> Look at the Arabs. They have no timing at all and have no respect for time. That is why if they fight with the Jews and plan for their attack at 9am, they would actually attack at 10am, some at 11am and at noon. Some even postponed the attack to the next day. How can they win? There was no discipline ... therefore, they often lose.⁴⁸

Further examples of these lines of Mahathir's thinking would provide updates to contemporary developments but the general point was evident from Mahathir's arguments in *The Malay Dilemma* and *The Challenge*.⁴⁹ Anxious as ever to secure the survival of the Malays, Mahathir was prepared to see the end of Malayness, where others might have wanted to preserve it – in linguistic or educational or even religious ways.

Sometimes Mahathir required a return to history to justify a departure from present policy. When Mahathir wanted to reinstate English-language schools after three decades of Malay-medium education, he recalled, partly from his knowledge of his father's attempts to persuade Malay parents to let their children study in the Government English School, the first English-medium school in Kedah: 'While the Chinese and Indians pursued education in English schools, the Malays rejected English schools because they were afraid of being Christianized. Hence the Malays became weaker and poorer.'⁵⁰ Mahathir's plan for reintroducing English schools was not to be: UMNO's Supreme Council turned it down in May 2002 in favour of a weak compromise, namely, the teaching of Science and Mathematics in English. Sometimes Mahathir negotiated between present and future in trying to ward off the 'terror of history' as when he pleaded that 'mastering English will not make us any less Malay or Islamic':

> English is a universal language. If we do not learn the language, we will not be able to read and if we want to wait for the translation [into the Malay language], it will take time.
>
> Let us not, due to this narrow perspective towards the Malay language, allow the Malays to miss out on the Information Age revolution, thereby regressing and be looked down upon and made to look stupid.
>
> Believe it, we will once again be colonised if we fail to master the language.⁵¹

Even people (and especially Malays) who accepted that 'the world is not going to learn Malay in order to understand the Malays',⁵² and

The Coming of the Second Dilemma 193

who would support new policies to reverse the declining standards of English in the country, would baulk at this direst of Mahathirist predictions. And yet the prediction was not alien to the thoughts of Mahathir. He had never freed himself of the nightmare that re-colonization could happen if the Malays 'failed'.

In fact, Mahathir suspected them to have already failed. At the opening of the 2002 UMNO General Assembly, Mahathir rather emotionally apologized to the Malays for having failed them. One month later, at the Harvard Club of Malaysia Dinner, Mahathir seemed to plumb the depths of his despair. He bitterly submitted that 'if we discount the non-Malay contribution to the nation's economy, Malaysia would be not much better than some of the African developing countries'.[53] Had Mahathir's remark been issued in 1969-70, it might have been sympathetically received, the way *The Malay Dilemma* resonated within the Malay community despite various rejections of the book's core arguments about Malay weaknesses. Or had Mahathir made the remark in the mid-1970s, he would have been regarded as anticipating the scale of the mission awaiting the Malays, just as his essays in *The Challenge* laid out new directions for the Malays under the NEP. Hearing the remark in mid-2002, many non-Malays (including foreigners) applauded Mahathir for the forthrightness of which he was ever so proud. But could anyone imagine that the statement would not infuriate or humiliate most Malays who were within earshot? Still, the statement has to be taken as the culmination of Mahathir's lengthy post-1999 reflection on the 'Malay condition'. To what then would one trace its apparent despair?

One source can be eliminated straight away. Unlike the circumstances in which Mahathir originally framed the 'Malay dilemma' (actually way back in 1950[54]), one cannot properly trace this formulation of a 'second dilemma' to the contemporary state of ethnic politics or relations. Ethnicity cannot be removed from Malaysian politics, but the indications rule out a replication of the interethnic politics of the past when serious Malay-Chinese disagreements over economics, culture and language dominated the political terrain. After the 1995 and 1999 general elections, it has become clear that non-Malay politics has reached what might be regarded either as a historical cul-de-sac or a point of settled realism. 'Chinese politics' in particular has been truncated into a minority politics according to which the 'Chinese-based parties' will strategically support the strongest of Malay parties – UMNO for the foreseeable future – but can hardly influence the 'big picture' despite Mahathir's tease that 'one day we'll have a non-Malay PM [prime minister]'.[55] Indeed, if MCA, the largest Chinese-based party, could perform very well in the 1995 and 1999 elections, it was precisely because it had lowered its political sights and ambitions. As UMNO's adjunct, a latter-day 'Protector of the Chinese', MCA's role is to 'swell a progress, start a scene or two'. Not even that role is available to Gerakan for whom an insecure claim on the chief minister's post in the Penang state government compensates its loss of national significance. And DAP, lacking the outreach to the Malay voters that only a firm coalition with a major 'Malay-based party' can offer, has been confined to islets of dissidence. The historical conditions that raised fears and resistance over the assimilation of non-Malays into Malay culture have passed. UMNO has sufficiently eased its pressures on the Chinese community over questions of language, education and culture, while PAS has actually been supportive of 'minority rights' in such areas. When a dispute arises in one of these areas now and then, it tends to be a sign of mismanagement along the 'negotiation-pressure' spectrum rather than being characteristic of the intractable ethnic politics of the past. For example, the controversies over the Vision Schools and the teaching of Science and Mathematics in English in Chinese schools were minor disputes. They arose out of the residual distrust between the state and the Dongjiaozong, and probably bureaucratic ineptitude as well, rather the regime's intent to 'change the character of the Chinese schools'. And even if Mahathir attacked Suqiu in 2000, his frequent praise of Chinese parents and students, and of Chinese culture and business, in contrast to his vitriolic comments on Malay attitudes and dependence, pointed to Suqiu's minor significance. Suqiu's lashing stemmed from Mahathir's reluctance then to be distracted from his futile soliloquy on Malay unity.

The real clue to appreciating the significance of Mahathir's apology to the Malays lies in turning the apology on its head: surely Mahathir meant that the Malays had failed him! The immensity of the Malays' unfulfilled task left him diffident about their culture and values once more, and weary as well:

> The dilemma faced by those few who want to build a strong, resilient and independent Malay race without crutches is that they are most likely to end up becoming unpopular and losing the ability to influence the changes in the culture and the value system which are necessary.[56]

Here one can leave alone Mahathir's disingenuous reference to his and UMNO's loss of popularity that makes no mention of their mauling of Anwar. It was suggested in *Paradoxes of Mahathirism* that 'Mahathir knows no other class to whom the Malay future can be entrusted' except the *Melayu Baru* – 'historically the "new" class of Malay capitalists and the "new" Malay middle class which were largely "engineered" by the state according to the logic of Malay parity with the non-Malays in a capitalist economy'.[57] By that assessment, Mahathir would have been consistent in vision and analysis to direct his regrets at the state-sponsored and UMNO-linked conglomerates. The winners he picked and pampered had not realized his grandest ambitions. But while Mahathir castigated many segments of the Malay community, he defended the conglomerates' captains and helmsmen as good businessmen and managers whose positions were undermined by currency speculators.

This was confirmation that Mahathir, who personified his class while personifying his race, advanced the ambitions of a class as the ideals of a nation. When the good times rolled, he exuded confidence:

> The Malays of today are not like the Malays of the old days. We have changed and so have [sic] our culture. We are now capable of doing things which we were unable to do before, and have ventured into and achieved success in many fields.[58]

The converse held during hard times. The failures of class were passed off as the weaknesses of culture. With his 'second dilemma', Mahathir cast the specific shortcomings of the Malaysian conglomerates as the generalized inadequacies of the Malay race.

It is not difficult to understand, then, why Mahathir decided that too many Malay (male) students, academicians, civil servants, professionals and smaller businessmen had 'underachieved' in a milieu bounded by Malay supremacy, restructuring targets, NEP quotas, and 'dual track meritocracy'. He was not alone in thinking so. He also had an axe to grind with many of them in the wake of the anti-UMNO turn. But their 'underachievement' would not be startling to those who regard it as one by-product of a 'soft political environment' that was shaped by 'constructive protection' – exactly as Mahathir had predicted in *The Malay Dilemma*. Neither would these segments of the BCIC, like any other social group in power, voluntarily surrender privileges they had habitually received. If, 'unfortunately, their view is that their crutches are symbols of their superior status in the country',[59] that, too, was comprehensible. That flowed from an ideological framework that justified the NEP's affirmative action in terms of the 'relative backwardness' of the Malays who needed a 'special position' guaranteed by UMNO's political dominance.

Less obvious and potentially more difficult to manage was the outline of a future etched by July 1997 that lurked behind Mahathir's diagnosis. The NEP originally envisaged the attainment of social equity – via poverty eradication and restructuring – in a global environment where 'reforms' meant state intervention to reduce social and economic inequality and improve mass living conditions. One can see this from Tun Razak's defence of the NEP before an UMNO Youth seminar:

> In the era of the 1950s and 1960s, we yielded to private industry to achieve the goals of that era, but now we have 'State Participation' to achieve the goals and objectives that are different and are suitable to our situation and aspirations of the Bumiputera.
>
> If that is what is called the 'Doctrine of Welfarism', then we have not only clung to but implemented the 'Doctrine of Welfarism' via Bank Bumiputra, Pernas, MARA, Bank Pertanian and National Electricity Board, Malayan Railways and bodies such as the Urban Development Authority and other bodies that will be established before long.[60]

As the NEP's principal architect, Razak was not afraid to argue that the NEP went beyond 'state participation' or 'welfarism':

> our [New Economic] Policy does not differ from the meaning of Paul Sigmund's Concept of the 'Socialism' in new and developing nations: According to Sigmund, this socialism is 'fed by a passion for social equality, and by a desire for rapid economic development.... It is a nationalist socialism....'[61]

Razak had been a member of the British Labour Party and the Fabian Society while he was a student in the United Kingdom. When he delivered the above argument in 1971, during the Cold War period, and having to tackle mass poverty and ethnic economic imbalances, Razak understandably chose to present state capitalism under the NEP in the ideological garb of a 'nationalist socialism' that 'reject[ed] the Marxist-Leninist theory of the class struggle'.[62] So expounded, Razak's concept of the NEP would find little in common with the current concept of 'reform' that has been corrupted by the neoliberal obsession with competition to refer invariably to pro-market and anti-welfare measures. More to the point, by the end of Mahathir's era, the early NEP's reliance on state-guided 'Malay trusts' had yielded to its Malaysia Inc. association with state-patronized 'Malay conglomerates'. An emphasis on social equity had given way to a preoccupation with competition. If Mahathir now wanted the Malays to discard their state-provided 'crutches' and become competitive, he spoke an idiom of 'Malay self-reliance' that was more attuned to an era of privatization than of the NEP's early 'state participation'.

The most critical interpretation of this twist to Mahathir's endless appraisal of the 'Malay condition' must imagine Mahathir to be ideologically preparing the Malays – those not yet successful or comfortably entrenched – for a cessation of the large-scale subsidies, targets and quotas they had once taken for granted. The fundamental reason is economic. The past three decades formed the period of greatest Malay social mobility. It should be plain that the pace of social mobility of the past three decades may not be sustained despite Vision 2020's projections of growth. Future generations of Malays can hardly expect to enjoy the same scale of socio-economic gains offered by the NEP's state-led high growth, privatization and Malaysia Inc. The 1985-86 recession was the NEP's first major crisis. Mahathir's regime resolved it by 'holding NEP in abeyance', reducing public spending, and attracting an influx of (East Asian) foreign direct investment. Then the Mahathir regime chose 'growth' over 'distribution' in ways that favoured big Malay businesses. A major political consequence of that policy choice was UMNO's internal turmoil. The July 1997 'meltdown' was the NEP's second and, arguably, greater crisis. It has ended with the preservation of the conglomerates as a way of saving, in effect, the NEP. The political fall-out from that crisis was Anwar's fate and *Reformasi*'s challenge to UMNO.

Despite all that, individual Malay ownership of corporate capital stood at only *seven* per cent, according to Mahathir's estimate.[63] Mahathir was rightly scornful of the IMF's prescriptions of stringent structural adjustment and drastic pro-market reforms. These would have brought a destabilizing end to the nationalist-capitalist project without, as in Indonesia, offering trickle-down relief for the vulnerable, mass, non-corporate sections of the populace. But, more importantly in the long run, the regime's 'economic shield' portended a more contentious interface with the global economy at the next economic crisis. Then the state may not find a politically acceptable resolution based on increased FDI inflows, given the changing volume and structure of global FDI flows, and the trends of industrial relocation from formerly valued sites like Malaysia. Nor can a small and open economy keep shielding itself with semi-autarkic measures against the vagaries and cycles of the global capitalist system. Internally there had always been a defensive Malay perspective on the NEP that wanted to 'hold back' the non-Malays (that is, the Chinese) if the Malays were 'not ready' for whatever it was they should be ready to assume. Two days before Mahathir announced his resignation, he firmly indicated that he did not see how Malay weaknesses could be resolved by keeping down the non-Malay community: 'If we take out the Chinese and all that they have built and own, there will be no small or big towns in Malaysia, there will be no business and industry, there will be no funds for the subsidies, support and facilities for the Malays.'[64]

When Mahathir is not posturing, he understands as few Malay politicians do (or will publicly admit), that one earns no respect by taking refuge in one's inadequacies, past suffering or present pain. One earns respect by attaining the standards set by those who had arrived – the developed countries, successful communities, progressive races or competitive individuals. Of course, one can lament one's 'relative backwardness', rely on state power, and employ social engineering to 'distort the picture a little in order to help [oneself]'. But until one succeeds by sheer effort and genuine accomplishment, one can have no pride or dignity. And above all else, Mahathir valued pride and dignity, as he intimated once more at the 2002 UMNO General Assembly: 'I realized I was a Malay some 65 years ago, at which time I realized that I was from a race that was looked down upon, a colonized race, a race without honour, a race with a feeling of inferiority when set against other races.'[65]

Are things any different now? Within the world, despite its political insignificance, Malaysia can claim a taste of achievement: the country does not suffer the terrible misery of most developing countries; the society is more 'progressive' than other Muslim countries; and the economy may yet keep apace of a rising Asia if indeed Asia keeps rising. Within Malaysia, ironically, the Malays, despite their political dominance, cannot quite compete in fact or imagination without 'crutches'. Mahathir has not repudiated the NEP, as some who were present at the Harvard Club Dinner were quick to hope and approve. He anticipated a scenario of diminishing options that might force the 'party of the Malays' to choose: between imposing measures of 'self-reliance' upon large segments of the Malay population *now*, or risk a *future* collapse of legitimacy should UMNO's ability to 'deliver development' be impaired. Echoing Mahathir, the *New Straits Times* warned that

> post-NEP Malays should not wholly embrace the victim status that results in blaming all failings on other races, the elites and the Government.... The Government's affirmative action was never meant to infantilise the race. Self-help and, yes, bootstrap capitalism, will add respect and honour to the Malays' collective civic self. The Malays must rise to the challenges of self-help and competition.[66]

What lies beneath this discourse of crutches and infantilism, self-help and bootstrap capitalism, respect and honour, and 'collective civic self' and competition? To put matters painfully, whereas the original 'Malay dilemma' required that 'some non-Malays will have to be sacrificed in order to bring the Malays up',[67] as Mahathir bluntly insisted in 1976, the 'second dilemma' foresees that some 'post-NEP Malays' will have to be sacrificed to keep the rest up.

Can anything be more tragic for Mahathirism than this dissolution of its grandiosity in a second Malay dilemma that is a devil's choice between crutchless competitiveness and self-reliant sacrifice? Maybe Mahathir arrived at this pitiable conclusion out of frustration at the collapse of the Malay conglomerates, or in anger at the Malay recalcitrance that was his reward from *Reformasi*. At any rate, only he would have expressed it so, having striven his political life to detect and resolve Malay dilemma after Malay dilemma as the world changed over and over again.

Since *Reformasi*'s advent in 1998, Mahathir has criticized the Malays for 'easily forgetting' their debts, for being ungrateful to those who advanced their cause, and for 'instilling hatred' among young Malays towards UMNO. Mahathir himself sets great store by history. He will be the among the first to remember that several turning points of Malaysian politics were set by mass Malay intrusions upon the political stage: witness 1946 and the Malayan Union; 1969 and May 13; and 1998 and *Reformasi*. The first instance brought UMNO into being. The second forced UMNO to alter radically the structure of political economy. The third threatened to render UMNO irrelevant. The question for future Malay, and Malaysian, politics is whether those who rule after Mahathir will forget or are allowed to forget.

Notes

[1] Mahathir (2000f).
[2] 'Dr Mahathir: It's Malay Dilemma II', *New Straits Times*, 22 June 2001.
[3] For example: '… there are still others who speculate that between now and October 2003, Malaysia might be hit by a huge crisis of some kind and sorry, Dr M, you just have to stay on indefinitely, the country needs you' (June H. L. Wong, 'Waking up to an imminent loss', *The Star*, 28 June 2002).
[4] To be accurate: 'On June 22, 2000, the American intelligence community organized a conference in Washington entitled "Prospects for a Post-Mahathir Malaysia", attended by officials from the Central Intelligence Agency and the departments of State and Defence.' See 'U.S. Thinks Post-Mahathir', *Far Eastern Economic Review*, 13 July 2000, p. 8.
[5] 'Interview: Mahathir on race, the West and his successor', *Time*, 9 December 1996, p. 28.

6   Mahathir (2001a).
7   Mahathir (2000f).
8   Mahathir, quoted in Rehman Rashid, 'Why I Took to Politics', *New Straits Times*, 5 July 1986; original emphasis.
9   *Ibid.*
10 *Ibid.*
11 Halim (1999: 187).
12 I feel obliged to say I have not borrowed from George Bush Jr's self-serving so-called 'axis of evil' here, having myself analyzed this notion of an axis in Malay politics in an academic essay that predated 11 September 2001. See Khoo (2001).
13 Crouch (1980: 17, 32-33).
14 Searle (1999).
15 Mahathir (2000a).
16 See the *malaysiakini* debate involving: Farish A. Noor, 'The failure of reformasi thinkers' (26 April 2003); Fathi Aris Omar, 'Memurnikan makna kesedaran berpolitik' (28 April); Marissa Dell, 'Reformasi "thinkers" should examine themselves' (30 April); and Umar Mukhtar, 'Reformasi is alive and well' (30 April). For comparison, see Khoo (2002a).
17 Mahathir (2000f).
18 *Ibid.*
19 Mahathir (2002c).
20 Ahmad (2002).
21 Mahathir (2002b).
22 *Ibid.*
23 Mahathir (2000e).
24 Armstrong (2000).
25 Wain (2000).
26 Mahathir (2002b).
27 *Ibid.*
28 'Datuk Seri Dr Mahathir Mohamad yesterday said the multitude of problems faced by the Malays now can be likened to "Malay Dilemma II"' ('Dr Mahathir: It's Malay Dilemma II', *New Straits Times*, 22 June 2001).
29 Mahathir (2000c).
30 Mahathir (2000d).
31 'Anak Melayu bukan bodoh', *Harian Metro*, 26 August 2001.
32 Mahathir (2000d).
33 'Dr M: Assert supremacy', *The Star*, 22 June 2000.
34 Mahathir (2000d).
35 'PM: In business, we must sell to all and not be selective of race', *Straits Times*, 27 February 2000.
36 'PM on downfall of entrepreneurs', *The Star*, 6 December 2000.
37 Mahathir (2001a).
38 *Ibid.*
39 *Ibid.*

40 'Examine why we fail, PM tells Malays', *The Star*, 16 January 2001.
41 And 'Thank God. If not for female students, the number of Malay students in universities would be reduced by half.' See 'PM: Malay girls holding up quotas', *The Sun*, 22 June 2001.
42 Mahathir (2001a).
43 'PM: Malay girls holding up quotas', *The Sun*, 22 June 2001.
44 'Dr M: Where have the *bumi* male students gone to?', *The Star*, 4 November 2000.
45 'PM: Malay girls holding up quotas', *The Sun*, 22 June 2001.
46 Mahathir (2001b).
47 'PM: In business we must sell to all and not be selective of race', *Straits Times*, 27 February 2000.
48 Mahathir (2001b).
49 Mahathir (1986).
50 Mahathir (2000c).
51 'Master English for your own good, Malays urged', *The Star*, 22 June 2001.
52 'We work by consensus, says Dr M', *The Star*, 29 December 2000.
53 Mahathir (2002c).
54 Khoo (1995: 85).
55 'Dr M: One day we'll have a non-Malay PM', *The Star*, 18 June 2000.
56 Mahathir (2002c).
57 Khoo (1995: 338).
58 Quoted in 'Malays can be successful in IT', *Business Times*, 27 February 1997.
59 Mahathir (2002c).
60 Abdul Razak (1971).
61 *Ibid*.
62 *Ibid*.
63 Montagnon (2000).
64 'PM: Easy to split the Malays', *The Star*, 21 June 2002. On 17 May 2001, Mahathir held a meeting with selected (predominantly Malay) academic staff from public universities and colleges. At one point, while criticizing the Malay students' lack of achievement, purportedly because of their distraction by political activities, Mahathir remarked: 'There's already a suggestion … don't let them (the Chinese) study while we [Malays] are playing. No! We cannot stop the Chinese.' This quote is drawn from an unofficial and incomplete translation of Mahathir's talk (Ucapan di Majlis Perjumpaan Perdana Menteri Dengan Para Akademik IPTA) (Speech at a Meeting with Academic Staff of Public Institutions of Higher Learning), Putrajaya), posted at (http://members.tripod.com/~mahazalimtwo/210501zaf.html).
65 Mahathir (2002b).
66 'No one to blame but themselves', *New Straits Times*, 21 June 2002.
67 Quoted in Sonny Yap, 'The Prodigal Who Made His Way Up', *New Nation*, 9 March 1976.

Bibliography

Entries for non-western names are cited and arranged alphabetically according to surnames or first names, without the use of commas, except where the first name is an honorific, or where the name follows western convention in the original source. Sources for quotations from newspapers and articles without authors' names in periodicals are given in the endnotes together with bibliographic details.

I. Writings by Mahathir Mohamad

_____ (1970) *The Malay Dilemma*, Singapore: Donald Moore for Asia Pacific Press.

_____ (1986) *The Challenge*, Petaling Jaya, Selangor: Pelanduk Publications; translated from *Menghadapi Cabaran*, Kuala Lumpur: Pustaka Antara, 1976.

_____ (1991) 'Malaysia: The Way Forward', Working Paper presented at the Inaugural Meeting of the Malaysian Business Council, Kuala Lumpur, 28 February, reprinted in *New Straits Times*, 2 March 1991.

_____ (1993) 'The Second Outline Perspective Plan, 1991-2000', in Ahmad Sarji Abdul Hamid (ed.) *Malaysia's Vision 2020: Understanding the Concept, Implications and Challenges*, Petaling Jaya, Selangor: Pelanduk, pp. 421-447.

_____ (1998a) 'Call Me a Heretic', *Time*, 14 September, p. 21.

_____ (2000a) 'Of Malays, mega projects and democracy', *New Straits Times*, 11 January.

_____ (2000b) 'Tackling problems methodically', *New Straits Times*, 2 May.

_____ (2002a) *Globalisation and the New Realities*, Putrajaya: Prime Minister's Office.

Mahathir Mohamad and Shintaro Ishihara (1995) *The Voice of Asia*, Tokyo: Kodansha International; translated by Frank Baldwin.

II. Speeches by Mahathir Mohamad

_____ (1995a) Speech at the National Summit on 'Achieving Zero Inflation', Kuala Lumpur, 12 September, reproduced as 'Towards Zero Inflation: A New National Agenda', in Hashim Makaruddin (ed.) (2000) *Managing the*

Malaysian Economy: Selected Speeches by Dr Mahathir Mohamad, Prime Minister of Malaysia, Vol. 2, Putrajaya: Prime Minister's Office, pp. 213-17.

_____ (1995b) Speech at the Dialogue on The Malaysian Economy and Capital Market, London, 26 September, reproduced as 'The Malaysian Economy and Capital Market', in Hashim Makaruddin (ed.) (2000) *Managing the Malaysian Economy: Selected Speeches by Dr Mahathir Mohamad, Prime Minister of Malaysia*, Vol. 2, Putrajaya: Prime Minister's Office, pp. 207-11.

_____ (1996a) Speech at the New Asia Forum, Kuala Lumpur, 11 January, reprinted as 'An Asian Renaissance for a New Asia', in Hashim Makaruddin (ed.) (2000), *Politics, Democracy and the New Asia: Selected Speeches by Dr Mahathir Mohamad, Prime Minister of Malaysia*, Vol. 2, Putrajaya: Prime Minister's Office, pp. 173-80.

_____ (1996b) Speech at St Catherine's College, University of Oxford, Oxford, 16 April, reproduced as 'Market Economy and Moral and Cultural Values', in Hashim Makaruddin (ed.) (2000) *Managing the Malaysian Economy: Selected Speeches by Dr Mahathir Mohamad, Prime Minister of Malaysia*, Vol. 2, Putrajaya: Prime Minister's Office, pp. 197-205.

_____ (1996c) Speech at the 29th International General Meeting of the Pacific Basin Economic Council, Washington, 21 May, reprinted as 'It's time Asia be accorded due respect', *New Straits Times*, 22 May 1996.

_____ (1996d) Speech at the Second Langkawi International Dialogue, Pulau Langkawi, 29 July, reprinted as 'Business partnership a success story' in *New Straits Times*, 30 July 1996.

_____ (1996e) Speech at the Beijing Dialogue, Beijing, 26 August, reprinted as 'Dawn of Asian Century is a myth', *New Straits Times*, 27 August 1996.

_____ (1997a) Speech at the Conference for Investors in the Multimedia Super Corridor, University of California, Los Angeles, 15 January, reproduced as 'A Global Bridge to the Information Age', in Hashim Makaruddin (ed.) (2000) *Regional Cooperation and the Digital Economy: Selected Speeches by Dr Mahathir Mohamad, Prime Minister of Malaysia*, Vol. 2, Putrajaya: Prime Minister's Office, pp. 97-109.

_____ (1997b) Speech at the 5th Gulf Economic Forum, Bahrain, 8 April, reprinted as 'Towards a Global Commonwealth', *New Straits Times*, 10 April 1997.

_____ (1997c) Speech at the National Congress on Vision 2020, Kuala Lumpur, 29 April, reprinted as 'Our Vision 2020 wins over nations', *The Star*, 30 April 1997.

_____ (1997d) 'MSC: A Global Bridge from Europe to Asia for the World Century', Speech at Imperial College, London, 20 May, reproduced as 'A Global Bridge to the World Century', in Hashim Makaruddin (ed.), *Regional Cooperation and the Digital Economy: Selected Speeches by Dr Mahathir Mohamad, Prime Minister of Malaysia*, Vol. 2, Putrajaya: Prime Minister's Office, pp. 75-83.

_____ (1997e) Speech at the 30th ASEAN Ministerial Meeting, Subang Jaya, Malaysia, 24 July, reprinted as 'An Asean of peace and prosperity', in *The Star*, 25 July 1997.

_____ (1997f) Speech at the Multimedia Asia 1997 Conference, Kuala Lumpur, 16 September, reproduced as 'Reinventing Our Common Future', in Hashim Makaruddin (ed.) (2000) *Regional Cooperation and the Digital Economy: Selected Speeches by Dr Mahathir Mohamad, Prime Minister of Malaysia*, Vol. 2, Putrajaya: Prime Minister's Office, pp. 61-66.

_____ (1997g) Speech at the Annual Seminar of the World Bank, Hong Kong, 20 September, reprinted as 'Asian Economies: Challenges and Opportunities', *Foreign Affairs Malaysia*, Vol. 30, No. 3, pp. 61-69.

_____ (1997h) Speech at the Canadian Investment Conference, Ottawa, 21 November, reproduced as 'On the Threshold of the Cyber Revolution', in Hashim Makaruddin (ed.) (2000) *Regional Cooperation and the Digital Economy: Selected Speeches by Dr Mahathir Mohamad, Prime Minister of Malaysia*, Vol. 2, Putrajaya: Prime Minister's Office, pp. 39-48.

_____ (1998b) Speech at the UMNO General Assembly, Kuala Lumpur, 19 June, reprinted as 'All Malaysians should defend our sovereignty', *New Straits Times*, 20 June.

_____ (1998c) 6th Prime Ministerial Lecture of the Harvard Club of Malaysia, Kuala Lumpur, 5 October, reproduced as 'Managing an Economy in Turmoil', in Hashim Makaruddin (ed.) (2000), *Managing the Malaysian Economy. Selected Speeches by Dr Mahathir Mohamad, Prime Minister of Malaysia*, Vol. 2, Putrajaya: Prime Minister's Office, pp. 77-87.

_____ (2000c) New Year's Day Speech 2000, reprinted as 'Globalisme mengancam negara', *Utusan Malaysia*, 1 January 2000.

_____ (2000d) Speech at the Official Ceremony of the Congress of Young Malay Professionals, Kuala Lumpur, 26 February, reprinted as 'Kekalkan Tamadun Melayu moden', *Mingguan Malaysia*, 27 February 2000.

_____ (2000e) Speech at the UMNO General Assembly 2000, Kuala Lumpur reprinted as 'The party's unfinished struggle', *The Star*, 12 May 2000.

_____ (2000f) Winding-up Speech at the UMNO General Assembly 2000, Kuala Lumpur, 14 May, reprinted as 'Dr Mahathir: Important for leaders to meet grassroots', *New Straits Times*, 15 May 2000.

_____ (2001a) Ucapan Perdana Menteri pada Konvensyen Perdana Pendidikan Kebangsaan 2001, Institut Aminuddin Baki, Genting Highlands, 19 April, reprinted as 'Pendidikan penentu kejayaan bangsa, negara', *Berita Harian*, 20 April 2001.

_____ (2001b) Winding-up Speech at the UMNO General Assembly 2001, 24 June, reprinted as 'Dr M: Important to obey the president', *New Straits Times*, 25 June 2001.

_____ (2002b) Speech at the UMNO General Assembly, Kuala Lumpur, 20 June, reprinted as 'Good values destroyed by hate' in *New Straits Times*, 21 June 2002.

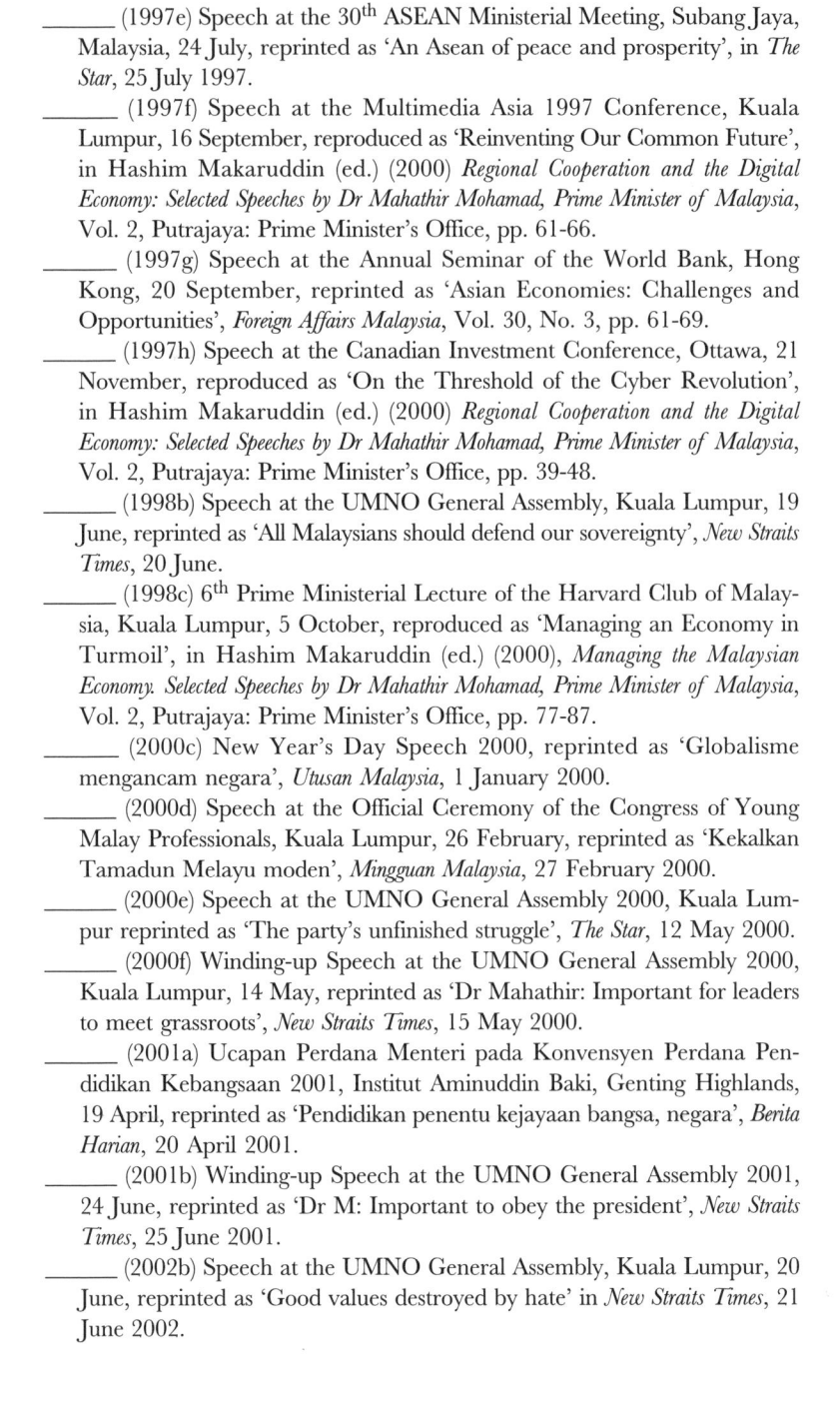

_____ (2002c) Speech at the Harvard Club of Malaysia Dinner, Kuala Lumpur, 29 July, reprinted as 'The New Malay Dilemma', *New Straits Times*, 30 July 2002.

III. Books and Articles

Abdul Razak, Tun (1971) Speech at the Development Seminar organized by UMNO Youth, Morib, Selangor, 25 July, reprinted in *Dasar Ekonomi Baru: hikmat, kebajikan dan peranan parti*, Petaling Jaya: UMNO, pp. 3-21.

Adam, Christopher and Cavendish, William (1995) 'Early Privatization', in Jomo K. S. (ed.) *Privatizing Malaysia: Rents, Rhetoric, Realities*, Boulder, Colorado: Westview Press, pp. 98-137.

Ahmad Hussein, Syed (2002) 'Muslim Politics and the Discourse on Democracy', in Francis Loh Kok Wah and Khoo Boo Teik (eds) *Democracy in Malaysia: Discourses and Practices*, Richmond: Curzon Press, pp. 74-107.

Amin, Samir (1993) 'Replacing the International Monetary System', *Monthly Review*, Vol. 45, No. 5, pp. 1-12

Anderson, Benedict (1998) *The Spectre of Comparisons: Nationalism, Southeast Asia, and the World*, London and New York: Verso.

_____ (2001) 'Asian Nationalism', *New Left Review*, 9 (May-June): 31-42

Anwar Ibrahim (1996) *The Asian Renaissance*, Singapore: Times Books International.

Appell, Douglas and Lopez, Leslie (1997) 'Foreign Funds to Shun Choreographed Buying', *Asian Wall Street Journal*, 2 September.

Armstrong, Karen (2000) *Islam: A Short History*, London: Phoenix Press.

Bank for International Settlements (1999) 69th *Annual Report* (1 April 1998 – 31 March 1999), Basel.

Bank Negara Malaysia (1998) *Annual Report 1997*, Kuala Lumpur.

_____ *Monthly Statistical Bulletin*, Kuala Lumpur; various years.

Beeson, Mark (2000) 'Mahathir and the Markets: Globalisation and the Pursuit of Economic Autonomy in Malaysia', *Pacific Affairs*, Vol. 73, No. 3 (Fall): 335-51.

Bhagwati, Jagdish (1998) 'The Capital Myth: The Difference Between Trade in Widgets and Trade in Dollars', *Foreign Affairs*, Vol. 77, No. 3.

Camus, Albert (1956) *The Rebel*, New York: Vintage Books; translated by Anthony Bower.

Case, William (2003) 'The Anwar Trial and its Wider Implications', in Colin Barlow and Francis Loh Kok Wah (eds) *Malaysian Economics and Politics in the New Century*, Cheltenham: Edward Elgar, pp. 119-31.

Cheah Boon Kheng (1998) 'The Rise and Fall of the Great Melakan Empire: Moral Judgement in Tun Bambang's *Sejarah Melayu*', *Journal of the Malaysian Branch of the Royal Asiatic Society*, LXXI, Part 2, 275 (December): 103-21.

_____ (2002) *Malaysia: The Making of a Nation*, Singapore: ISEAS.

Crouch, Harold (1980) 'The UMNO Crisis: 1975-1977', in Harold Crouch, Lee Kam Hing and Michael Ong (eds) *Malaysian Politics and the 1978 Election*, Kuala Lumpur: Oxford University Press, pp. 11-36.

Elegant, Simon (2000) 'Maverick Reformer', *Far Eastern Economic Review*, 22 June, p. 34.

Farish A. Noor (1999) 'Looking for Reformasi: The Discursive Dynamics of the Reformasi Movement and its Prospects as a Political Project', *Indonesia and the Malay World*, Vol. 27, No. 77 (March): 5-18.

Financial Times (1995) *Banking in the Far East 1995*, London: FT Financial Publishing.

Funston, John (1998) *Political Careers of Mahathir Mohamad and Anwar Ibrahim: Parallel, Intersecting and Conflicting Lives*, Bangi: Institut Kajian Malaysia dan Antarabangsa (IKMAS) Working Papers No. 15.

―――― (2000) 'Malaysia's Tenth Election: Status Quo, *Reformasi*, or Islamization?', *Contemporary Southeast Asia*, Vol. 22, No. 1 (April): 23-59.

Ghani Ismail (1983) *Razaleigh Lawan Musa, Pusingan Kedua, 1984*, Taiping, Perak: IJS Communications.

Godement, Francois (1998) 'The Politics of a Crisis', *Far Eastern Economic Review*, 8 January, p. 28.

Gomez, Edmund Terence and Jomo K. S. (1997) *Malaysia's Political Economy: Politics, Patronage and Profits*, Cambridge: Cambridge University Press.

Halim Salleh (1999) 'Development and the Politics of Social Stability in Malaysia', *Southeast Asian Affairs 1999*, Singapore: ISEAS, pp. 185-203.

―――― (2000) 'PAS and UMNO in Kelantan and Trengganu', Paper presented at the Workshop on the Malaysian General Election of 1999, Universiti Sains Malaysia, Penang, 1-2 April.

Henwood, Douglas (1997) *Wall Street: How It Works and for Whom*, London and New York: Verso.

Hiebert, Murray and Jayasankaran, S. (1997) 'What Next?', *Far Eastern Economic Review*, 18 September, pp. 62-64.

Higgott, Richard (2000) 'The International Relations of the Asian Economic Crisis: A Study in the Politics of Resentment', in Richard Robison, Mark Beeson, Kanishka Jayasuriya and Hyuk-Rae Kim (eds) *Politics and Markets in the Wake of the Asian Crisis*, London: Routledge, pp. 261-82.

Hilley, John (2001) *Malaysia: Mahathirism, Hegemony and the New Opposition*, London and New York: Zed Books.

Husin Ali, Syed (1996) *Two Faces*, Petaling Jaya, Selangor: INSAN.

Hwang, In-Won (2001) "Changing Conflict Configurations and Regime Maintenance in Malaysian Politics: From Consociational Bargaining to Mahathir's Dominance", PhD dissertation, Australian National University, Canberra.

Jayasankaran, S. (1996) 'Equal Opportunity', *Far Eastern Economic Review*, 25 July, p. 16.

―――― (1997) 'High-Wire Act', *Far Eastern Economic Review*, 9 October.

―――― (1998) 'Art of the Bail', *Far Eastern Economic Review*, 30 April, pp. 62-63.

Jayasankaran, S. and Hiebert, Murray (1998), 'Calling for Daim', *Far Eastern Economic Review*, 19 February, p. 14.

Jomo K. S. (1995) 'Overview', in Jomo K. S. (ed.) *Privatizing Malaysia: Rents, Rhetoric, Realities*, Boulder, Colorado: Westview Press, pp. 42-60.

_____ (2001a) 'Capital Controls', in Jomo K. S. (ed.) *Malaysian Eclipse: Economic Crisis and Recovery*, London: Zed Books, pp. 199-215.

_____ (ed.) (2001b) *Malaysian Eclipse: Economic Crisis and Recovery*, London: Zed Books.

Khoo Boo Teik (1995) *Paradoxes of Mahathirism: An Intellectual Biography of Mahathir Mohamad*, Kuala Lumpur: Oxford University Press.

_____ (1997) 'Malaysia: Challenges and Upsets in Politics and Other Contestations', in *Southeast Asian Affairs 1997*, Singapore: ISEAS, pp. 163-84.

_____ (1998) 'Reflections on the 1998 UMNO General Assembly', *Aliran Monthly*, Vol. 18, No. 6 (July): 2-7

_____ (1999a) 'The Value(s) of a Miracle: Malaysian and Singaporean Elite Constructions of Asia', *Asian Studies Review*, Vol. 23, No. 2 (June): 181-92.

_____ (1999b) 'Mahathir and foreign media no bitter foes', *The Nation*, Bangkok, 5 August.

_____ (2001) 'The State and the Market in Malaysian Political Economy', in Garry Rodan, Kevin Hewison and Richard Robison (eds) *The Political Economy of South-East Asia: Conflicts, Crises, and Change*, 2nd revised edition, Melbourne, Oxford University Press, 2001, pp. 178-205.

_____ (2002a) 'Can There be Reformasi Beyond BA?', *Aliran Monthly*, Vol. 22, No. 1, pp. 2-7.

_____ (2002b) 'Writing Reformasi', *Kyoto Review of Southeast Asia*, Issue 1, *Power and Politics* (http://kyotoreview.cseas.kyoto-u.ac.jp/issue0/index.html), March.

Khoo, Philip (1999) 'Thinking the Unthinkable: A Malaysia Not Governed by the BN?', *Aliran Monthly*, Vol. 19, No. 5 (June): 2-8.

Kua Kia Soong (1996) *Inside the DAP, 1990-95*, Petaling Jaya, Selangor: PB.

Kulkarni, V. G., Hiebert, Murray and Jayasankaran, S. (1996) 'Tough Talk', *Far Eastern Economic Review*, 24 October, pp. 23, 26-27.

Lim Chong Eu (1983) Speech at the Cultural Congress, Chinese Town Hall, Penang, March 27, 1983, reproduced as 'Malaysian Culture', in Lim Choon Sooi (1990), *Towards the Future: Selected Speeches and Statements of Lim Chong Eu 1970-1989*, Penang: Oon Chin Seang, pp. 122-26.

Lim Kit Siang (1998) *Economic and Financial Crisis*, Petaling Jaya, Selangor: Democratic Action Party.

_____ (2003) 'The Challenges of Opposition Politics in Malaysia – Checking Growing Authoritarianism and Ethnic Re-polarization', in Colin Barlow and Francis Loh Kok Wah (eds) *Malaysian Economics and Politics in the New Century*, Cheltenham: Edward Elgar, pp. 159-71.

Loh Kok Wah, Francis (1997) '"Sabah Baru" dan Pujukan Pembangunan: Penyelesaian Hubungan Persekutuan-Negeri Dalam Malaysia', in Francis Loh Kok Wah (ed.) *Sabah and Sarawak: The Politics of Development and Federalism*, Special Issue, *Kajian Malaysia*, Vol. XV, Nos 1 and 2 (December): 175-97.

_____ (2001) 'Where Has (Ethnic) Politics Gone? The Case of the BN Non-Malay Politicians and Political Parties', in Robert Hefner (ed.) *The Politics of Multiculturalism: Pluralism and Citizenship in Malaysia, Singapore and Indonesia*, Honolulu: University of Hawaii Press, pp. 183-203.

_____ (2002) 'Developmentalism and the Limits of Democratic Discourse', in Francis Loh Kok Wah and Khoo Boo Teik (eds), *Democracy in Malaysia: Discourses and Practices*, Richmond: Curzon Press, pp. 19-50.

Lopez, Leslie (1997) 'Malaysia Plans Stock-Purchase Initiative That Alienates, Alarms Foreign Investors', *Asian Wall Street Journal*, 4 September

Lopez, Leslie and Pura, Raphael (1997) 'Mahathir Tightens Control of Market', *Asian Wall Street Journal*, 2 September.

McCarthy, James (1994) 'Asia's Future Wall Street', *Malaysian Business*, 16 March.

Malayan Law Journal (1999) *The Anwar Ibrahim Judgement*, Kuala Lumpur.

Malaysia (1998), National Economic Action Council White Paper, *Status of the Malaysian Economy* (http://www.topspot.com/NEAC/).

Mahani Zainal Abidin (2000) 'Malaysia's Alternative Approach to Crisis Management', in *Southeast Asian Affairs 2000*, Singapore: ISEAS, pp. 184-99.

Maznah Mohamad (2000) 'The UMNO Malaise', *Aliran Monthly*, Vol. 20, No. 2, pp. 2-6.

_____ (2002) 'Puteri UMNO: Sound and Fury Signifying Nothing New', *Aliran Monthly*, Vol. 22, No. 8, pp. 2-6.

_____ (2003) 'The Contest For Malay Votes in 1999: UMNO's Most Historic Challenge?', in Francis Loh and Johan Saravanamuttu (eds) *New Politics in Malaysia*, Singapore: ISEAS, pp. 66-86.

Mohamed Ariff (1996) 'Effects of Financial Liberalization on Four Southeast Asian Financial Markets', *ASEAN Economic Bulletin*, Vol. 12, No. 3 (March): 325-38.

Montagnon, Peter (2000) 'Mahathir attacks US pressure', *Financial Times*, 6 October.

Musa Hitam (2000), Speech at the Annual General Meeting of UMNO Branches in the Johor Baru Division, February 19, 2000, reprinted as 'What has happened to UMNO?' in *Aliran Monthly*, Vol. 20, No. 2, 2000, pp. 7-10.

Ng Tien Eng (2003) 'The Contest for Chinese Votes: Politics of Negotiation or Politics of Pressure', in Francis Loh and Johan Saravanamuttu (eds) *New Politics in Malaysia*, Singapore: ISEAS, pp. 87-106.

Ong-Giger, Kim (1997) 'Malaysia's Drive into High Technology Industries: Cruising into the Multimedia Super Corridor?, in *Southeast Asian Affairs 1997*, Singapore: ISEAS, pp. 185-201.

Patomäki, Heikki (2001) *Democratising Globalisation: The Leverage of the Tobin Tax*, London: Zed Books.

Petra Kamarudin, Raja (2000) *When Time Stood Still*, no place of publication.

Pura, Raphael (1997) 'Tough Talk by Mahathir Rattles Overseas Investors', *Asian Wall Street Journal*, 2 September.
Rajah Rasiah (2001) 'Pre-Crisis Economic Weaknesses and Vulnerabilities', in Jomo K. S. (ed.) *Malaysian Eclipse: Economic Crisis and Recovery*, London: Zed Books, pp. 47-61.
RAM (1997) 'Malaysia Inc. Falters', *Aliran Monthly*, Vol. 17, No. 7, pp. 2-7.
K. J. Ratnam and R. S. Milne (1970) 'The 1969 Parliamentary Election in West Malaysia', *Pacific Affairs*, XLIII, 2 (Summer), pp. 203-26.
Robison, Richard (1996) 'The Politics of Asian Values', *Pacific Review*, Vol. 9, No.3, pp. 309-27.
Rodan, Garry and Hewison, Kevin (1996) 'A "Clash of Cultures" or Convergence of Political Ideology?', in Richard Robison (ed.) *Pathways to Asia: The Politics of Engagement*, St Leonards, New South Wales: Allen and Unwin, pp. 29-55.
Sabri Zain (2000) *Face Off: A Malaysian Reformasi Diary (1998-1999)*, Singapore: BigO Books.
Sachs, Jeffrey (1998) 'Global Capitalism', *The Economist*, 14 June, p. 19.
Saludo, Richard and Shameen, Assif (1998) 'How Much Longer?', *Asiaweek*, pp. 36-44.
Peter Searle (1999) *The Riddle of Malaysian Capitalism: Rent-seekers or Real Capitalists*, St Leonards, New South Wales: Asian Studies Association of Australia in association with Allen & Unwin.
Singh, Ajay (1999) 'The New Malay Dilemma', *Asiaweek*, 10 December, p. 34.
Spaeth, Anthony (1997) 'Man in the Middle', *Time*, 6 October, pp. 16-22.
_____ (1998) 'Broken Dreams', *Time*, 15 June, pp. 24-28.
Suh, Sangwon and Shameen, Assif (1998) 'Battle of Wills', *Asiaweek*, 18 September, pp. 40-41, 44, 49.
Suh, Sangwon, Ranawana, Arjuna and Oorjitham, Santha (1999) 'The Struggle Goes On', *Asiaweek*, 23 April, pp. 22-26.
Tan Liok Ee (1997) *The Politics of Chinese Education in Malaya 1945-1961*, Kuala Lumpur: Oxford University Press.
Tan Tat Wai (2003) 'The Impact of the 1997 Financial Crisis on Malaysia's Corporate Sector and its Response', in Colin Barlow and Francis Loh Kok Wah (eds) *Malaysian Economics and Politics in the New Century*, Cheltenham: Edward Elgar, pp. 29-45.
Thillainathan, R. (2003) 'Malaysia and the Asian Crisis: Lessons and Challenges', in Colin Barlow and Francis Loh Kok Wah (eds) *Malaysian Economics and Politics in the New Century*, Cheltenham: Edward Elgar, pp. 13-28.
Toh Kin Woon (2003) 'Machang Bubuk: Changes in Voting Patterns, 1995-99', in Francis Loh and Johan Saravanamuttu (eds) *New Politics in Malaysia*, Singapore: ISEAS, pp. 141-57.
Tripathi, Salil and Saywell, T. (1998) 'Out of Controls', *Far Eastern Economic Review*, 17 September, p. 52.

Wain, Barry (1998) 'Why Doesn't Mahathir Bow Out?', *Asian Wall Street Journal*, 12-13 June.
_____ (2000) 'The Doctor Divides Malaysia', *Asian Wall Street Journal*, 18 August.
Zaharom Nain (2000) 'Hacks and Hussies', *Aliran Monthly*, Vol. 20, No. 1, pp. 2-5.
Zainal Aznam Yusof, Awang Adek Husin, Ismail Alowi, Lim Chee Sing and Sukhdave Singh (1996) 'Financial Reform in Malaysia', in Gerard Caprio *et al* (eds) *Financial Reform: Theory and Experience*, Cambridge: Cambridge University Press, pp. 276-320.
Zunar (2000) *Kerana Mu Hidung!*, Batu Caves, Selangor: Oneside Network.

IV. Newspapers and Periodicals

Aliran Monthly
Asian Wall Street Journal
Asiaweek
Berita Harian
Business Times
The Economist
Fortune
Far Eastern Economic Review
Harakah
harakahdaily.net
malaysiakini.com
Malaysian Business
The Nation, Bangkok
New Nation
New Straits Times
New Sunday Times
Newsweek
The Star
The Straits Times
The Sun
The Sunday Times
The Sydney Morning Herald
Time
Utusan Malaysia

Index

Entries for non-western names are cited according to surnames or first names, without the use of commas, except where the first name is an honorific, or where the name follows western convention in the original source.

Abdul Ghani Harun, 163
Abdul Hadi Awang, Haji, 149, 151
Abdul Rahman, Tunku, 99, 121, 129, 168
Abdul Razak, Tun, 168, 174, 177, 196
Abdullah Ahmad Badawi, 167-68, 171
ABIM, *see* Angkatan Belia Islam Malaysia
ADIL, *see* Pergerakan Keadilan Sosial
Afghanistan, 186-87
Ahmad Hussein, Syed, 183
Ahmad Lufti Othman, 129
Ahmad Mohd Don, 66
Ahmad Zahid Hamidi, 80-82, 84, 107, 122
Aib, 104
Al Arqam, 184
Al Ma'unah, 125-26
Al Qaedah, 186
Algeria, 186
Aliran Kesedaran Negara, 112
Aliran Monthly, 124
Alliance, 8, 30, 144, 161, 182
Amir Muhammad, 105
Amnesty International, 100
Anak Bukit by-election, 183
Anarchy, 38, 40, 67, 93, 108, 188
Anderson, Benedict, 15, 17

Angkatan Belia Islam Malaysia, 86-89, 92, 98, 157, 174, 184
Angkatan Perpaduan Ummah, 161
Anwar Ibrahim, Datuk Seri
 and ABIM, 86-89, 92, 157, 174
 accused of being foreign agent, 102
 Acting Prime Minister, 72
 'agenda', 91, 94, 96
 aib and Malay revolt, 104
 alleged sexual misconduct, 72, 101-103, 109, 111, 122
 'anointed successor', 4, 9, 72, 78, 82-83, 87, 94
 anti-establishment phases, 87
 The Asian Renaissance, 174
 assaulted by Inspector-General of Police, 72, 108-11
 at Baling, 88
 battered face, 88
 career, 10, 73, 86-87, 96
 civil society, 75, 89, 94-96
 convictions and prison sentences, 9, 72, 110, 113, 116, 129, 138, 154, 157, 174
 defeated Ghafar Baba, 7, 21, 71, 83-84
 Deputy Prime Minister, 4, 10, 30, 49, 71, 82, 86
 detention under ISA, 88

different from Razaleigh, 139
dismissed from office, 4, 9, 11, 66, 72, 80, 82-83, 85-86, 105, 174
expelled from UMNO, 72, 88
'father-and-son' relationship, 73
icon of *Reformasi*, 10, 87, 95
Keadilan's advantage, 157
management of financial crisis, 49, 51, 57, 60-63, 67
multiculturalism, 88, 96
party base, 84-85
Permatang Pauh Declaration, 95
'plot to overthrow Mahathir', 81-82
politics of uneasy conscience, 90
populism, 95
praised by international media, 74-76, 78
putative anti-Mahathirist, 93
rumoured rift with Mahathir, 72-73, 76, 80, 83, 91
supported Mahathir's Islamization, 89, 184
supported Zahid, Siti Zaharah, 122
suspected arsenic poisoning, 111
target of vilification, 77-78
trial for corruption, 9, 108, 110
trial for sodomy, 9, 108-109, 111
UMNO phase, 89, 92
visionary quality, 174
Wawasan Team, 84, 90
and Zahid's criticism of Mahathir, 80-82
Anwar Online, 106
Armstrong, Karen, 186
Asian century, 24
Asian Renaissance, The, 89, 93, 174
Asian values, 10, 14, 25-26, 93, 96, 103, 175
Asian Wall Street Journal, The, 55, 76, 187
Asiaweek, 71, 147
Authoritarianism, 4-5, 93, 95, 117, 172, 188
Azizan Abu Bakar, 78, 108
Azmin Ali, 78

BA, *see* Barisan Alternatif
Badaruddin Ismail, 163
Badrul Amin Bahron, 163
Baling, 88
Bank Bumiputra, 58
Bank Negara Malaysia
  bank lending policies, 51, 59
  capital controls, 52-53
  classification of NPLs, 51, 59
  confidence-building, 51, 58, 62
  conservatism, 63
  criticized by Mahathir, 58, 61
  economic orthodoxy, 58
  economistic solutions, 58
  faith in fundamentals, 63
  foreign exchange losses, 58
  initial response to contagion, 48
  monetary policy, 57-58, 63
  offshore banking licences, 41
  regulation of financial sector, 58
  relationship with IMF, 58, 63, 67
  removal of ringgit peg, 48
  resignation of Governor and Deputy Governor, 66
  support from Anwar, 57
Bangsa Malaysia, 5, 34
Banking and Financial Institutions Act, 45
Barisan Alternatif
  1999 election, 9, 11, 112, 116-19, 181
  against erosion of constitutional government, 89, 161
  and Anwar Ibrahim, 157
  budget strategy, 116-17, 156
  by-elections, 158, 163
  coalition, 117-18, 135, 138, 157-58, 160-61
  and DAP, 9, 140, 142-44, 163, 183
  electoral disadvantages, 118
  formation, 4, 11, 88, 116, 153, 160, 162
  issue of Islamic state, 12, 143
  joint manifesto, 116, 139, 156, 163
  and Keadilan, 155-56
  leaders, 120, 124-25, 127, 143, 157-58
  non-Malay fears, 119-20, 141, 144

Index

and PAS, 142, 151
political experiment, 116, 134, 142
and *Reformasi*, 12, 140, 162
repression against, 12, 124, 126, 182
significance of resistance, 12, 162, 164, 188
street protests, 126, 159
Barisan Nasional, 17, 94, 113, 128, 138, 141, 145, 151, 161, 183-84
2/3 majority, 115, 119, 140
14-member coalition, 160
1999 election, 9, 11, 117-120
against BA, 115-16, 134, 140, 145, 154
compromise with Suqiu, 126, 139
electoral victories in 1990 and 1995, 9, 18, 26, 29
Lunas by-election, 129, 162-63
monopoly on state power, 117-18, 161, 173
non-Malay leaders and parties, 140, 142, 184
non-Malay support, 119-20, 130, 135-36, 141
opposed by *Reformasi*, 100, 118
Penang, 137
propaganda, 118-19, 130, 141, 143
Sabah state election 1999, 117
Teluk Kemang by-election, 158
UMNO's dominance, 116, 123
Berita Harian, 126
'Black 14', 110, 114, 124
BN, *see* Barisan Nasional
BNM, *see* Bank Negara Malaysia
Bretton Woods, 64
Bumiputera Commercial and Industrial Community, 7, 19-20, 122, 176-78, 195
Bureaucracy, 13, 46, 65, 176-78, 185

Camus, Albert, 22
Capital controls, 4, 9, 10, 50, 53-56, 58, 63-67, 107, 116, 171, 173, 176, 180-81
Capital flight, 49, 51, 53-54
Capital strike, 49, 62

Capitalist rationalization, 10, 65, 67, 181
Ceramah, 100, 124, 126, 155
Chaebol, 44, 180
Challenge, The, 192-93
Challenger: Siapa Lawan Siapa, 77
Chandra Muzaffar, 112-113, 119, 141-42, 154-55, 158-59
Chechnya, 186
Chen Man Hin, 119, 140
Chia Kwang Chye, 120
Chia Lim Thye, 124
China, 52, 54, 56
Chinese
  anti-Chinese violence in Indonesia, 139
  attitudes towards Anwar Ibrahim, 139
  contribution to national economy, 193, 198
  declining dissidence, 137-40
  fear of 'Islamic state', 141
  language, 27, 29
  praised by Mahathir, 194
  politics of negotiation, 135-36, 139
  politics of pressure, 135-36, 139
  schools, 27-29
  support for UMNO, 130-41
  under PAS rule, 153
  urban constituencies, 28-29, 115, 120
Cintai IT!, 31, 105
Civil society, 11, 75, 89, 93-96, 107, 114, 124, 138, 145, 155, 160-61, 174, 181
Coalition building, 12, 134, 159, 161, 164
Commonwealth Games 1998, 100
Communist Party of Malaya, 6
Communitarianism, 30
Confucianism, 93
Conglomerates, 42-44, 46, 50-51, 53, 57, 59-60, 64-67, 92, 177, 179-80, 195-97, 199
Constitutional crisis, 18, 73, 188
Contagion, 47-48, 56
Corporate Debt Restructuring Committee, 53, 66

Currency depreciation, 39-40, 50-51, 56, 60, 62
Currency peg, 52-56, 59
Currency trading and traders, 39, 42, 47, 65-66

Daim Zainuddin, Tun, 17, 49, 51, 53, 60-61, 65-66, 82, 112, 177, 180
Danaharta, 53, 66, 180
Danamodal, 53, 66, 180
DAP, *see* Democratic Action Party
Decolonization, 15, 34-35
Democratic Action Party
  1986 election, 6, 138
  1990 election, 18, 116, 137-38
  1995 election. 9, 29, 115
  1999 election, 115, 119-21, 135
  'catastrophic loss', 135
  defeats of leaders, 119, 140
  differences with PAS, 9, 12, 143-44
  intra-party fight, 138
  islets of dissidence, 139
  Malay attitudes towards, 113, 135
  'Malaysian Malaysia', 114
  membership in BA, 9, 12, 138, 143-44
  pendulum of minority politics, 12, 136
  principal opposition party
  and *Reformasi*, 113-15, 120, 140
  Tanjung campaigns, 137
  'unholy alliance', 141
Detik, 105, 124
Developmentalism, 29
Dongjiaozong, 194

East Asian Economic Caucus, 25
East Asian Economic Group, 25
East Asian financial crisis, 4, 8-9, 38, 45, 50, 56, 75, 93, 100, 107, 138, 174-75, 177-78, 185, 189, 196-97
East Asian miracle, 8, 24, 30, 92, 175, 180
East Asian model of development, 25, 39, 56, 64, 66
Economic nationalism, 62, 65
Economic orthodoxy, 50, 56, 58, 63-65

Economic shield, 9, 10, 54, 139, 159, 180, 197
Economist, The, 48, 74
Eksklusif, 105, 124
Election Commission, 118
Employees Provident Fund, 53, 60
Ethnic politics, 14, 29, 126, 145, 151, 193-94
External debt

Fadzil Noor, 127, 183
Far Eastern Economic Review, 74
Financial liberalization, 41-42
Fitnah, 77
Fong Weng Phak, 66
Fortune, 75
Freemalaysia, 106
Funston, John, 123

GAGASAN, *see* Gagasan Demokrasi Rakyat
Gagasan Demokrasi Rakyat, 113-14, 138
Gagasan Rakyat, *see* Gagasan Rakyat Malaysia
Gagasan Rakyat Malaysia, 114, 136-37, 144, 161
GERAK, *see* Majlis Gerakan Keadilan Rakyat
Gerakan, *see* Parti Gerakan Rakyat Malaysia
Ghafar Baba, 6, 7, 71, 83-84, 101, 122
Ghani Ismail, 79
Globalization, 41-42, 73, 175, 180, 189
Gobalakrishnan, N., 154, 163
Gomez, Terence, 47
Gong Xi Raya, 30
Governance, 39, 42, 46-47, 50-51, 57-58, 61, 66, 71, 80, 153
Groupe Islamique Armée, 186

Halim Saad, 180
Halim Salleh, 23, 176
Hamas, 186
Harakah, 105, 123-24, 126

Index

Harakahdaily, 106
Harun Hashim, 110
Harvard Club of Malaysia, 167, 182, 188, 193, 198
Hezbollah, 186
Hilley, John, 21, 153
Hishamuddin Hussein, 167, 174
Hishamuddin Rais, 163
Hong Kong, 42, 56
Husin Ali, Syed, 141
Hussein Onn, Tun, 85
Hwang, In-Won, 80

IMF, *see* International Monetary Fund
Indonesia, 39, 50, 55-56, 59-60, 62, 74, 81, 94
Information Technology, 27, 31
Interest rates, 48, 50-51, 58, 60, 62
Internal Security Act, 103, 113, 124, 151, 155, 162
International financial system, 38-39, 50, 64
International Monetary Fund, 10, 47, 49, 50-52, 54, 56-63, 66-67, 79-80
Internet, 105-107, 112-13, 123
Investor confidence, 8, 39, 47, 49, 51, 57-58, 62, 64, 95
Iran, 186
Iraq, 186-87
Islam, 4, 5, 13
    Anwar and, 82, 86-89, 93, 96
    'fundamentalism', 141, 151
    global *ummah*, 186
    Islamic resurgence, 86
    Islamic state, 12-13, 114, 117, 141, 143-44, 151, 153-54, 163, 181-87
    PAS-Islam, 152, 181, 184
    root causes of extremism, 187
    topography of suffering, 186-87
    Vision Islam, 152
    war against, 186
Islamic Jihad, 186

Jammu, 186
Japan, 26, 44, 52-53, 81, 179
Jemaah Islah Malaysia, 114, 156

Jeyakumar Devaraj, 142
Jiwa Merdeka, 106
Jomo K. S., 47, 54, 61-62
Kamarudin Jaffar, 157
Kampung Baru, 104
Kamunting, 88, 162
Karpal Singh, 119, 124, 140
Kashmir, 186
Keadilan, *see* Parti Keadilan Nasional
Kelantan, 12, 124, 144, 155, 163
    1999 election, 9, 117-19, 147
    financial deprivation, 125, 146
    Nik Aziz government, 146, 153
    PAS's economic populism, 148
    PAS-S46 coalition, 7, 28
    PAS-S46 split, 9, 29, 121, 145
    poverty, 125, 146, 150
    simple living, 146
    Syariah Criminal Code (11) Enactment 1993, 147, 151
    UMNO defeats, 119
    UMNO-PAS divide, 120, 137, 147, 152
Kesas Highway demonstration, 162
Khalil Jafri, 78
Khalil Yaakob, 168
Kini, 106
KLSE, *see* Kuala Lumpur Stock Exchange
Kolusi, korupsi, nepotisme, 81, 100
Konsortium Perkapalan Berhad, 49
Krugman, Paul, 54
Kuala Lumpur Stock Exchange, 41, 44-45, 47-49, 51, 54-55, 61
Kumpulan Militan Malaysia, 163

Labuan, 41
Labour Party, 157, 161
Labour Party, Britain, 196
Laman Reformasi, 106
Lee Kuan Yew, 25
Lim Chong Eu, Tun Dr, 137
Lim Guan Eng, 112-13, 116, 137-38, 140, 142, 161
Lim Kit Siang, 113, 119-20, 138, 140, 142-44
Loh Kok Wah, Francis, 29, 140

Lokman Adam, 163
Lunas by-election, 162-63
Mahafiraun, 106, 134, 188
Mahathir Mohamad, Datuk Seri Dr
  ambitions of class, 195
  anarchy, 38, 40, 93, 108, 188
  announced retirement, 13, 167
  Arabs, 192
  Asian values, 25-26, 93, 175
  assessment of NEP, 19-21
  attitude towards Malay culture, 99
  authoritarianism, 4-5, 7, 91, 93, 103, 172-73, 188
  balance of power, 180
  being fragmented, 173
  capital controls, 4, 10, 50, 53-56, 65-66, 171, 173, 180-81
  capitalist rationalization, 65, 67
  The Challenge, 192-93
  C. H. E. Det, 1, 5
  civil service, 46
  control of state power, 86
  cooperation with USA, 187
  criticism of Malay business, 190, 195
  criticism of Malay students, 191, 195
  criticized by international media, 75-76
  criticized by Zahid, 80-82
  currency trading, 42, 50, 66
  defended Melayu Baru, 185, 195
  democracy, 5, 182
  East Asian financial crisis, 38, 57, 66, 178, 189
  end of NEP, 22
  English language, 193-94
  Fadzil Noor, 127
  failed by the Malays, 194
  failing the Malays, 193
  failures of class, 195
  Harvard Club Dinner 2002, 167, 182, 188, 193, 198
  history, 190, 192, 199
  ideas on economy, 63-64
  ideals of nation, 195
  interest rates, 58, 60, 62
  International Monetary Fund, 50, 52, 57, 60, 62, 67

Islam, 4-5, 89, 172-73, 181, 184-85, 190-91
Kuala Lumpur Stock Exchange rules, 61
'last Malay rebel', 129
Mahafiraun, 106, 134
Mahathirism, 4-5, 13, 21, 34-36, 170-72, 174-76, 181, 185, 199
Mahathirist vision, 34, 170
Mahazalim, 106, 134
The Malay Dilemma, 5, 167, 170-71, 192-93, 195, 197
Malay unity, 127
Malaysia Incorporated, 10, 42, 44, 46-47, 57, 65-66
managed 1980s' recession, 19
Multimedia Super Corridor, 31-35
nationalist-capitalist project, 5, 8, 10, 14, 39, 92, 175-76, 197
nationhood and national unity, 30
no lame duck, 85, 168, 171
opposed punishment of apostasy, 171
original Malay dilemma, 167, 199
personal victory in 1995 election, 26, 29
personalized hegemony, 13, 169, 172-73
picking winners, 180
plot by Anwar, 81
political intuition, 10, 55
praise of Chinese, 194
problems of instability, 188
psychology of decolonization, 35
qualities of leaders, 172
reform of international financial system, 50
relations with Anwar, 71-73, 75-76
rescuing companies, 49, 60
response to UMNO's losses, 123
root causes of extremism, 187
sandiwara, 169
second Malay dilemma, 4, 189
'September 11', 169, 187
Shahrir Samad, 129
solutions to cultural issues, 28, 92
Soros, George, 39, 50, 62

succession, 80, 83, 85-86, 168
Suqiu, 126, 194
technophile, 31
vis-à-vis Bank Negara, 57-58, 61-63
Vision 2020, 20-22, 26, 29, 34, 36
UMNO reform, 128-30
weaknesses of culture, 195
will to power, 169
Mahazalim, 106, 134, 188
Mainichi Daily News, 81
Majlis Gerakan Keadilan Rakyat, 113-16, 134, 138, 157, 160-61
Malay Dilemma, The, 5, 167, 170-71, 192-93, 195, 197
Malays
  competitiveness, 20
  conglomerates, 42-44, 46, 177, 179-80, 195-96, 199
  dilemma, 1, 13
  disunity, 126-28
  failing Mahathir, 194
  Melayu Baru, 5
  political turning points, 199
  second dilemma, 4, 13-14, 189, 193, 195, 199
  students, 82, 87, 89, 94, 104, 108, 124, 126, 181, 186, 190-91, 194-95
  swing against UMNO, 119-20, 141, 147
  'thinking the unthinkable', 117, 162
  UMNO's strategic constituencies, 130
  underachievement, 195
  unity, 127-28, 142, 151
  women, 101, 104, 130, 191
Malaysia Incorporated, 8, 10, 39, 42, 44, 46-47, 51, 57, 65-67, 90, 92, 170, 175, 177, 189-81, 196-97
Malaysiakini, 158
Malaysian, The, 106
Malaysian Business Council, 36, 47
Malaysian Chinese Association, 6, 29, 135, 137-39, 194
Malaysian Indian Congress, 162
Malaysian International Shipping Corporation, 49
Malaysian Solidarity Convention, 161

Maluku, 186
Marina Yusof, 154-55, 158-59
Maznah Mohamad, 120, 130
MCA, *see* Malaysian Chinese Association
Merdeka, 15, 174
Milne, R. S., 128
Minority politics, 140, 144, 183, 193,
Mirzan Mahathir, 49
Mohamad Ezam Mohd Nor, 114, 124, 154-55, 161, 163
Mohd Anuar Tahir, 155, 158
Moody's, 53
Morgan Stanley Capital International, 54-55
MSC, *see* Multimedia Super Corridor
Muhammad Muhammad Taib, 84, 174
Muhyiddin Yassin, 84, 174
Multimedia Super Corridor, 8, 30-34, 36, 105
Munawar Ahmad Anees, 101, 103, 108
Murad Khalid, 112
Musa Hassan, 101
Musa Hitam, 6, 65, 73, 77-80, 83, 86, 121, 123, 129, 177

Najib Tun Razak, 83-84, 174
Nallakaruppan, S., 101, 108-109
National Development Policy, 8, 9, 20, 27, 39, 190
National Economic Action Council, 49, 61-62, 66
Nationalist-capitalist project, 8, 10, 14, 47, 92, 175-76, 197
NDP, *see* National Development Policy
NEP, *see* New Economic Policy
Neoliberalism, 40
New Economic Policy, 4-8, 10, 13, 16-22, 24, 26-30, 35, 39-40, 42, 46, 81, 87-88, 122, 136, 139, 151, 159, 161, 170-71, 174-78, 180, 185-86, 188, 190, 193, 195-99
New Straits Times, The, 71, 101, 105, 198
New Sunday Times, The, 103
Newsweek, 74

Newly industrializing countries, 24
Nik Abdul Aziz Nik Mat, 146, 163, 186
Non-governmental organizations, 11, 88, 105, 112, 155-57, 187
Non-performing loans, 51, 60

Official Secrets Act, 89, 154
Offshore banking, 41
Offshore financial centre, 41
Offshore ringgit accounts, 52-53

Palestine, 186
Paradoxes of Mahathirism, 4-5, 170, 172, 195
Parti Berjaya, 157
Parti Bersatu Sabah, 6-7, 18, 28-29, 116, 118, 125, 157
Parti Gerakan Rakyat Malaysia, 120, 126, 135, 137-39, 141, 157, 194
Parti Islam SeMalaysia
   1990 election, 1, 18, 115-16, 146
   1995 election, 115, 146
   1999 election, 9, 119-20, 123, 129, 134, 146-47
   and Anwar, 81-82, 89, 113, 145, 154, 157, 184
   and Barisan Alternatif, 115, 119, 134-35
   'building Islam', 125, 151
   coalition building, 153, 160-61
   conservatism, 147, 150-52
   democracy, 182-84
   denied petroleum revenue, 124-25, 149
   economy, 149-50
   government of Kelantan, 28-29, 121, 144-46, 152-53
   government of Trengganu, 119, 144-45, 148, 151-53
   Islamic state, 117, 141, 182-83
   Majlis Gerakan Keadilan Rakyat, 114
   Malay heartland, 120, 126, 128, 146, 148
   Malay unity talks, 127
   non-Muslims, 141-43
   PAS-Islam, 116, 147, 150, 152, 181, 184, 186-87
   political liberalism, 151
   programmatic bifurcation, 12, 151-52, 154
   Reformasi, 113
   relations with DAP, 9, 12, 120, 140-44, 160, 163-64, 183
   relations with S46, 9, 29, 145
   rise of, 13, 145, 147, 180
   'September 11', 164, 169, 183, 186-87
   simple living, 146, 185
   Syariah Criminal Offences (Hudud and Qisas) Bill, 151
   Taliban, 164
Parti Keadilan Nasional (Keadilan)
   1999 election, 119-20,129, 142, 146, 148, 154
   'Anwar's party', 114-15, 13, 154, 156-57
   by-elections, 158, 163
   formation, 114
   in BA, 12, 115, 140, 153, 156, 158, 160-61, 164
   leadership, 154-55
   membership, 155-57
   merger with PRM, 158
   multiethnic politics, 115, 138, 141, 155
   organizational stresses, 154, 157-59
   rejected 'Malay unity' talks, 127
   repression against leaders, 9, 12, 124, 154, 159, 163
Parti Rakyat Malaysia, 113-15, 119-20, 127, 129, 158, 161
Parti Semangat 46, 7, 9, 18, 28, 83, 116-19, 121
Party-bureaucracy-class axis, 176-78, 181, 185
PAS, *see* Parti Islam SeMalaysia
PBS, *see* Parti Bersatu Sabah
Patomäki, Heikki, 63
Paul, Augustine, 109-11
Pemuda UMNO, 84, 90, 122, 126-27, 130
Penang, 28-29, 137, 141

Index

Pendang by-election, 183
Pergerakan Keadilan Sosial, 113, 154
Permatang Pauh, 86, 119
Permatang Pauh Declaration, 95, 100, 113
Persatuan Bahasa Melayu, 86-87
Persatuan Kebangsaan Pelajar-pelajar Islam, 86
Petra Kamarudin, Raja, 94, 106, 153, 155, 163
Petronas, 49, 53, 149-50
Philippines, The, 15
Portfolio investment funds, 40-41, 45
Privatization, 5-6, 8, 17, 27, 39, 42-43, 57, 65-66, 71, 116, 175, 177, 196-97
PRM, *see* Parti Rakyat Malaysia
Putera-AMCJA, 161
Puteri UMNO, 130

Rafidah Aziz, 112, 167, 174
Rahim Noor, 110-11
Rahim Tamby Chik, 112
Ratnam, K. J., 128
Razaleigh Hamzah, Tengku, 6, 7, 9, 18, 27, 29, 73, 79, 83-84, 118, 121-23, 139, 160
Recapitalization, 9, 54, 59, 66
Reflation, 9, 10, 54-55, 59, 62, 66-67
Reformasi, 4, 9, 12, 67, 82, 96, 99, 103, 123-24, 129, 138, 143, 160, 168-69, 174, 181, 185-86, 188
   and 1999 election, 112-16, 118-20, 181
   cultural revolt, 9, 11, 100, 152-53, 176
   dissent and alternative media, 11, 14, 88, 104-105, 160-62, 181, 188
   erosion of hegemony, 11-12, 104, 107-108, 197, 199
   in Indonesia, 11, 81, 94, 100
   and non-Malays, 138-40, 156
   and opposition parties, 145, 155, 157-59
   websites, 105-106
Reformasi Diary, 105
Renong Berhad, 49, 53, 66

Rukunegara, 16, 21
Ruslan Kasim, 155, 158
Russia, 56
Rustam Sani, 127

Saari Sungib, 163
Sabah, 6-7, 15-16, 18, 28-29, 117, 125, 136, 145
Sabri Zain, 105-106, 113, 161
Saifuddin Ismail Nasution, 163
Sandiwara, 125-26, 169
Sanusi Junid, 122
Sarajevo, 186
Sarawak, 15-16, 117
Searle, Peter, 178-79
Second Outline Perspective Plan, 19
Sejarah Melayu, 103
September 11, 2001 incident, 163, 168-69, 182-83, 186-88
Shahnon Ahmad, 105
Shahrir Samad, 129
SHIT@PukiMak, 129
Short-selling of shares, 48, 58
Siddiq Ghouse, 102
Sime Bank, 53
Siti Zaharah, 122
Socialist Front, 161
Soros, George, 39, 50, 62, 67
South Africa, 56
South Korea, 10, 24, 26, 39, 50, 56, 59-60, 74
Spaeth, Anthony, 74
Special Branch, 103-104, 109
Standard and Poor's, 53
Stiglitz, Joseph, 54, 56
Structural adjustment, 66
Surat layang, 77-78, 82
Suara Rakyat Malaysia, 113
Suhaimi Kamaruddin, 90
Suharto, 80-81, 94
Sukma Darmawan Sasmitaat Madja, 101, 103, 108
Suqiu, 126-27, 139, 142, 194

Taiwan, 24, 56, 26
Tajudin Ramli, 180
Taliban, 186

Talkin Untuk Anwar Ibrahim, 78, 82
Tamadun, 105
Tan, Joceline, 103
Tan Tat Wai, 49
Teoh Teik Huat, 138
Teluk Kemang by-election, 156
Templeton, 55
Thailand, 10, 39, 47-48, 50, 59, 60, 62
Trengganu
    1999 election, 118-19, 146-48
    1999 General Election Manifesto, 148-49
    denied petroleum revenue, 124-26, 149, 184
    PAS's return to power, 9, 12, 119, 147, 184
    poverty, 150, 185
    predominant Muslim population, 147, 152
    social conservatism, 144, 150, 163
    Syariah Criminal Offences (Hudud and Qisas) Bill, 151
Thomas, Tommy, 149
Tian Chua, 119, 124, 138, 154-55, 163
Time, 74
Tohmah, 77
Towards a Just Malaysia, 116

Ummah, 182, 186-87
Ummi Hafilda, 78
UMNO, *see* United Malays National Organization
Undur Mahathir!, 108, 129, 156, 174
United Democratic Party, 157
United Malays National Organization
    1986 election, 6
    1990 election, 28, 137
    1995 election, 28
    1999 election, 7, 11, 118-20, 135
    Chinese support, 130, 141, 193
    hegemonic stability, 12, 121, 123
    factionalism and party elections, 6-7, 10, 13, 18, 21, 71, 77, 79, 83-84, 90, 93, 121-23, 177, 188, 197
    General Assembly, 76, 79, 80-82, 168, 185, 198
    intra-Malay conflict, 13
    involvement in business, 49, 53, 65, 176-77
    'irrelevance', 117
    leadership succession, 11, 13, 73, 82-83, 85, 121, 168, 175
    Malay disunity, 128
    and Malay masses, 172, 176, 181, 183, 187, 194-95, 199
    Malay unity talks, 127
    power behind NEP, 176
    reaction to Mahathir's resignation, 167-69
    resistance to reform, 12, 123, 128-31
    split, 7, 27, 147, 169
    Supreme Council, 72, 84, 86, 122, 129, 192-93
Utusan Malaysia, 105, 126

Vision 2020, 5, 7-8, 11, 20-22, 26-27, 29-30, 33-36, 39, 91-92, 107, 120, 128, 145, 170, 174-75, 190, 197
Vision Schools, 142, 194

Wade, Robert, 39
Wain, Barry, 76
Wan Azizah Wan Ismail, 91, 94, 113-14, 119, 127, 138, 154-55, 157
Wanita UMNO, 84, 122, 131
Washington consensus, 39, 56, 173, 178
Wasilah, 105, 124
Wawasan 2020, see Vision 2020
Wawasan Team, 7, 21, 64, 90, 121
Wee Choo Keong, 137-38
Wo men do shi yi jia ren, 30
World Bank, 53, 56

Yayasan Anda, 87, 92
Yayasan Salam, 92
Yusof Rawa, Haji, 144

Zaibatsu, 44, 180
Zainur Zakaria, 109, 119, 141, 154-55
Zaitun Kassim, 142
Zunar, 105, 130